Improving Student Learning

Applying Deming's Quality
Principles in Classrooms

Second Edition

Also available from ASQ Quality Press:

Continuous Improvement in the Science Classroom
Jeffrey Burgard

Continuous Improvement in the Primary Classroom: Language Arts K–3
Karen Fauss

Continuous Improvement in the Mathematics Classroom
Carolyn Ayres

Continuous Improvement in the History and Social Sciences Classroom
Shelly Carson

Successful Applications of Quality Systems in K–12 Schools
The ASQ Quality Education Division

Futuring Tools for Strategic Quality Planning in Education
William F. Alexander and Richard W. Serfass

Insights to Performance Excellence in Education: An Inside Look at the Baldrige Award Criteria for Education
Mark L. Blazey, Karen S. Davison, and John P. Evans

Tools and Techniques to Inspire Classroom Learning
Barbara A. Cleary, PhD and Sally J. Duncan

Thinking Tools for Kids: An Activity Book for Classroom Learning
Barbara A. Cleary, PhD and Sally J. Duncan

To request a complimentary catalog of ASQ Quality Press publications, call 800-248-1946, or visit our Web site at http://qualitypress.asq.org .

Improving Student Learning

Applying Deming's Quality Principles in Classrooms

Second Edition

Lee Jenkins

ASQ Quality Press
Milwaukee, Wisconsin

Improving Student Learning: Applying Deming's Quality Principles in Classrooms
Lee Jenkins

Library of Congress Cataloging-in-Publication Data

Jenkins, Lee.
  Improving student learning : applying Deming's quality principles in classrooms / Lee Jenkins.—2nd ed.
    p. cm.
  Includes bibliographical references and index.
  ISBN 0-87389-569-X (Hardcover : alk. paper)
  1. School improvement programs—United States. 2. Learning. 3. Total quality management—United States. 4. Deming, W. Edwards (William Edwards), 1900– . 5. Educational tests and measurements—United States. I. Title.

LB2822.82.J46 2003
371.2'00973—dc21   2003000299

10 9 8 7 6 5 4 3 2

ISBN 0-87389-569-X

Publisher: William A. Tony
Acquisitions Editor: Annemieke Koudstaal
Project Editor: Paul O'Mara
Production Administrator: Gretchen Trautman
Special Marketing Representative: David Luth

ASQ Mission: The American Society for Quality advances individual, organizational, and community excellence worldwide through learning, quality improvement, and knowledge exchange.

Attention Bookstores, Wholesalers, Schools, and Corporations: ASQ Quality Press books, videotapes, audiotapes, and software are available at quantity discounts with bulk purchases for business, educational, or instructional use. For information, please contact ASQ Quality Press at 800-248-1946, or write to ASQ Quality Press, P.O. Box 3005, Milwaukee, WI 53201-3005.

To place orders or to request a free copy of the ASQ Quality Press Publications Catalog, including ASQ membership information, call 800-248-1946. Visit our Web site at www.asq.org or http://qualitypress.asq.org .

Printed in the United States of America

♾ Printed on acid-free paper

American Society for Quality

Quality Press
600 N. Plankinton Avenue
Milwaukee, Wisconsin 53203
Call toll free 800-248-1946
Fax 414-272-1734
www.asq.org
http://qualitypress.asq.org
http://standardsgroup.asq.org
E-mail: authors@asq.org

This book is dedicated to Rev. Kenneth L. Jenkins, my father.

Somewhere in my teens I asked, "Dad, if you moved to a new church wouldn't you have it real easy? You could re-preach all the same sermons and wouldn't have to work so hard." He responded, "It doesn't work that way, because all your life you grow and develop. The sermons of a couple years ago just aren't good enough today." My appreciation for quality and continuous improvement started young and is due, to a large extent, to this wonderful man who lives all week the sermons he preaches on Sunday.

Table of Contents

Section V   Beyond the Three Basic Graphs

Section VI   Reflection

Section VII   Accountability

Section VIII   Conclusion

Section IX   Appendixes (also included on CD-ROM)

List of Figures and Tables

Preface

Improving student learning is the aim of this book; it is written for teachers and others who have a passion for teaching and learning. The classroom is center stage.

Improvement occurs because somebody's theory is proven accurate. All innovation is first in the mind before it is created in actuality. Thus, improved learning occurs because a teacher has a theory in his or her head, tries out the theory, and notes that student learning has improved. If an educational theory does not improve classroom learning, it matters not how many legislators, editors, or other leaders ascribe to the theory; it is useless.

The management theory of Dr. W. Edwards Deming improves student learning. Some may ask, "Didn't he advise manufacturers? What does that have to do with teaching school?" Dr. Deming advised owners of manufacturing firms on how to better manage their people to create an improved manufactured product. He gave the same advice to educators on how to better manage their people to create improved learning. It matters not that a person is managing 25 people producing brakes or 25 people producing better learning. It matters not that some people are tall and some are short. The theories of Dr. Deming are as powerful for teachers and their leaders as they are for businesses.

Most of *Improving Student Learning* is set in the classroom. How can teachers know if the changes made in instructional strategies really do result in improved learning? Can teachers document that this year's students are learning better than last year's students? Can parents and students clearly see growth themselves, or do they have to take somebody else's word that learning has taken place? Is there improved learning that parents and students can understand? Dr. Deming told leaders that they have the responsibility to create joy in the workplace. How can educators know if they are maintaining the joy of learning contained inside their kindergartners?

Teachers are typically treated like members of a bowling team. Faculty members enter their own classrooms, teach as they see fit, and the scores are added up once each year. When teachers see the power of thinking about their students as a team working toward a common goal, they naturally desire to become a team member themselves. But, can teachers be treated like orchestra members rather than bowling team members? Yes, they can, so there's a chapter on schoolwide improvement. This chapter is not a treatise on how the principal can leverage more work from a staff, but how teachers can work together with their principal to create a powerful team. And what is the energy that fuels this orchestra of educators? It is improvement. People become addicted to the joy of knowing that their school is improving every year and to the understanding that, most likely, next year will be even better than this year.

One chapter is included on districtwide improvement. Why? Because teachers and principals want the team to include everyone. Again, this chapter is not about how the superintendent and school board can strategize to wring more effort from people, but how to maximize effort and talent. Much energy is wasted in every school district because one employee or school, in pursuit of an individual objective, is undoing the work of another employee or school. Districtwide improvement is not top-down, nor is it site based. It is the group agreeing on an aim, having in-depth discussions on methods, and collecting the data to know when improvement has actually occurred.

Improving Student Learning includes more than 100 figures. Because education degrees often include never-used statistics courses and many have been taught by newspapers to see statistics as harmful, educators often wince at graphs and statistics. Dr. Deming would have educators replace useless and harmful statistics with useful, helpful statistics. The graphs in this book are simple and profound. Shirley Chenoweth of Arnoldsburg, West Virginia, had an idea regarding improving her students' learning, tested out the idea, and in three weeks possessed the data proving that the concept worked—no hoping, no guessing, but *knowing* her idea worked. (See chapter 7 for details.) Dr. Deming's statistics for learning are revolutionary, simple, and yet, profound. As Herlina Leggins of Oklahoma City put it, "Who would have thought a dot on the wall could accomplish so much?" This type of data and joy has never before been available to teachers.

As you read *Improving Student Learning,* I hope you capture the enthusiasm from each of the classrooms and understand that you, too, can improve the lives of your students with Dr. Deming's quality principles.

The enclosed CD is provided to allow readers to print out the complete appendixes for use in their respective schools.

Classroom graphs included in *Improving Student Learning* may be produced by From LtoJ Software, www.fromLtoJ.com

Lee Jenkins
Scottsdale, AZ
LtoJ@earthlink.net
www.fromLtoJ.com

Acknowledgments

In 1990, Lew Rhodes introduced me to Dr. Deming's theories. He helped organize the four-day seminar with Dr. Deming, in 1992, that provided the basis for this book. Special thanks go to Dr. Susan Leddick, who has mentored me along this path of continuous improvement since 1993.

Administrators often provide the leadership behind continuous improvement implementation. Administrators to whom I am especially grateful, in the preparation of this second edition, are Tom Armelino, Nancy Ayres, Jim Barkman, Cheryl Downs, Dennis Eller, Rick Fauss, Jerry Fowler, Brian Grenell, Orv Huffman, Scott Mills, Laurel Moore, Ron Nash, Kerry Newman, Darren Overton, Bob Poffenbarger, Carolyn Roettger, Dave Scragg, Dave Stickrod, Thomas Tan, and LeRoy Walser. Much appreciation is due to them.

Numerous teachers have participated in this second edition by providing living examples that Dr. Deming's concepts work with children. You will see their credits adjacent to their cited work.

Four teachers from Enterprise District (Redding, California) wrote books on continuous improvement in 2000. They inspired me greatly then, and continue to assist with their creativity. They are Karen Fauss, *Continuous Improvement in the Primary Classroom: Language Arts;* Carolyn Ayres, *Continuous Improvement in the Mathematics Classroom;* Shelly Carson, *Continuous Improvement in the History/Social Science Classroom;* and Jeff Burgard, *Continuous Improvement in the Science Classroom.* Debi Molina-Walters is currently writing another book for this series; her creativity and talents are equally inspiring.

If it were not for the professional competence and attitude of Quality Press, I would never have considered the prospect of a second edition. Thank you, Annemieke Koudstaal.

Sandy Jenkins had no idea 40 years ago when she married a college student preparing to be a teacher that extensive travel and publishing deadlines were a part of the deal. She has been my partner in every aspect of this endeavor. First as a wife and secondly as a teacher extraordinaire, she is always there to be of help.

Introduction to First Edition (With One Slight Addition)

E ducation has undergone change after change accompanied by subsequent reversal to former practices. Continual changes must be replaced with improvement. Education can no longer afford expensive changes and the ensuing debates over the efficacy of each change.

The 20th century had just begun. France had already failed; the United States was almost ready to call it quits. The problem was not money, talent, technology, or determination. It was dropouts. People were dropping out completely—six feet under.

The location was Panama; the challenge was the Panama Canal.[1] The problem: yellow fever. Up to 50 percent of each new shipload of workers died from yellow fever. Nobody knew the cause of yellow fever, but conventional wisdom was to blame the worker. People thought those who contracted yellow fever had a deficiency either in character or health habits. But blame did not eradicate yellow fever.

If blame could improve schooling, American K–12 education would be the envy of the world. Everybody is blaming everybody, but few are looking for root causes of educational problems. In the midst of the Panama yellow fever crisis, blaming seemed reasonable. Looking back, however, blaming appears quite silly. Yellow fever was built into the Panamanian system; it was not the fault of the workers. Ants in Panama were biting people in their sleep, so people placed dishes of water under each bedpost. The nightly ant bites stopped, but, of course, the mosquitoes spreading yellow fever had more breeding water. The solution to an irritant caused death.

It is hoped that America will be able to look back on the current crisis in K–12 education and laugh at the practice of blaming workers—administrators, teachers, students, and parents. Just like Panama, America will find that failure is not coming from the workers, but from the system. What is education's counterpart to the bedpost water bowls of Panama? Dr. W. Edwards Deming clearly identified the counterparts and solutions. First, however, is a look at blaming. What's wrong with blaming?

1. *It fixes nothing.* The legislature and press blame the education establishment, the school board blames the superintendent, the superintendent blames the principals, the principals blame the teachers, the teachers blame the parents, and nothing improves for the students.

2. *Blaming lets those in charge escape responsibility.* As long as blaming persists, everyone's job is to convince the boss that he or she is not the one responsible for the problem. For example, school cooks know that the person who buys the food, develops the menu, and sets cafeteria policies has the most control over the profit-loss statement for the food service program of the school district. But if cooks, who have no power to change the system, are blamed for a cafeteria loss, the situation continues with those in charge escaping responsibility. The food service supervisor has escaped responsibility by convincing the business manager that the cooks are at fault.

3. *Blaming stops the search for underlying causes.* Usually current problems are caused by yesterday's solutions to former problems. If nobody is looking for underlying causes, then today's problems are not being connected to yesterday's solutions. For example, suppose a middle school changes from a seven-period day to a six-period day to solve a school problem. Everything seems to be OK, except that Band cannot fit into the six-period day and must be taught before school. That seems satisfactory to parents and students, but nobody wants students to arrive at school in the dark. So, the school starting time is moved ahead 20 minutes. This also seems fine, but now the bus system cannot handle the change and an elementary school has one bus that is late 20 minutes each day. The staff at the elementary school blames the transportation department for running an inefficient system, without knowing that the root cause of the problem is a decision to allow another school across town to alter its schedule. Today's bus problem is caused by yesterday's solution to an unpopular student schedule.

Here's the slight addition:

Betti Souther, a Farmington, New Mexico, educator, told me an interesting formula that inevitably surfaces when blaming is the constant. It is: Rules + Regulations − Relationships = Resentment + Rebellion. (R + R − R = R + R)

Improving Student Learning describes how to replace blaming and excuses with quality education.

ENDNOTE

1. D. McCullough, *The Path between the Seas* (New York: Simon and Schuster, 1977).

Introduction to Second Edition

The express purpose of the second edition of *Improving Student Learning: Applying Deming's Quality Principles in Classrooms* is to communicate with an international audience the wonderful ways educators have improved, revised, stretched, and applied the concepts since the first edition in 1997.

Chapter 3 of the second edition is a review of Dr. Deming's 1992 advice given at a Washington D.C. seminar sponsored by the American Association of School Administrators. During the 1992–93 school year, one teacher in Redding, California's Enterprise School District tested out the concept. His graphs are reprinted in chapter 3. I knew from this one example that Dr. Deming was right. Many other teachers in the Enterprise School District followed the concept, and in 1997 the first edition of *Improving Student Learning* was published. It cited many kindergarten through grade eight examples. Enterprise teachers followed up this book in 2000 with the publication of four additional titles. Carolyn Ayres wrote *Continuous Improvement in the Mathematics Classroom,* Jeff Burgard wrote *Continuous Improvement in the Science Classroom,* Shelly Carson wrote *Continuous Improvement in the History/ Social Science Classroom,* and Karen Fauss wrote *Continuous Improvement in the Primary Classroom: Language Arts.* There were now five books helping teachers in the United States and elsewhere implement Dr. Deming's continuous improvement concept.

It is now 2003, 11 years later, and teachers from preschool to graduate school have found such success with continuous improvement that the editors at ASQ Quality Press suggested this edition. If the examples were the same except for different states and countries, then no second edition would be warranted. However, this is not the case: the locales are all different, but the insights provided by so many other educators are profound. I hope the readers can sense the pride I feel in my colleagues who have submitted so much to their students and the world through their examples and stories.

When I was writing the first edition it felt like a "push." This is because I was promoting Dr. Deming's concept in as many different classrooms as possible. This second edition feels like a "pull." My responsibility is to pull in—from as many locales as possible—the insights that will help the readers with their specific responsibilities.

This second edition is even more important than I could have conceived when writing the first edition. California was just emerging from a standardized assessment drought when the first was written. After the California Learning Assessment System (CLAS) came apart for political reasons, there was a long period with no state-mandated testing. Certainly this is not the case in 2003. Further, as more and more pressure is applied to raise test scores, solutions are needed. It seems there are several possible responses to this pressure:

1. Teach only reading and math, which triples the time for reading and doubles the time for math.

2. Teach test-taking strategies.

3. Provide student incentives for high scores.

4. Provide staff incentives for high scores.

5. Threaten staff with loss of jobs.

6. Buy scripted programs.

7. Align the curriculum.

Then, there is this book and the topic of continuous improvement. It pains me to see the first six strategies in use. The seventh solution, alignment, is a great partner for continuous improvement—if the alignment means alignment of curriculum based upon best practices, not merely alignment with test items.

While visiting the Henry Ford Museum, I was particularly intrigued by the description of the 1913 air races in Paris. It is well known what happened in North Carolina in 1903, but I was surprised to learn how much aeronautic progress had been made in 10 years. As I write this book I reflect upon an 11-year span. Six years ago, the first edition was published; the readers of this second edition will be able to sense much of what has occurred since then, because any example outside Redding, California's Enterprise School District is new to this edition.

Section I

Improvement Basics

1

An Aim for Education

Every system includes seven elements. An organization without each of the seven elements is a collection of parts, not a system. Brakes, engine, steering wheel, and transmission do not add up to a car that works. Likewise, teachers, buildings, budget, and instructional materials do not add up to a school system that works. Crucial to the understanding of Dr. Deming is the understanding of system. Dr. Deming was fond of citing the following example: you could bring to one location the dozen best cars in the world. The top automotive experts in the world could determine which car had the best engine, which had the best steering, which had the best brakes, and so on. These best parts could be collected from the best cars by the best experts, and what you would have is a collection of parts, but not one working automobile.

The automobile metaphor is crucial to understanding improvement. To have a working car, all the parts must be in place and they must work together. The seven components of a system are: aim, customers, suppliers, input, process, output, and quality measurement. If any component is missing or not in tandem with the other six parts, one has a collection of pieces, but not a system. Looking at education, one would have to conclude that it is a collection of pieces, not a system. Unfortunately, a mediocre school with one world-class part is often considered an above-average school. Never mind that the parts are not working together as a system.

The first requirement for a system is to have an aim. Without an aim the parts will never work together as a system. Spelling instruction is an example of an aimless segment of education. Spelling instruction in the United States has perfected its process. The process is a Friday test. But how do students know if they have accomplished success in spelling? They don't know, because nobody told them the *aim* in spelling. The spelling test in week one generally has nothing to do with week two spelling or any other week's spelling. It is merely a collecting of Friday tests that, when added up, equal a collection of tests. So, the first step in improving spelling instruction in any school district is to establish an aim. An example of a spelling aim is for students to know how to spell, by a particular grade, the 1000 words most often used in English.

Dr. Deming offered the following overall aim for education: "Increase the positives and decrease the negatives so that all students keep their yearning for learning."[1] He knew that if students could only keep the enthusiasm for learning that they had in kindergarten, then they could be successful in school. The aim of the educational system, for Dr. Deming, was to figure out which positives help students keep their joy and spread those positives to all classrooms. Conversely, educators must also determine the negatives that remove joy and eliminate those practices.

Over time I have come to believe the aim for education should be merely, "Increase success; decrease failure." School districts have several different divisions: personnel, finance, operations, and learning. The aim for education is to increase success and decrease failure in all four. What is success in personnel? What is failure? That is a value judgment for staff to agree upon and then work both to increase success and decrease failure. It might be agreed that success is hiring teachers who meet the needs of all or almost all students and failure is having teachers who meet the needs of nobody.

What is success and failure in finance? Success could be more money and failure could be spending money on items, such as trash pickup, that add no value to learning. The aim in finance, then, is to increase overall income and to decrease the money spent on items that add no value to learning. It's not that these items can go away completely, but they can be decreased.

Success and failure can be agreed upon for every aspect of schooling. *Improving Student Learning* is obviously about student learning, and little mention of operations, finance, and personnel will be made. An aim that encompasses all of education, however, is possible. Dr. Deming's aim for education can stand alone, or it can fit very nicely into the aim for learning.

Moving away from education's collection of parts to Dr. Deming's quality system requires an aim. Other system statements, such as a mission, tenets, and vision, are all valuable for planning, but a precise, all-encompassing aim is essential to beginning the process of educational improvement. The mission, tenets, and vision are rings on the organizational target; the aim is the bull's-eye.

ENDNOTE

1. W. E. Deming, American Association of School Administrators Conference, Washington, D.C. (January 1992).

2

Improvement Instead
of Change

E ducation in the United States is at the same place the automobile industry was several years ago. Every year a new model was intro- duced, but the car was essentially unchanged. A new chrome orna- ment, plus redesigned taillight, plus pinstriping, does not equal improvement. These are changes—maybe appealing changes—but nevertheless, merely changes. Likewise, education goes from change to change to change with little evidence of improvement. What comes to mind is a toddler on a rock- ing horse: lots of motion and spent energy, but the horse has not changed locations. Often these changes are written into law. For example, some states require new textbooks to be adopted every six or seven years. It is assumed that the change from the old textbook to the new textbook will be an improvement; but in fact it is only a change, without one shred of evi- dence that the new textbook results in any improvement. Change is a neu- tral word; it can represent a positive or a negative. Improvement, on the other hand, is defined as positive change.

How does one know if improvement has occurred? Two indicators must be in place before a change can be declared an improvement: fewer failures and more successes. Ideally, there is also less variation. Figure 2.1 displays two bell-shaped curves. The solid line represents the status of an organization before a change. The dotted line represents improvement.

The two curves could represent high school seniors, for example. In this case, the left of both curves represent students who are in prison or who have dropped out of school; the right of both curves represent students entering a university with advanced placement credit. An academic change

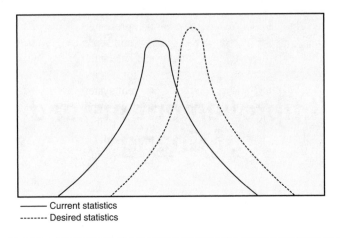

——— Current statistics
-------- Desired statistics

Figure 2.1 Improvement on the normal, bell-shaped curve.

at the high school can be declared an improvement when there are: (1) fewer dropouts, and (2) more students with advanced placement credit. Less variability in student accomplishment is also desirable, if this variation does not subtract from the successes of the most successful students. Again, Figure 2.1 is the desired picture of improvement.

Organizations often declare that an improvement has occurred when only the lower or the upper end of the curve has changed. For example, if a school has fewer dropouts, common sense would indicate this is improvement. One cannot tell, however, by looking at only the lower end of the curve. The school might have redirected resources to decrease dropouts but had far fewer students well prepared for the university. Such is merely a change in emphasis; it is not an improvement of the high school.

At other times, organizations declare that an improvement has occurred if the average exam score rises. This is a deceiving statistic. It is possible for a high school to raise the average score on an exam and at the same time have more dropouts. If five more students drop out of school and 10 more score slightly higher on an exam, the average might go up, but the high school has not improved.

Bright ideas appear constantly, but they should not be implemented right away. The bright idea decision must be delayed while the organization members gather data on the current situation. For example, somebody has a concept for improving school discipline. First the staff must gather data on what discipline the current system is producing. How many students are referred to the office in a year? How many students have had zero referrals, one referral, two referrals, three referrals, four, and so on, up to

10 or more referrals? The current system is represented by the solid line on the bell-shaped curve in Figure 2.1. The left end represents those students who are referred to the office up to 10 times. The right end represents those students who are never referred to the office for discipline. The appropriate time to listen to a bright idea is after the current system is documented.

If the changes from the bright idea result in improvement, then fewer students will be sent to the office a significant number of times, more students will have no referrals, and ideally the range will be narrower. Data from Pine Island, Minnesota, Middle School are shown in Figures 2.2 and 2.3.

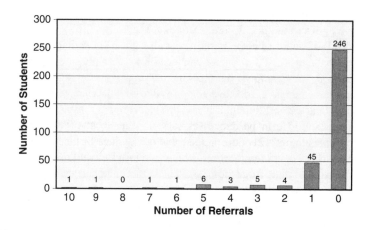

Figure 2.2   First three quarters of 2001–02, Pine Island Middle School.

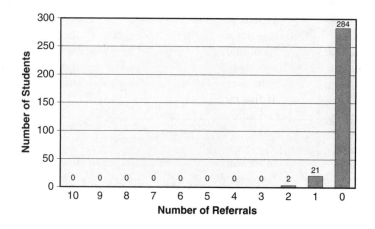

Figure 2.3   Fourth quarter referrals, Pine Island, 2001–02.

Figure 2.2 represents the educational output before any changes in discipline practice. The time period is the first three quarters of 2001–02. Figure 2.3 represents the output after changes in the fourth quarter of 2001–02. In this situation, it can be declared that improvement has occurred because fewer students are experiencing failure in discipline and more are experiencing success. The change was the development of a student leadership class taught by the principal, Darren Overton. All students with more than one referral during the first three quarters were in the class. Basically, the class was a time for the principal to listen and a time for the students to analyze causes of their behavior. They expected to be chastised but were awed that the principal desired to hear their input on improving the school as a whole, and discipline practices in particular. Figure 2.4 shows the totals for all of 2001–02 and thus is the baseline data for 2002–03 to determine if any changes made in '02–03 are mere changes or are actually improvements.

Improving Student Learning describes the process for achieving improved results. Figures 2.2 and 2.3 document improved results; the changes made during the school year *did* result in improvement. The central purpose of this book is explaining how to improve processes so that better results will be present. When administrators accept the premise that one of their jobs is to continually make the school a safer place, versus merely punishing whomever is sent to them, there is a definite process available to accomplish creating a safer school. Pine Island examples are shared during the remainder of this chapter, the purpose being to introduce readers to some of what is necessary when educators commit themselves to being involved only in change that has a chance of becoming improvement.

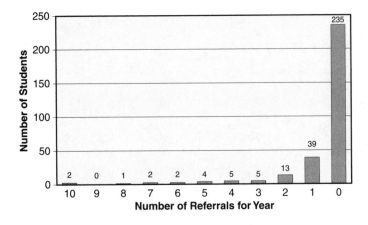

Figure 2.4 Referrals totals for 2001–02: Pine Island.

The first process step is publicly posting the numbers, in this case the number of weekly referrals. Students, parents, and teachers need to know this total: no details, just the totals (Figure 2.5 from Pine Island Middle School). Schools have a choice of posting referrals weekly or daily; then a simple dot and connecting line are added to the graph each week or each day. The next step is to reduce the number of referrals. The improvement process continually presented in *Improving Student Learning* is: (1) gathering data, (2) constructing graphs, (3) gaining insight from studying the graphs, (4) testing hypotheses, and (5) increasing knowledge from hypotheses testing.

In this discipline example, Darren has data (the stack of referrals), graphed data, and now he needs insight. Insight comes from studying disaggregated data. His student discipline committee generates hypotheses by discussing the insights gained from this disaggregated data. His discipline committee is composed of students randomly chosen from the total student body. Seventeen is approximately the square root of the Pine Island student body and is an adequate sample size. Figures 2.6 through 2.13 are examples of the disaggregated graphs produced by or for students in their committee.

In 2002–03, Pine Island added to the above list by correlating, with a scatter diagram, phases of the moon and temperature. One of the science teachers had students collect the moon phase and temperature data for the discipline committee. Also, the time of day was expanded beyond morning and afternoon, to include before school, morning class, morning passing period, lunch, afternoon class, afternoon passing period, and after school.

One of the most interesting discoveries, made from studying Figure 2.5 is that the last two weeks of each quarter were the most difficult behavior

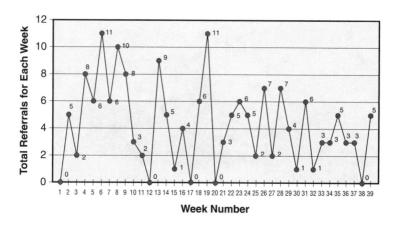

Figure 2.5 Referrals each week in Pine Island.

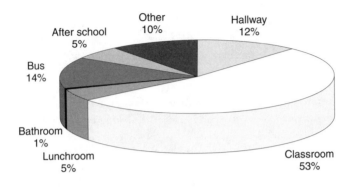

Figure 2.6   Pine Island Middle School discipline incidents by location, 2001–02.

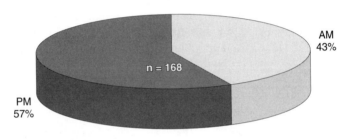

Figure 2.7   Pine Island Middle School referrals by time of day, AM or PM, 2001–02.

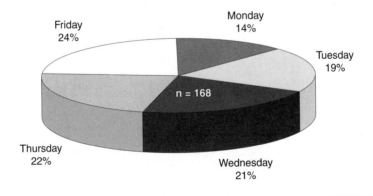

Figure 2.8   Pine Island Middle School discipline referrals by day of the week, 2001–02.

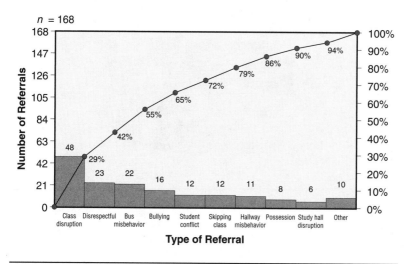

Figure 2.9 Pine Island Pareto chart—student discipline 2001–02.

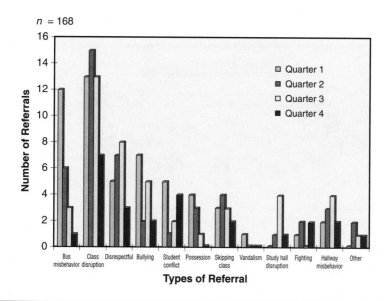

Figure 2.10 Pine Island grades 6–8 type and number of referrals by quarter, 2001–02.

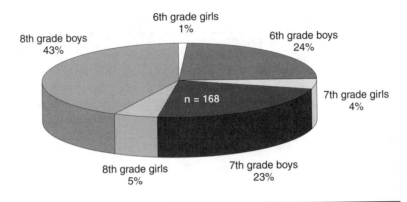

Figure 2.11   Pine Island Middle School discipline referrals by grade level and gender, 2001–02.

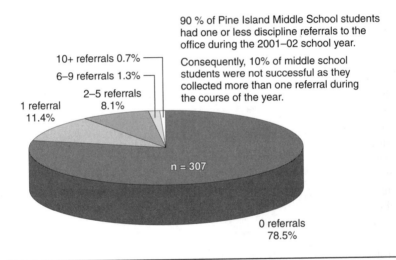

90 % of Pine Island Middle School students had one or less discipline referrals to the office during the 2001–02 school year.

Consequently, 10% of middle school students were not successful as they collected more than one referral during the course of the year.

Figure 2.12   Pine Island Middle School discipline referrals.

times for the school. This helped faculty see that the problem was the system (for which they are responsible), not the students. If the problems were student-generated, then the misbehavior would not consistently occur the last two weeks of the quarter, but would be evenly spread out.

In every instance, privacy of staff and students is to be protected. The goal is not to blame people, but to gain insight into how the discipline system can be improved.

From the graphed data, students on the discipline committee generate hypotheses regarding how safety and behavior can be improved. Agreement is reached regarding which hypotheses to test, the results are posted, and the committee comes together regularly to study overall results. Everybody concerned will know if changes result in improvement; the wait is only three to four weeks long.

Some readers will wonder if there's time to analyze data in such a manner. Everybody already has an overflowing plate full of duties. Chapter 2 is all about how to stop wasting time moving from change to change to change. If the downward spiral of change-but-no-improvement is to stop, some up-front time will need to be invested. Sometimes educators will just spend the evenings and/or weekends with the data in order to set up an improvement process. Other times, a principal with three assistant principals, for example, will say, "You two are to take care of the discipline problems while the third one is freed up to establish the process described in this book that will reduce misbehavior." Darren reports that the significant time savings occurred during year two (2002–03) of his continuous improvement efforts.

Many potentially great principals never become principals because they don't want to spend three to five years of their life punishing students who are sent to them. These great teachers, with such leadership potential, need to see that the job, if assigned discipline, is to establish a discipline improvement system as done in Pine Island by Darren Overton. With this attitude, the job of assistant principal has a whole new meaning. The new assistant principals now have laboratories; they are able to learn the improvement process. Once they are principals, they will know how to stop change after change after change and infuse continual improvement into the fabric of schooling.

Dr. Deming fully recognized that teachers and other leaders have much to manage. They cannot set aside all their time to work on improvement. He wrote, "We must of course solve problems and stamp out fires as they occur, but these activities do not change the system."[1] It is a deep sense of purpose that propels leaders to manage resources and time so that all energy is not used up stamping out fires.

ENDNOTE

1. W. Edwards Deming, *Schools and Communities Cooperating for Quality— Lessons for Leaders* (seminar sponsored by American Association of School Administrators, Alexandria, VA, 1990): 2.

Section II

Dr. W. Edwards Deming

3

Theory of Profound Knowledge

W hy do leaders need to know profound knowledge? Who are the leaders? First of all, teachers are the most numerous leaders in education. They have a significant number of people reporting to them. Although the people who report to teachers are sometimes shorter and almost always younger than they are, this should not detract from the fact that teachers have many direct reports. Everything Dr. W. Edwards Deming wrote about profound knowledge for leaders applies equally to teachers and administrators.

Without significant knowledge, teachers and administrators follow the exact same slippery path. They start their new position believing they have enough knowledge to be successful. When they find they don't, they then revert to personality. "If I am nice enough, the people who report to me will do what I say and we'll all be better off." It doesn't work, so the only alternative available is power. Dr. Deming states that leaders have only three assets: power, personality, and knowledge. Teachers and administrators who manage with knowledge have the most long-term success.

Some people, however, are blessed with an incredible personality; people like them and do what they ask. So, they begin their teaching career with personality and 25 years later are relying upon personality alone. It seems to work, but is not nearly as wonderful a tool as knowledge. Of course we should use our personalities, but they cannot be our foundation. All readers have probably observed a personality-based leader fail through a succession of promotions. Personality worked in the classroom; the kids responded. Mr. or Mrs. Personality became principal; personality still worked. Mr. or Mrs. Personality became the superintendent; personality was not enough. Why? Personality works well when the people for whom a leader is responsible are in the same building; it depends upon constant interaction. At the central office this daily contact is not possible, so personality becomes a very weak foundation.

Knowledge that the prevailing style of management (power or personality based) must change is necessary but not sufficient. We must know what changes to make. Profound knowledge appears in four parts: appreciation for a system, epistemology (theory of knowledge), psychology, and variation. In Dr. Deming's last book, *The New Economics*, he outlined his management philosophy as divided into these four categories. The four following descriptions are not intended to compete with the complete thoughts of Dr. Deming, but are meant as a commentary and bridge between Dr. Deming's thoughts and educational applications.

SYSTEM

Merit pay for teachers seems to make sense. Why not pay exemplary teachers more money? After all, in other professions those who work a 10- to 12-hour day generally earn more money than those who work a six- to eight-hour day. Some teachers are inferior and almost everyone knows who they are. Some teachers are average; they meet the needs of half of the students. But some teachers are exemplary; they meet the needs of all students with maybe an occasional failure. So why not pay them more?

The faulty logic behind merit pay proposals is the same inadequate thinking supporting most educational reform. The nonsystem thinker purports to improve the whole of education by tinkering with some parts of the system. Merit pay advocates naively believe that changing the salary schedule will improve learning. (Unions often have the same belief, just a different concept of change to the salary schedule.)

Several years ago, I spent a weekend with a membership organization's board of directors. For the last five years the organization had been losing members. Because of this failure, the board was most willing to listen to Dr. Deming's philosophy. A synopsis of my questions and the board's answers follows:

Q: What has your sales record been like the past five years?

A: Between 8 percent and 10 percent new customers each year.

Q: How about lost members?

A: We've been losing approximately 12 percent of our membership each year.

Q: What are your current plans to improve?

A: We are providing a free trip to Hawaii for each salesperson who meets his or her quota [merit pay]. If all sales staff meet their quota, we'll reverse the downward spiral.

Q: Is the trip incentive working?

A: It is too soon to tell, but 40 percent to 60 percent of the sales staff seem discouraged, believing they'll never meet their quota.

Q: What is your biggest problem? Obtaining new members or keeping current members?

A: Keeping members.

Q: Which members of your staff have the most to do with keeping members?

A: Office staff.

Q: Not the sales staff?

A: No.

Q: Is the office staff afforded the opportunity to win a trip to Hawaii?

A: No.

Q: Why?

A: We haven't looked at the whole company this way. We thought the solution to our problem was more sales.

Q: If the problem is net loss of members, wouldn't it be better if everybody could go to Hawaii when the five-year trend of losing members is reversed?

A: That means the secretaries might go to Hawaii? We hadn't considered this.

Q: Does this line of questioning help you understand a little of Dr. Deming's thinking about a system?

A: Yes.

I'm writing now at 30,000 feet. One requirement for completion of this book is a safe landing. The whole air transportation system must work together for a safe landing. I have little interest in a bonus for the pilot if the mechanics didn't do their job correctly. Everyone understands the need for the whole air transportation system to work together because the flights begin and end within a period of a few hours.

The school system, however, starts and ends over a 13-year period. Public schooling will survive the current crisis only when the whole system improves. Customers (students) and stakeholders (parents) must have a system that works together to produce quality high school graduates. Most reform efforts address only a subsystem. Merit pay, for example, makes only a few people happy. Charter schools allow some children to attend a different school (not necessarily better) for a few years. A charter school spanning all grades, K–12, has the opportunity to address system improvement, but other charter schools are only tinkering with a subsystem of education. Dropout prevention programs are also a subsystem. Special and bilingual education are subsystems. Anyone can cite attempts to improve subsystems, often at the expense of the whole system.

One recent reporting of improving a portion of education at the expense of the whole of education is California's recent class size reduction in grades K–3 from over 30 per class to 20. School administrators were given five weeks to implement class size reduction. Researchers have been asked to determine if this expenditure of $1 billion per year improved student learning at the end of third grade. The report states that yes, learning improved in many locales, but sometimes not in the places most in need. Why? Because so many jobs were available in the suburbs, teachers left their urban posts for jobs closer to their homes. A portion of the schools won at the expense of the whole. The teacher interns hired by the urban districts often could not help students as well as the departing teachers.[1]

Actually, it is my opinion that the researchers were given the wrong question to answer. A more important question would be, "Are students leaving elementary school more prepared for middle school because of class size reduction?" The limited data I have suggest they are not better prepared for middle school. The fourth and fifth grade teachers who did not change districts moved, over time, from their classrooms of 34 down the hall to second and third grades with 20 students. The huge teacher shortage created by class size reduction in California was filled by novices in many urban areas and suburban fourth and fifth grades. The point here is not to argue against 20 in a classroom versus 30 or more. The point is that leaders can easily make decisions, with the best of intentions, which suboptimize the system. A *portion* of the system wins, but the *whole* system does not.

Prakash Nair wrote, "But what is the system? In almost every case, it is an enterprise broken up into a predefined series of fields and compartments. There are groups responsible for transportation, food and nutrition, building construction and maintenance, curriculum, security, administration, technology, community relations, special education, early-childhood programs, and on and on. Maybe there was a distant time when these groups all operated under one set of guiding principles oriented toward improving student learning, but today they operate more or less as disparate entitites."[2]

When Dr. Deming suggested replacing the traditional organizational chart with a system view, he diagrammed a profound school restructuring vision. His system view of organizations published in 1986 is the foundation for the education system view shown in Figure 3.1.

Dr. Deming's system view had only one input location. My variation of his system view for education has two input locales—one for the supply and one for the K–12 system itself. Education improvement depends not only on improved input to the system, but improved input to the supply.

A system is a network of components within an organization that work together for the aim of the organization. Note that all seven system elements are included on the system diagram in Figure 3.1. The paragraphs that follow explain the seven elements and contrast the system diagram with the traditional organizational chart.

1. *Education has customers.* The word *customer* is not on traditional organizational charts. Education's customers are the students. As K–12 organizations study quality principles in more detail, their members identify more customers, such as universities, employers, teachers at the next grade level, and other external and internal customers. These discussions are healthy once consensus has been reached that the students are the prime customers: they live the rest of their lives with the services they receive in the K–12 school systems.

2. *Education needs an aim.* Aim is not on traditional organizational charts. Education currently has many people working toward their own aims. Increase success and decrease failure is my suggested aim for education.

3. *Education can improve its supply. Suppliers* are not on traditional organizational charts. Educators often think there's nothing they can do about supply. They must accept all children who live within their school district boundaries. The second sentence is true, but the first is not. Whatever the aim of education, it is in the best interest of school districts to assign some of their most talented teachers to helping parents and preschool teachers better prepare students for school success.

4. *Process: Grade levels must be linked.* Only the job classification of the teacher is on the traditional organizational chart, not the process and grade levels. The amount of time necessary to coordinate education between grade levels is no more than the amount of time necessary to coordinate the design of the components of an automobile. The term being used

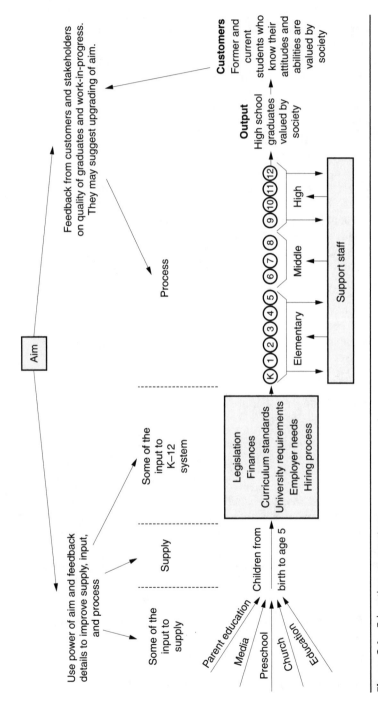

Figure 3.1   Education as a system.

for this linking is *alignment,* but because of the pressure to raise test scores, alignment has come to mean "align our work with the tests." Here I am not speaking of test alignment, but of aligning the work of teachers, grade levels, and schools. The other aspect of process is *methods.* Which combination of methods are we using in order to have all students improve?

5. *Education has output. Output* is not mentioned on traditional organizational charts. Education produces graduates qualified for universities, colleges, military and technical schools, and also produces graduates prepared neither technologically nor for college admission. Education also produces dropouts. The term *produce* is repulsive to educators because Americans live in a blaming society. Some students never had a book read to them prior to entering kindergarten; some have little or no love; some are abused; some move every three months; and many are full of alcohol, tobacco, and other toxins. Educators don't want to be blamed for society's failures. Educators do, however, have the responsibility to improve education, which quite simply means producing fewer unprepared graduates, fewer dropouts, and more prepared graduates. Nobody believes that all dropouts will be eliminated or that every student will graduate prepared for university education, but gradual, continual improvement in graduate production is attainable.

6. *Education needs quality measurement. Quality measurement* is not mentioned on traditional organizational charts. State laws mandate that principals evaluate their teachers. This has limited value. Instead, legislators should demand that school boards orchestrate the collection of quality measurements from their customers and stakeholders. Ranking is not quality measurement. If it was, this book would not be necessary.

7. *Education has input.* Most input is from state and federal government. *Input* is not mentioned on traditional organizational charts. Legislators need to view education as a system for which they are responsible. Educators are not in control of the education system; noneducators elected to the legislatures or placed in judicial chairs control it. Dr. Deming frequently asked, "Who has the most control over a ship crossing the ocean?" After captain, engine room boss, and navigator were rejected as answers, he said, "The designer of the ship. The ship can never do better than its design will allow."[3]

Legislators designed the education ship. They legislate what the government will pay for (attendance, collective bargaining, grant awards, and so on); the requirements to be a teacher or administrator; the requirements to fire a teacher or administrator; the number of school days the government will pay for each year; that the demands of special education attorneys must be met no matter what the effect on other students; and thousands of other rules that require compliance. Legislatures control most of the input.

The elements of a system are: aim, supply, input, process, output, customer, and quality measurement. If any one of the elements is missing, there is no system—only parts. Since improvement is the goal, all seven elements must be studied. All components of the system must work together toward the aim of the system. Dr. Deming called all components working together *optimization.* Suboptimization, as in merit pay or special interest legislation, is one part of the system winning at the expense of the whole.

EPISTEMOLOGY

Epistemology is the study of how people come to know; sometimes people are taught, sometimes they research, sometimes they observe, sometimes they learn through pain, and so forth. Jean Piaget spent his professional life documenting the learning process at all ages of childhood. Dr. Deming would not be considered a foremost epistemologist, as was Jean Piaget. Nevertheless, Dr. Deming has significant epistemological insights for educators.

Readers should not be surprised that Dr. Deming's epistemological theories run counter to prevailing practice. For example, he states that experience is not the best teacher. If experience were the very best teacher, then we'd have no more problems. A recent example of how true his statement is comes from the 2000 U.S. presidential election. The United States has significant experience conducting elections and yet had a problem only the Supreme Court could solve with a split vote. When people first hear that experience is not the best teacher, they think Dr. Deming said experience is not a teacher. He didn't say people don't learn from experience; it's just not the best teacher.

If experience is not the best teacher, then what is the best teacher? The best teacher is testing theory. This does not mean dissertation and thesis. What Dr. Deming wanted us to do was substitute the words *method, policy, rules, plan,* and *education law* with the word *theory.* He then wanted us to collect data to inform us if the new plan, method, or law brought about improvement. A new discipline policy should be called the new discipline theory; it is currently being tested. If the theory is accurate, then more students will behave and fewer will misbehave. After the theory is tested, then comes the opportunity to turn the theory into standard practice.

One of the most significant aspects of using the process outlined in chapters 4 through 7 is that a teacher can test an instructional practice and know in a few weeks if it works. Fifteen years in a classroom gaining experience is not what makes a teacher knowledgeable; the continual testing of theories creates the expert teacher.

The second aspect of Dr. Deming's epistemological theory is the distinction between information and knowledge. Often educators use the phrase "what students know and can do." Dr. Deming's use of the simple words *information* and *knowledge* is much more meaningful in designing educational improvement.

Dr. Deming defined *information* as facts about the past. A dictionary is full of information, yet it has no knowledge. Spelling is a subject studied in schools that relates the past to today's youth. It communicates how people in the past agreed to spell particular words. *Knowledge,* by contrast, is about the future. Writing is a subject studied in schools that is about the future: How can something be written so readers in the future will better understand? Students who become proficient in writing can help create a better future for themselves and others.

Every subject taught in schools has both information and knowledge. The educational pendulum swings to and fro, placing emphasis on information and then knowledge and then back to information. The reality is that both knowledge and information have importance and need clear aims. The following provides some examples of information and knowledge gained from school subjects:

Subject	Information	Knowledge
Mathematics	Concepts	Problem solving
Language	Spelling; pronunciation	Writing; reading with understanding
Art	Technique identification	Producing own work
Business Education	Check writing	Balancing an account
Science	Definitions	Using scientific method
History	Chronology	Relating current events to past
Geography	Locations	Relating economy to geography
Music	Composer identification	Producing or performing music

Dr. Deming's use of the words information and knowledge provides deeper insight into the meaning of "what students know and can do." In this second edition, however, I use the terms *essential information* and *performance.* Essential information and performance are more precise than other terms, but no matter which words are chosen, Dr. Deming's understanding of information and knowledge is powerful for educators.

How many examples contrary to a theory does one need prior to it being necessary to change the theory? For example, a theory I was told early in my teaching career was that students are more prolific in their writing when they write first and edit second. I accepted this theory as truth and taught as if it were true for all students. I learned later, with the help of my son Todd, that the theory is not valid for all. Some students must know how to spell the word *right now,* or the writing stops. So, how many examples contrary to the theory does one need before rewriting the theory? One example is all that is needed. If I had known Dr. Deming's epistemological theory, then I would have revised my theory instead of attempting to force students into an incorrect theory.

Examples abound regarding how school personnel persist with theories that don't fit all students. Three examples are: (1) punishment improves behavior for all students, (2) phonics is necessary in order for all students to read, and (3) all high school students must pass required courses before being enrolled in electives. Some children are so embittered through punishment that they behave worse; a minority of children are so confused by phonics generalizations that their reading success is damaged; and some ninth graders, scheduled for all core courses, drop out before having elective success.

Yes, most students are more prolific in their writing when they put down their thoughts first and edit second. Most students behave better because of the fear of punishment. Most students are helped by some phonics generalizations and most students progress nicely from general course requirements to specialty courses. But not all fit these patterns. Educators must remember: it takes only *one* example contrary to our theory to force us to rethink our theory. Coming up with the new theory is not easy, but knowing that one contrary example refutes the theory starts the learning process. Epistemology is about "coming to know."

Accepting the fact that "one example contrary to our theory" forces us right back to testing theories. A ninth grade counselor, for example, faced with a dozen incoming freshmen whose indicators predict they will not be successful in high school, could schedule the dozen in only one required course with a teacher known to be successful with at-risk students and then schedule the rest of the day in elective courses of interest to the students. When the students have success in these courses and are more mature, they then will be scheduled into the required graduation classes. The hypothesis, to be tested, is that more students will graduate after having a freshmen and sophomore year of credits than graduate with two years of D's and F's.

Maybe the hypothesis I've proposed is false; I don't know, but I do know that the current practice of scheduling *all* the students into general classes first is wrong. When we find one student who does not fit the theory, then we must change the theory.

The fourth component of Dr. Deming's epistemology is the admonition to learn from the masters; they are few. Only once was I given this advice in a formal way. It was as a doctoral student at The Claremont Graduate University. My major professor, Malcolm Douglass, asked, "Have you had a course from Peter Drucker?" I replied that I had not and was told, "You don't want to leave Claremont without at least one Drucker course. It doesn't matter which one, but you must learn from him." The reasons for reading professional books and attending conferences is to find the masters and learn, learn, learn.

Student teachers are assigned based upon the theory that experience is the best teacher. Universities spread out the student teachers so that everyone can have their two weeks of *experience* taking over the class on their own. Now, student teachers might not be ready to test many theories, but they are ready to learn from the masters. If education were to accept Dr. Deming's admonition to learn from the masters, then the universities might assign 12 student teachers and one professor to a single classroom for a semester. Students would not have the traditional two weeks of experience, but would be much better prepared for their first year of teaching by watching a genius at work. Twice in my career I was able to watch genius teachers at work. The first was Evelyn Neufeld and the second Marion Nordberg. Nobody provided time for this; it was snippets of time from lunch hours and so forth. Life was never the same after observing and questioning these masters. Dr. Deming was right: search for the masters and learn from them.

It is the responsibility of leaders to create more leaders. When school districts set out to invest in their teachers' learning, many become leaders. I have found that it takes from 50 to 100 days of staff development for a teacher to have the necessary knowledge to provide significant leadership in a district. It the money now spent adopting new programs, adopting more new programs, and adopting even more new programs were spent developing leaders, schools would be in a far better position. School districts need student leaders, teacher leaders, custodian leaders, secretary leaders, principal leaders, and yes, even superintendent leaders. We cannot have too many leaders because there are too many aspects of schooling for any one person to know it all. Some schools have formalized this aspect of epistemology by helping every student in the oldest grade of a school do something for the good of the whole school. In a school district organized K–5, 6–8, and 9–12, for example, all the fifth-, eighth-, and 12th-graders are expected to provide service for the good of the whole school.

Epistemology, as stated earlier in this chapter, is the study of how people "come to know." By applying the theoretical statements of Dr. Deming into the very fabric of people and institutions, much more learning will take place and thus the system will possess much more student success and much less student failure.

PSYCHOLOGY

Never did I expect to pick up books written by a person who spent most of his career advising manufacturers and clarify my thinking on child psychology. Prior to reading Dr. Deming, I had questions but no coherent theory. I questioned the motivation admonition given to teachers. I seriously wondered if it was the responsibility of teachers to artificially motivate students. When my preparation matched student interests, students were motivated; and when my preparation had nothing to do with what the students wanted to learn, my motivation tricks failed. Dr. Deming provided a coherent, simple psychology theory.

Instead of thinking that one must motivate children, Dr. Deming reminded us that all children are born motivated to learn. Educators are meant not to motivate children to learn, but to discover what demotivates them, and stop those practices. He wrote, "We have been destroying our people, from toddlers on through the university, and on the job. We must preserve the power of intrinsic motivation, dignity, cooperation, curiosity, and joy in learning that people are born with. . . . All the qualities that have been traditionally and erroneously applied to competition actually apply better to cooperation. Cooperation builds character, is basic to human nature, and makes learning more enjoyable and productive."[4] America's obsession with competition is destroying the inborn motivation to learn.

The basic tenets of Western-society management destroy natural motivation. All of the tricks that are designed to motivate children actually have the opposite effect—they demotivate. Examples of such tricks are prizes for reading, stickers for completed work, grades, money for grades, and graphs comparing children's progress. Audiences from every U.S. state generally agree that students between kindergarten and grade 12 receive over 10,000 incentives (five per day times 180 school days times 13 years). If the extrinsic theories were correct, America's seniors should be the most motivated people on the face of the earth.

I am often asked why systems are in place that systematically demotivate students. I believe David Elkind gave us the most significant answer to this question. He wrote, "One of the most serious and pernicious misunderstandings about young children is that they are most like adults in their thinking and least like us in their feelings. In fact, just the reverse is true, and children are most like us in their feelings and least like us in their thinking."[5]

It really isn't difficult to determine what has the long-term effect of destroying student motivation. Try out the practice on the teachers first. If it demotivates teachers, then it will demotivate students. Even if children are initially excited about a prize, the long-term effect on children will be the same as the long-term effect on teachers. For example, if a school has a problem with teachers forgetting their duties, the principal could put up a chart in the staff room with the name of each teacher. Stickers would be placed daily next to the names of the teachers who remember their duties. If the staff room chart motivates teachers to dedicate themselves even more deeply to their profession, then the same technique will help children keep their inborn motivation for learning.

Once teachers internalize that: (1) everyone is born motivated, (2) the management techniques they have observed throughout their lives demotivate, and (3) whatever demotivates adults also demotivates children, then they are ready to use with students only the management techniques they want their principals to use on them.

Students are on a 13-year, K–12, formal learning train. Those who reach the graduation depot, having completed advanced placement courses, are extremely well prepared for the world-class economy. The name of the track that takes the learning train to the depot is *motivation*. Students enter kindergarten with a complete track ahead of them. Adults and the culture of schooling systematically dismantle the railroad ties until few students have a working track by age 18. It's very simple—no track equals a derailed learning train.

Beyond the facts that all children are born motivated to learn and educators have the responsibility to maintain this enthusiasm, Dr. Deming provides five other key psychological truths:

1. Most people, once discouraged, stay that way. How often do people say, "I loved math in grades 2, 5, and 8?" What everybody normally hears is, "I loved math until grade X, and then I never liked it again."

2. Children don't destroy their own motivation; adults do. These adults can be teachers, cooks, secretaries, church leaders, scout volunteers, parents, or relatives.

3. There's no shortage of good people unless people create it. No teachers set out to create a shortage of good adults. It is safe to say, however, that

almost every teacher is part of a K–12 system using Western-society management techniques that systematically creates shortages of good people. For example, the typical school district with 1000 first-graders rarely has 100 in calculus. We systematically destroy the love of mathematics and then import mathematicians from other countries.

4. Ranking destroys joy. No adult I'm aware of wants to be publicly and badly ranked in anything. Even in a simple game of Scrabble, no one wants to be ranked last. Sure, the pain of losing at Scrabble is over in two minutes, but adults still don't like it. Consider being ranked for something important. The major way educators rank is with grades. Grades destroy joy. Destruction of joy destroys learning. Built into Dr. Deming's complete theories are the necessary tools to eliminate ranking through grades while, at the same time, being more accountable to the public.

5. The customer defines joy. When I am the customer at a restaurant, I determine whether the dining experience is joyful. I am the customer. In schools, the students define joy. It is the students' morale that must be of prime importance.

The memory of Education 101 must disappear. Future teachers need no longer be admonished to motivate as a part of every lesson plan. Dr. Deming's simple psychology must replace Education 101. Life comes with built-in motivation.

VARIATION

Every teacher knows the frustration caused by the wide range of ability in a single classroom. Kindergarten teachers face five-year-olds who know how to read and other five-year-olds who don't know if a book is upside down or not. High schools have both students reading like an average third-grader (usually these become dropouts) and students earning college credit while still in high school.

Some students attend the same school system for the 13 years of their K–12 education. Some students attend 50 or more schools in 13 years. Some students are rarely absent; others are rarely present. Members of service clubs know this. After spending their entire lunch complaining about the morning's poorly-written job applications, they award a $1000 college scholarship to an incredibly talented 17-year-old senior.

Variation is the enemy of education; it is also the enemy of business. The quality of service and product varies among different stores in the same chain. Not all products manufactured from the same factory, on the same day, operate equally well.

Variation is such a problem that Dr. Deming wrote, "The central problem of management . . . is to understand the meaning of variation, and to extract the information contained in variation."[6]

Understanding variation means educators must accept that variation will always be present. No amount of educational research, reform, or referendum will eliminate variation. Some variation is caused by unusual events; some variation is built into the system; and some is just probability, both good and bad. Variation just *is.*

Even though variation *is,* leaders have the responsibility to reduce it. When teachers first hear this they are repulsed because they think uniqueness is to be reduced. Nothing could be further from the truth. Uniqueness is prized. Uniqueness is not a problem; variation is the problem that must be reduced.

For example, a fifth grade teacher might have students whose reading abilities range from that of an average first-grader to that of an average 11th-grader. Reducing variation in reading would improve education.

Not so, say the parents of students who are reading at high levels. The picture they have of reducing variation is Figure 3.2, which is the opposite of Dr. Deming's view of improvement and reducing variation (see Figure 2.1 in chapter 2).

Yes, the poorest students are to be helped, but not at the expense of the better readers. Figure 3.2 is not what Dr. Deming meant by reducing variation. Decisions that take away from one part of the organization and give to another part of the organization are not improvement; they are merely a shift of resources. Figure 3.2 represents an economic picture of socialism, which in no way represents Dr. Deming's thinking.

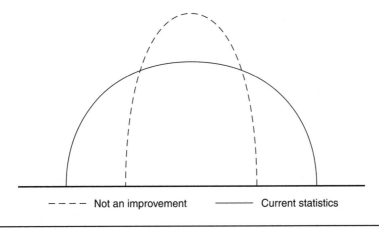

‒ ‒ ‒ ‒ Not an improvement   ───── Current statistics

Figure 3.2 The opposite of Dr. Deming's view of reduced variation.

In Figure 2.1, fifth-graders' reading ability (first grade through 11th grade level) is represented by the solid line. The dotted line represents Dr. Deming's idea of reduced variation, which shows that after an improvement, fifth grade classes had students reading between the third and 12th grade levels. The variation is reduced from 10 grades (11–1) to 9 grades (12–3). Dr. Deming's concept of reducing variation encompasses improvement whereby there is not only a reduction of variation, but fewer failures and more successes.

The seven key elements of Dr. Deming's statistical thinking are:

1. Variation is always present.

2. Variation is the enemy.

3. The purpose of statistics is to help decision-makers reduce variation.

4. The key responsibility of management is to reduce variation.

5. Through the use of statistical control charts, managers can determine whether variation is caused by special events outside the system or by common causes within the system (see chapter 22).

6. Ninety-seven percent of what occurs in organizations cannot be measured but must be managed anyway.

7. Through statistics, one can more nearly predict the future. For example, if one knows the number of dropouts in a school district for the past 10 years, one can predict the number of dropouts next year with greater precision. It is very easy to predict the number of D's and F's that any particular teacher will give next year; look at the records for the last few years.

8. Do not set numerical goals. Setting political numbers for growth does great harm. The July 10, 2002 edition of *Education Weekly* reports, "State officials are frustrated and worried over a lack of federal guidance on setting annual performance targets for schools, as required by the nation's major education law."[7] Dr. Deming would not have us "pull numbers out of the air" but only hold schools accountable for a pattern of improvement. This means that in most years there will be fewer students experiencing failure and more students experiencing success.

"Management is about the future; nobody should be paid much for counting up the past."[8] The required statistics in most undergraduate and graduate courses help educators count up the past. Quality measurement is completely different; it's about creating a better future.

Successful managers of people do develop their personality and their knowledge. They rarely rely upon power. They have, nevertheless, an obligation to use power, as this source of power enables them to change the system—equipment, materials, methods—to bring improvement. They are in authority, but if they lack knowledge or personality then they must depend upon their power. They unconsciously fill a void in their qualifications by making it clear to everybody that theirs is a position of authority.[9]

Teachers, principals, superintendents, board members, and other leaders are all tempted to use power too often. It is well understood in education that personality and persuasion are valuable tools, but knowledge is the key resource to keep from abusing power. Dr. Deming's profound knowledge fills a vacuum in educational knowledge. Table 3.1 provides a summary of profound knowledge.

Table 3.1 Summary of profound knowledge.

System	Epistemology	Psychology	Variation
Aim	Information about the past	People are born motivated	Always present
Customers	Knowledge for a better future	Once discouraged, most stay that way	The enemy
Supply	Learn from Masters	Adults destroy motivation	Statistics reduce variation
Input	One contrary example equals wrong theory	Society creates a shortage of good people	Primary responsibility of management
Process	Better predict the future with knowledge	Ranking destroys joy	Special and common cause variation
Output	Create more leaders	Customer defines joy	97% of occurrences cannot be measured
Quality measurement	Experience alone provides limited knowledge		Statistics help managers better predict the future

ENDNOTES

1. D. Hoff, L. Olson, and J. Sack, "Teaching and Learning," *Education Week* (July 10, 2002): 60.
2. P. Nair, "But Are They Learning?" *Education Week* (April 3, 2002): 60.
3. W. E. Deming, American Association of School Administrators Conference, Washington, D.C. (January, 1992).
4. W. E. Deming, *Schools and Communities Cooperating for Quality—Lessons for Leaders* (seminar sponsored by American Association of School Administrators, Alexandria, VA, 1990): 1, 14.
5. D. Elkind, *Children and Adolescents* (New York: Oxford University Press, 1974): 51.
6. W. E. Deming, *Out of the Crisis* (Cambridge, MA: MIT Press, 1986): 20.
7. L. Olson and E. Roelen, "Frustration Grows as States Await 'Adequate Yearly Progress' " *Education Week* (July 10, 2002): 1, 41.
8. See note 3.
9. See note 4.

4

Dr. Deming's 1992 Advice and the Three Basic Graphs

In a 1992 seminar sponsored by the American Association of School Administrators, Dr. Deming suggested a radically different way to manage learning. It has now been used from preschool to graduate school in many different U.S. states and beyond. His simple suggestion, that soon becomes profound and not quite so simple, is:

1. Provide the students the information they are expected to learn by the end of the course.

2. Each week, randomly select a sample of the total amount of information and quiz the students on these items. The square root is an ample sample size.

3. After correcting the quiz, count up the total correct for the whole class and make a class run chart.

4. Next, use the same data to make a scatter diagram.

During the 1992–93 school year, Damon Cropsey of the Enterprise District in Redding, California, completed the first-ever complete run chart and scatter diagram according to Dr. Deming's educational advice. He selected 100 locations in the United States that he wanted his fifth grade students to know. In addition to the 50 states, he selected 50 rivers, cities, mountains, and lakes.

Figures 4.1 and 4.2 are reproductions of the class run chart and scatter diagram Damon constructed.

The exact process Damon used was to provide the students with the list of 100 locations. He related that this was the most difficult aspect of the task, determining exactly what he wanted the students to know at the end

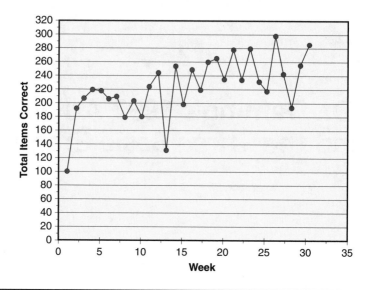

Figure 4.1   Class run chart for fifth-grade Geography.

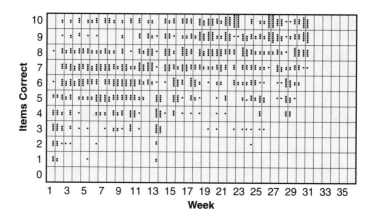

Figure 4.2   Class scatter diagram for fifth-grade Geography.

of the year. He could have selected 75, 250, or any other number of locations, but 100 seemed reasonable to him. He also used a 100-sided die,[1]
which the students loved. It is worth noting that Damon did not select the
50 capitals. Common sense says that it is more important for students in
California to know where Chicago is than to know where Springfield,
Illinois, is located. In addition, students in the United States need to know

the location of the Rocky and Appalachian Mountains; the Great Lakes; and the Mississippi, Ohio, and Missouri Rivers. They certainly need to know what a capital is and what occurs in a nation's or state's capital that occurs in no other cities, but they don't need to memorize the capitals.

The first week of school, Damon gave the students a quiz on 10 of the locations. Ten was chosen based upon Dr. Deming's advice that the square root is an ample sample size when assessment is done weekly. The y axis on Damon's graph ends at 320 because he had 32 students. Should every student answer every question correctly, then the class, as a whole, would have answered 320 questions. The graph shows that the students answered approximately 100 questions correctly. Obviously they came into fifth grade with some prior knowledge of geography.

Damon provided the students with a blank United States map each week. He then had a student roll the 100-sided die and read off the number. He looked at the list to see which location matched the number. If the student rolled 73, and 73 was the Appalachian Mountains, then students were to sketch on the map where the mountains were located. This process was repeated 10 times. Damon then went over the quiz, correcting the map. He collected the papers and constructed the two graphs.

The scatter diagram in Figure 4.2 shows each student. The y axis is from zero to 10 because students can answer from zero to 10 correctly each week. The first week of school no students missed all 10 questions, five students answered one correctly, six students answered two correctly, eight students answered three correctly, and the others answered either four, five, six, or eight correctly. The scatter diagram matches "the heart of a teacher" because the teacher can see the class as a whole and also see each individual student.

By studying the two graphs it can be observed that learning was constant throughout the year; the range of items correct the last week of school was 7 to 10. Damon was asked how continuous improvement was any different from prior years. He stated that this was his first attempt to have students learn 100 locations; he had expected only the 50 states prior to this experiment. In prior years, Damon said his typical results were that three students knew California, Florida, and Oregon, about seven students knew half of the states, and the remainder knew them all. At the end of this year, three students knew half of the states and the rest knew them all. These results were obtained with no more classroom or preparation time given to geography locations.

Damon attributed the higher rate of success to the fact that he knew every week where the students were in their learning journey. Locations that he expected all to know were missed by some. Likewise, locations that he hadn't taught yet were known by all or almost all. This caused him to slightly adjust his instruction. He credits this ability to fine-tune to the higher levels of learning. When I heard an astronaut speak, he described how an airplane was always slightly off course and the purpose of the instruments in the cockpit was to help the pilot bring the plane back on course. He said the space shuttle is also always off course, but is moving so much faster, that many more corrections are needed to keep it from ending up in "never-never land." It seems that teaching is also always off course and this feedback system is the instrument panel for teachers.

Another look at the class run chart shows three distinct patterns. It's a coincidence that Damon's example is geography and the terms used to describe the patterns are geographical. There are inclines, valleys, and plateaus. Inclines are exciting and there's nothing to do except enjoy the moment. Valleys can be depressing, except for the fact that they don't last long. Valleys are caused by student absences, bad luck, other interests, or maybe periods of absence, such as Christmas vacation.

In week 13, Damon's class hit a valley. It could have been the flu, but actually was probability. By the roll of the die, 10 nonstate locations were quizzed. Normally, students could expect five states and five nonstates. It is important for teachers and students to discuss the valleys. If it is caused by illness or bad luck, there's nothing for them to do. However, if it is caused by lack of attention or extended absences, then students can plan ways to avoid such future problems. Debi Molina-Walters, another California teacher in a year-round school with three one-month-long vacations during the year, was able to lead the students in a plan to avoid the after-break valley.

The most exciting location on the graph is the plateau. Why? This is a picture of going nowhere fast. The reason the plateau is so exciting is that it gives the teacher the opportunity to further engage the students. In a class meeting, the teacher merely asks, "Why hasn't our graph gone up for the last four weeks and what can we do about it?" It is this engagement that has such power. We all know that, for ourselves, intrinsic motivation is a much more powerful motivator than external motivation from the boss. The planning by the students, at any grade, regarding how to improve their learning graph is intrinsically motivating to students and to staff. In over 11 years of studying class run charts from hundreds of classrooms, the inclines, plateaus, and valleys are always present. When students analyze their class graphs they often comment that valleys occur throughout the year, but the new lows are not as low as prior valleys.

Very soon after teachers hear Dr. Deming's suggestion, somebody asks, "You mean we quiz the students on concepts we have not yet taught?" The answer is yes. Teachers call this the review–preview process. No justification is needed for review, but preview needs discussion. First of all, these quizzes are not graded; it would be unfair to grade students on content they had not been taught. Secondly, the preview is essentially what the

English teachers would call "narrative hook." Students like this short introduction to new topics, what is coming up later, and what they'll be learning later in the year. Tom Cook, a Carlisle, Pennsylvania, math teacher and cross country coach, tells us that preview is the reason for much of his success as a cross country coach. The day prior to the meet, he and his team walk the course. This preview is very helpful the next day at the meet. He sees adding preview to his math teaching as exactly the same concept.

Early in the continuous improvement process, teachers began to inform parents of this process. Back-to-school nights became more about what we were going to learn, rather than being limited to classroom procedures, homework, discipline, and so on. Appendix D is a sample letter from teachers in Clarksville, Iowa. The letter plus the format the teachers used to share the basic reading vocabulary (Dolch) words is but one of many ways teachers are communicating expectations (a preview); the charts then communicate results.

Dr. Deming did not suggest the third graph—the student run chart. It soon became apparent, however, that this was needed. It's not a matter of having class records versus students' records; both are needed. Figures 4.3, 4.4, and 4.5 are example student run charts, the first from an elementary school, the second from a middle school, and the third from a high school. The process is exactly the same. The elementary example is 200 words in second-grade spelling. Students are not told before the quiz which 14 words will be on the test; they know it will be 14 (square root of 200) words, but not which 14. The middle school students are assessed on 10 essential science facts each week from a total of 100. Again, they do not know which 10 will be on the

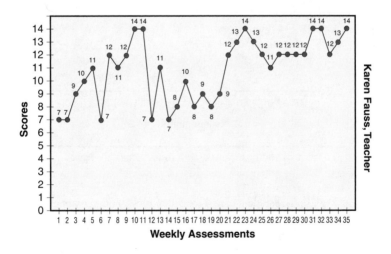

Figure 4.3 Spelling student run chart for Allen.

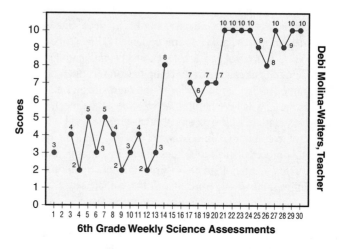

Figure 4.4   Science essential facts student run chart for Adam.

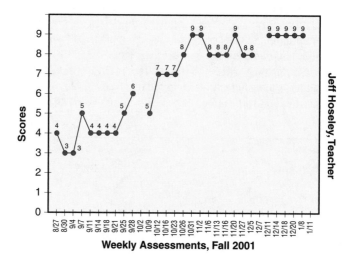

Figure 4.5   Third-period economics student run chart for Travis.

quiz. The high school students are quizzed on nine of 80 essential economics facts in a senior semester course.

Shortly after implementation of Dr. Deming's concepts, Dan Flores, of the Enterprise School District (Redding, California) combined the scatter diagram and student run chart. His graph, Figure 4.6, displays one student's

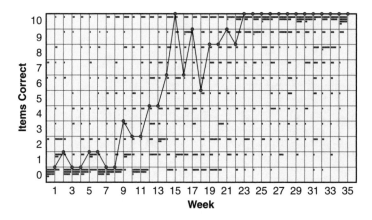

Figure 4.6   First-grade student reading run chart, overlaid with class scatter diagram.

progress in reading 10 randomly selected Dolch sight words, as compared to the remainder of the class. The student overlay has proven valuable in elementary, middle, and high school classrooms.

The three basic graphs are the class run chart, class scatter diagram, and the student run chart. Combined, they provide a very complete picture of the classroom learning journey.

ENDNOTE

1. Dice from Game Science, 7604 Newton Drive, North Biloxi, MS 39532, 228-392-4177.

Section III

Improving Learning: The Details

5

Performance without Rubrics

It took Dr. Deming less than five minutes to outline the contents of the prior chapter. No mention was made of performance. It is known that he was concerned about the teaching of information as well as performance, based upon his writings in epistemology. However, no mention was made of measuring performance in his comments cited in the prior chapter. Nevertheless, since 1992 many educators have adapted the basic strategy into the processes described in this chapter. Here, some of these innovations for measuring performance without rubrics are described.

Deborah Welch, an Oklahoma third-grade teacher, measures her students' reading fluency monthly. Her expectation is 120 words per minute (WPM) on grade level material by year's end. Each student reads to her one minute per month for this assessment. When students cannot read a particular word, she provides the word for the student and makes a tally mark. At the end of the minute, she counts up the total words read for the minute and subtracts the words she provided for the total WPM. Figures 5.1, 5.2, and 5.3 are the class run chart, scatter diagram, and one of her student's run charts. The power of these three graphs is that the students, teachers, administrators, and parents all know that improvement is occurring. They can see the growth develop before them.

Karen Fauss, a California teacher and author of *Continuous Improvement in the Primary Classroom: Language Arts,* did some of the early work with continuous improvement and reading fluency. She realized that monitoring her second grade students up to 200 WPM was not a productive use of her time. What she wanted was for all of her students to read at least 100 WPM on second-grade material. This is an important insight, because if she

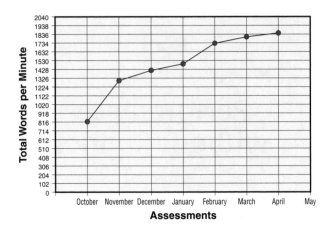

Figure 5.1 Mrs. Welch's reading class run chart.

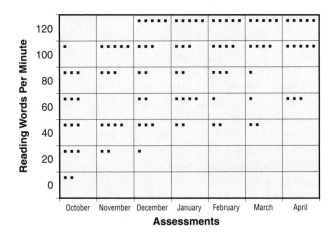

Figure 5.2 Mrs. Welch's reading class scatter diagram.

records up to 200 WPM and has 20 students, the *y* axis on her graph would extend to 4000 WPM. In Figure 5.4, readers can see that her class almost made the total of 2000 WPM (20 students times 100 WPM) for the whole class. Changing the graph to 4000 WPM because a couple of students might read at 200 WPM discourages many and is not the realistic objective.

I have suggested in numerous seminars that once students have read the WPM expectations for their grade level, their fluency need not be checked again that school year. The class is given credit for their speed (so

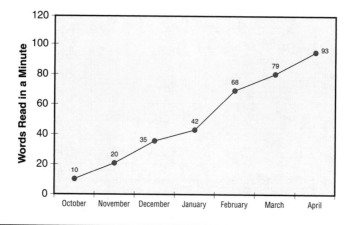

Figure 5.3 One student's fluency record.

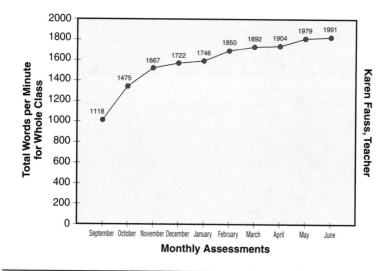

Figure 5.4 Reading fluency class run chart.

the class graph doesn't go down), but no official check is needed. Figure 5.5 is the record from which Karen's charts were made. (Student numbers replace the names for privacy reasons.) Readers can see that once students read the 100 WPM, then 100 was entered in the computer for the remainder of the year.

Recently, Southwest Iowa educators working in Area Education Agency (AEA) 13 suggested to me that students should be checked again,

	September	October	November	December	January	February	March	April	May	June
Student 1	73	98	100	80	70	96	100	100	100	100
Student 2	28	62	100	100	100	100	100	100	100	100
Student 3	100	100	100	100	100	100	100	100	100	100
Student 4	14	46	57	72	59	78	71	78	100	100
Student 5	100	100	100	100	100	100	100	100	100	100
Student 6	100	100	100	100	100	100	100	100	100	100
Student 7	37	100	100	100	100	100	100	100	100	100
Student 8	14	29	39	78	56	64	80	74	98	91
Student 9	41	71	93	52	63	68	70	75	88	100
Student 10	81	100	45	72	72	74	100	100	100	100
Student 11	29	74	99	100	100	100	100	100	100	100
Student 12	55	63	91	98	99	100	100	100	100	100
Student 13	67	74	85	85	84	100	96	98	100	100
Student 14	19	19	56	59	68	71	75	79	93	100
Student 15	61	69	88	100	100	100	100	100	100	100
Student 16	85	88	90	100	100	100	100	100	100	100
Student 17	17	40	52	63	75	99	100	100	100	100
Student 18	100	100	100	100	100	100	100	100	100	100
Student 19	55	87	100	100	100	100	100	100	100	100
Student 20	52	85	99	100	100	100	100	100	100	100

Figure 5.5   Reading fluency data.

even after reaching the goal for the year, using a different genre of litera-ture. It is especially important, they said, for fluency to be measured with nonfiction text. Good advice. The grade 1–8 reading fluency recommenda-tions for grade level text are:

Grade 1   60 WPM

Grade 2   100 WPM

Grade 3   120 WPM

Grade 4   130 WPM

Grade 5   140 WPM

Grade 6   160 WPM

Grade 7   180 WPM

Grade 8   200 WPM

At each grade level, increased expectations are present both in fluency expectations and difficulty of text.

Kevin Baker, a Grants, New Mexico, teacher, measures fluency in his high school English classes on a weekly basis. He uses the 400-word passages from *Timed Readings in Literature,* edited by Edward Spargo.[1] Each passage is accompanied by 10 comprehension questions. The process

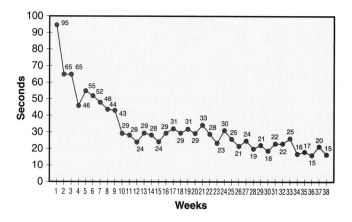

Figure 5.6   Seconds to read a 400-word passage.

Kevin describes is that students raise their speed and comprehension falls. He advises the students to hold the new speed as a constant until their comprehension reaches 80 percent. Then he suggests they raise their speed again. Of course the same pattern reoccurs. The comprehension drops. Students must again work to build their comprehension back up to 80 percent or higher. Kevin is continually testing hypotheses to help the students. His most recent one is, "Would students be able to increase their comprehension faster if I had them read the questions prior to reading the passage?" The fact that teachers can have hypotheses, share them with the students, and all together they can carry out an experiment is thrilling. Figure 5.6 is a high school junior's example from Kevin. The student quickly met the expectation of 400 WPM (60 seconds) and ended the year at 1800 WPM.

One of the most intriguing examples of performance measurement is from Cincinnati, Ohio, music teacher Dave Bell. Each student in his four high school choirs and ensembles receives the two sheets of rhythm patterns in appendix B. The four levels of rhythm patterns on the two sheets match the four levels of his choirs. For example, the chorus is expected to know the first 16 patterns on the 2/4 sheet and the first 12 patterns on the 6/8 sheet. The Chorale students are expected to know the first 19 rhythm patterns on the 6/8 sheet and the first 24 on the 2/4 sheet. Students are expected to know the new patterns as well as those from the prior year. The Ensemble is expected to know all 73 patterns on both pages.

Freshmen were quizzed on four in 2/4 time and two in 6/8 time

Girls Chorale were quizzed on four in 2/4 time and two in 6/8 time

Concert Choir was quizzed upon six in 2/4 time and four in 6/8 time

Varsity Ensemble was quizzed on six in 2/4 time and four in 6/8 time

Figure 5.7 is a class run chart for his chorus; it is shown with percent correct.

About halfway through his first year of implementation, his graph flatlined. It was going nowhere. When he asked his students for help, they gave suggestions for 60 minutes, nonstop, on ways to improve their learning. Dave says that this is when he really understood the power of continuous improvement. Students were not talking about grades or other rewards and punishments; they were focused upon learning of rhythm patterns.

Rochester, Indiana, principal Cheryl Downs, along with the district's classroom connections coordinator, Mary Bohr, have worked with K–2 teachers to record reading levels. Books are leveled according to Marie Clay's Reading Recovery Levels. They expect kindergarten students to read at level four by the end of the year and first graders to be at level 24. Each quarter, the reading levels of all students are added up and posted in the hallway. In this way, everyone entering the building can see that the learning-to-read process is working. Figure 5.8 is the first-grade run chart for 2001–02.

Citrus County, Florida assesses first-graders each quarter on how many words they can read from a 100-word passage. They have agreed upon the passages to be used, how to count words read (that is, self-correcting, and so on), and recording the results. Figures 5.9 to 5.12 are a set of histograms

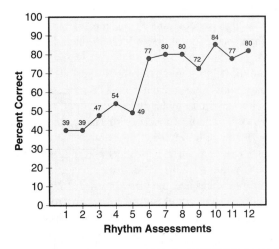

Figure 5.7 Third-period freshman chorus class run chart.

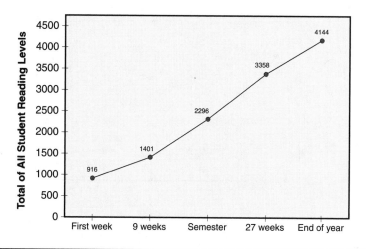

Figure 5.8   First-grade school run chart: reading levels.

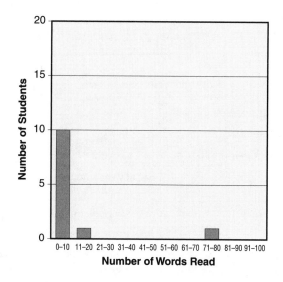

Figure 5.9   First-quarter 100-word passage first grade Title 1.

from Jean Jaworski, showing the results for her Title I reading students. Some schools have students read sight words, some schools select fluency, and others select reading passages while errors are counted. It doesn't seem to matter; what counts is that the teachers, parents, and students all know the students' reading is improving.

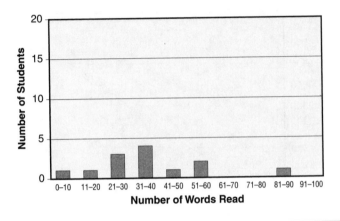

Figure 5.10   Second-quarter 100-word passage first grade Title 1.

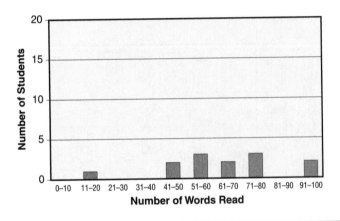

Figure 5.11   Third-quarter 100-word passage first grade Title 1.

Fitness monitoring is perfect for continuous improvement. Indiana teacher Katie Felke tells how her weekly fitness day in high school was such a problem. The students saw no reason for sit-ups, push-ups, pull-ups, or running. The class total graph changed their mind. Once the students could see the graph go up and understood that their hard work paid off, their resistance was greatly reduced. Appendix P contains the blank student run charts used by her students. Other teachers have used a recording from the American Fitness Alliance[2] to monitor running endurance. The width of the gym is used and students receive a score based upon how long they run.

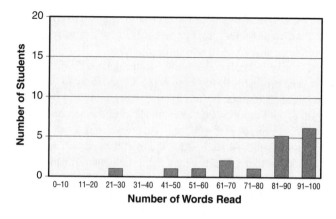

Figure 5.12   Fourth-quarter 100-word passage first grade Title 1.

Other examples of continuous improvement implementation of performance, without rubrics, are typing speed, editing (daily oral language), and competencies from vocational education. No adjustment in basic classroom procedures is needed to implement continuous improvement for typing speed or for counting up checked competencies in vocational education. In business classes, students are usually working with spreadsheets, so making a graph of their own typing speed progress as well as one for the whole class can be a regular part of the class assignments. Vocational teachers document, often for future employers, the competencies each student has met. In continuous improvement classrooms, the total competencies checked off are added up biweekly or monthly.

Slight changes are needed in daily oral language (editing) procedures in order to implement continuous improvement. Each time students are given a paragraph to edit, educators need to prepare the writing sample with the same number of errors. For example, if a class has 27 students, and the paragraph has 10 errors, the class is looking for 270 errors. By graphing this on a weekly basis, students and teachers will know if they are becoming better editors. Daily oral language will become an activity with an aim that all understand. The other change is to include from the very beginning of the year all of the error types to be known at the end of the year. For example, if semicolons are to be used correctly by the end of the year, then they must be one of the errors included in any example of writing to be edited. This editing practice also works in classrooms learning languages other than English.

One of the most interesting uses of performance without rubrics comes from Carolyn Ayres, a California teacher and author of *Continuous*

Improvement in the Mathematics Classroom. Her first-graders had nine graphs in their data folders; eight made perfect sense to me, but I didn't understand the significance of skipping rope.

"Why," I asked, "are you graphing skipping rope?"

"Well," she replied, "all my first-graders knew how to do at recess and lunch was chase each other. I wanted to influence how they used their recess and lunchtime, but I didn't want to be outside with them in order to have that influence. So I started assessing the students weekly in jumping rope. Students jumped twice—once holding the rope themselves, and once having the rope turned for them. The higher total was counted for the week."

"Did it work?" I asked.

"Yes, the major activity of my students at lunch was jumping rope."

What Carolyn wanted is what we all want. We want more positive influence upon the lives of our students without having to be there all of the time. We want students practicing reading fluency, times tables, typing speed, sit-ups, and rhythm patterns without it being necessary for the teacher to be present on the weekends and evenings.

ENDNOTE

1. Edward Spargo, ed., *Timed Readings in Literature* (Chicago: Jamestown Publishers, 1989).
2. Pacer cassette tape, American Fitness Alliance, www.humankinetics.com , 800-747-4457.

6
Performance with Rubrics

ubrics are scales of quality. When an endeavor cannot be measured by counting, such as reading fluency (chapter 5) or essential science information (chapter 7), a scale must be developed. Examples from sports include diving, figure skating, and gymnastics.

Every subject has within its content both essential information and performance expectations. Educated people are to know the information and be able to demonstrate the performance. Often, educators use the phrase "what students know (essential information) and what they can do (performance)."

The most difficult aspect of teaching is increasing performance. This is true for any subject. Take reading, for example: it is much simpler to teach a student the names of the letters and sound(s) of each letter than it is to teach the child to read. Every subject is the same. How do teachers know when students are better writers, better solvers of math problems, better science researchers, and better artists? And if this isn't difficult enough, how does a teacher know if a whole class is improving?

Essentially, the answer to these questions and the core of this chapter is five words: add up the rubric scores.

Jeff Burgard's science students had eight assignments measured on the 0–6 rubric in appendix T. The total scores for each student were added up. Figure 6.1 is his class run chart for the assignments and Figure 6.2 is the accompanying scatter diagram. The two graphs together give a picture of improved writing and understanding of scientific principles over the course of a year. Jeff also did an item analysis (chapter 13) for each writing assignment.

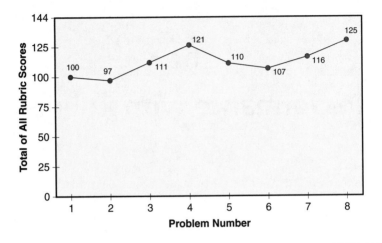

Figure 6.1   Science essay problems: class run chart.

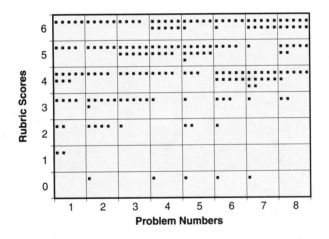

Figure 6.2   Science essay problems: class scatter diagram.

Even though "add up the rubric scores" is accurate advice, secondary teachers have so many papers to evaluate that more help was needed. What follows is quite exciting for all of the secondary teachers so buried with papers and papers and papers.

Helping secondary English teachers with writing has been of particular interest to me. Any suggestions for them had to address the "full plate" caused by the obligation to read all the papers. Any new ideas, no matter how wonderful, ran up against the time demand to grade all those papers.

The theoretical statement from Dr. Deming that applies to English teachers is that we cannot inspect quality into any process; we must build in the quality. Spending Saturday after Saturday after Saturday scoring papers is essentially an attempt to inspect quality into student writing. It doesn't work. The problem is what to do.

Susan Leddick first started my thinking about writing sampling and continuous improvement. She told me that with essential information we sample content, but with performance expectations we sample students. She went on to work with New Mexico elementary teachers to document that sampling papers, scoring them on a rubric, analyzing errors, graphing the results, and working to improve the total on the graph improved writing, as measured by state writing tests. The average writing score in the New Mexico example improved from 2.2 to 3.4, on a four-point scale, on the state's standardized writing sample for grade four.

Readers can imagine the response I received when I shared with secondary English teachers that they need not read every paper. The square root of the total papers, randomly selected, was enough. The audience said, "But I have to put a grade on every paper." In other words, the pressure to inspect overwhelmed the teachers' desire to improve writing. What to do?

Jana Vance, a Rochester, Indiana, high school teacher, has given me the very best help in fine-tuning a practical way to actually implement continuous improvement in the secondary English classroom. Quality can be built into the writing process. These steps are based upon an ongoing conversation.

Step 1 Provide the students with the rubric(s) by which their papers will be evaluated. Elicit student help in clarifying the language of the rubric and provide sample papers from prior years (with names removed). The sample papers are scored according to the rubric(s). Often, English teachers have different rubrics for each genre of writing, rather than one for all assignments.

Step 2 Explain to students that the first eight weeks of each quarter is writing practice. The teacher is the coach and will be doing everything possible to help them improve their writing. The ninth week is "game week;" practice is over. The teacher becomes the referee for the last week of each quarter, and assigns grades to student papers. The grade is based upon comparison to the rubric(s) provided in step 1.

Step 3   Assign the first writing paper. After writing is complete, all students are to reflect upon possible errors or trouble spots in their writing. They share their perceptions by placing paper-punch size Avery dots upon 8½ × 11 sheets of paper. The sheets are labeled with error types such as lack of subject/verb agreement, colons and semicolons, and fragmented sentences. A quick look at the various dots tells the teacher how the students perceive their problems. Teachers will all design unique methods of collecting students' perceptions of their errors; using paper-punch dots is only one technique.

Step 4   The teacher randomly selects five students (approximate square root of the total students in each class) from each period for a 1:1 conversation regarding their papers. The randomness is done in front of the class, so that students know it is probability that chose them. In this 1:1 conference, teachers tally errors and give the quality of help they'd like to provide for all students for all assignments. They also give the paper a rubric score. After five students have had their conference, the teacher adds and graphs the total for the five. As with any random selection process, the graph will vary based upon who is selected, but if the class writing is improving, a general upward trend will occur. The teacher also goes over to the 8½ × 11 sheets of paper to add different colored dots to the error analysis.

Step 5   Based upon the error analyses on the 8½ × 11 sheets and observations from the 20 papers (four periods of five students each), teachers prepare lessons for their writing instruction. The time for this preparation comes from not having to read and score approximately 100 papers.

Step 6   Teachers repeat this process four times each quarter. Up to this point, there is still no grade recorded for writing; practice time is for eight weeks. Grades have been recorded for other aspects of the English curriculum, but not for writing.

Step 7   During the last week of the quarter, on a designated day, students bring all four papers to class. They can revise any paper, based upon instruction given, up until the due date. Jana has an eight-sided die (1, 1, 2, 2, 3, 3, 4, 4). She rolls the die in front of the students and they hand in their paper. If a three is rolled, for example, every student hands in the third assignment of the quarter. Her next Saturday is gone; she's the referee now, and one paper from each student is graded for that portion of the English grade.

The goal is to improve writing by building quality into the process instead of attempting to inspect quality in. Jana says, "When I first began learning from Lee and Susan (Leddick), I was excited about many of their ideas and was anxious to begin putting into practice those things I was learning; however, like many others I was hesitant about not looking over each paper the students wrote. It wasn't until I had practiced Lee and Susan's methods for a few years with essential facts that I realized that it was very possible to implement this into the writing process. It is so exciting to see how much the students are learning about writing and are sincerely putting forth the effort needed to make their writing better. For so many years of my teaching, I would introduce a paper with enthusiasm, assign a paper, we would go through all of the writing process steps, and they would turn their papers in. Then I would spend hours grading them, only to pass them back to the students and see students just look at their final grade and shove them in their folders. I would become so aggravated and disappointed to think that I had spent so much time trying to help them improve their writing and they cared only about their final grade. As time would progress I would become more aggravated with the students' lack of effort and focus on improving their writing. The idea of grading about one-quarter of the papers I normally did was appealing, but I wondered how 'fair' it was to the students.

"However, at the same time I was seeing so much progress and excitement from the students in the areas where I was following Deming's theory. I finally decided to give it a try with the writing process. My only complaint was, why did I wait so long to use this in the writing process? My students were given more responsibility for their own learning, taking some of the burden off of my shoulders. I then saw them make a concerted effort to improve their writing because they were identifying the areas they need help with instead of me putting the red marks on the paper and telling them what was wrong. The time I got to spend with students was quality time on what they needed most. The students began to feel more responsible for their own learning and I became more and more of a facilitator rather than a teacher. I found students coming into my room asking for additional help and their questions were sincere and quite focused. I found they were taking their writing a step further and I was simply a resource for information rather than the giver of information. The quality of writing was unbelievable and their dedication did not falter as the year progressed, but instead grew. For the first time I had students taking their papers with them as a resource for future writing instead of throwing them into my trash can at the end of the hour. And, by the way, did I mention I had more free time on the weekends to spend with my family—making me a better teacher when the students needed the most out of me!"

Mary Kaser of Rochester, Minnesota's Lourdes High School, after hearing about Jana's process in English, adopted for her 2002–03 Chemistry students a process that is almost identical. Her Post-Lab Assessment Rubric is included in appendix K. Mary scans all lab reports briefly, giving a 1–5 score, but then randomly selects the five students from each period for the complete 1–20 scoring and item analysis of errors. At the end of each nine weeks, she selects one lab report to be gathered from each student. This is randomly selected from the eight to 12 lab reports written each quarter. Then, as does Jana, she grades this lab report from all students; nothing is random. She wrote to her students upon initiating this process, "I'd like to try being a coach most of the quarter, and a referee during the last week before grades are due . . . during the last week of the quarter, I will collect one lab report (my choice) from each student that will be graded in detail and recorded as part of your quarter grade. This is the refereeing period."

Elementary teachers Tim Sheppard and Nancy Hunter, working with the other third-grade teacher at their school in Wenatchee, Washington, have agreed to randomly select sample stories by grade level. The teachers agreed upon the 11 essential skills below. They wrote them as a check sheet for students to self-monitor their writing. They called their process "wacky writing."

A. I made and used a plan to help my writing.

B. I worked with my sentences. I made sure that my sentences were not all the same length; some are short and some are long. My sentences don't all sound the same.

C. I worked with spelling in my writing. I was able to tell when words were spelled wrong and corrected as many as I could.

D. I revised and edited my writing. I used a red pen; I crossed out writing I didn't need any longer in order to make it better. I fixed my writing to make it as perfect as I could.

E. I used details in my writing. I made sure to include enough details so that the reader could understand and enjoy my ideas.

F. I thought how my writing was sequenced as I wrote. I made sure to include a clear beginning, a middle, and an end in my writing.

G. I thought about punctuation while I was writing. I worked on using capitals, periods, commas, quotation marks, and complete sentences.

H. I organized my writing into paragraphs. I used indents and blank lines to separate my writing into clear groups of ideas (paragraphs).

I. Character and setting: when writing a narrative story I made sure to write enough to introduce and explain the characters and the setting (where the story took place). I made sure that the reader knows all about the characters.

J. I used transition words to connect my ideas together. I used words like: first, next, then, finally . . . and others.

K. All of my writing is focused on the topic and follows the idea of the prompt (what you are writing about). I only wrote about things that matched the topic.

At regular intervals the three third-grade teachers have their students write on the same topic. The papers are collected from the students and 15 are randomly selected. Each teacher scores five; there's no need to read all papers; the 15 scored give all the necessary information. (See chapter 13 for an example Pareto chart used for item analysis.) The teachers say that their "wacky writing" provides an avenue for regular conversation among grade three teachers regarding their understanding of the essential writing skills and the writing process. Again, these teachers are no longer attempting to inspect quality into student writing, but are systematically building quality into the writing.

Before providing other examples of the use of continuous improvement with performance rubrics, I've inserted here an observation regarding the teaching of performance. How does one actually go about helping students with math problem solving? With artistic creation? With scientific investigation? As I observe teachers who are competent in this most difficult aspect of teaching and learning, the one constant is the teachers' ability to "hear the students think." They then interact with the thinking and this leads the students to higher levels of thinking.

For example, West Virginia teacher Sue Steinbeck does not have her high school math students work at their desks. They work in groups at the white board around the perimeter of her room. She can stand anywhere in the room and observe what is occurring, but more importantly she can stand adjacent to any small group and listen to the math conversation. It is through this listening that she knows how to assist the students.

In *Continuous Improvement in the Mathematics Classroom,* author Carolyn Ayres describes a similar process. Students are given a math problem (sample in appendix O). The students solve it on their own, Carolyn scores it according to a rubric (appendix A), and the results are graphed (Figure 6.3). The teaching comes the following day when her second-graders are placed in groups of four and given the same problem again, along with a blank transparency. The students solve the problem again, this

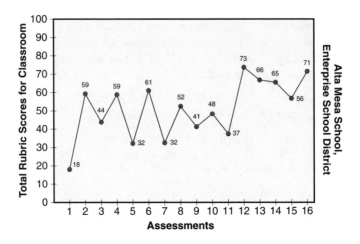

Figure 6.3   Carolyn Ayres' problem-solving class run chart.

time allowing her to listen to their thinking. Each group, using their transparency, presents their solution to the remainder of the class. The ensuing discussion with the whole class and the teacher is a primary method that Carolyn uses to assist them in reaching higher levels of performance.

Figure 6.4 is a class run chart and Figure 6.5 is the accompanying scatter diagram from Debi Molina-Walters, an Antioch, California, sixth-grade science teacher. Her process for recording the results of science labs is described here along with her means of listening to student thinking.

The school year begins with students receiving the rubric for science lab reports (appendix N). Students are then given their first lab assignment and they record their results. They self-edit, using the rubric, then they have their peers edit their lab write-up. Finally, Debi edits the labs so students have a model to work from for the year. This lab is not graded; it is used as the foundation for future learning.

The process continues throughout the year in the same manner. Experiments are conducted in groups of four, students write up their lab report, they self-edit the report, they have the report peer-edited, and then they save the report. After four labs, each student selects their two best lab reports for their portfolio, and then one of the two to be handed in for Debi to score on the rubric and record as a grade.

It is very significant that she is not scoring all of the lab reports. When do many teachers score period one lab reports? During period two. When do they score period two lab reports? During period three. Since Debi is only scoring 25 percent of the labs herself, what is she doing with the time?

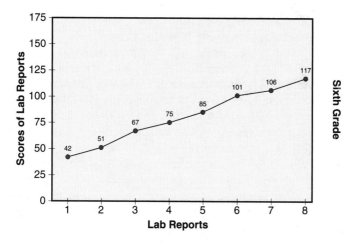

Figure 6.4   Science Labs class run chart.

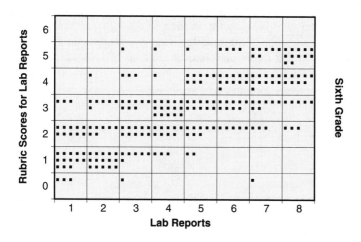

Figure 6.5   Science Labs class scatter diagram.

She is listening. She is listening to the discussion of each group of four while they are conducting the labs and she is listening to the peer-editing of the lab write-ups. She says that listening to the peer-editing is one of her favorite activities. Her students know that if a lab is perfectly written, a reader will be able to "see in his or her mind's eye" exactly what occurred in the lab. Listening to students coach each other through the process gives her the information necessary to further develop their performance levels.

If all there was to continuous improvement was adding up the total of rubric scores and graphing it, life would be much simpler. The graphing tells the teacher and the students if improvement is occurring. It tells if the methods being used are working. So, the discussion of the methods used to improve performance learning is essential. The four teachers mentioned above have clearly developed ways to hear their students think—Jana with the 1:1 conversations, Sue with math on the white boards, Carolyn with math on transparencies, and Debi with labs and peer-editing.

What could be a better climax for this chapter than art? How do art teachers and their students know they are improving? Is it always a feeling? Do students obtain better grades because the teacher likes their work? Dave Brown, a Florida art teacher, uses a set of four rubrics (See appendix U for an example) to evaluate all of his art projects. Each student has a potential of 20 points per project; the graph shows the percentage of the total possible points earned by the class. For example, for the stamp project the students earned 52 percent of the possible points for the whole class (see Figure 6.6). Note on the graph that the type of assignment is listed, rather than the date or assignment number. In this way, Dave can compare progress from like assignment to like assignment as well as overall progress. Photographs of three student examples are shown in Figures 6.7, 6.8, and 6.9, giving the reader some concept of the complexity of evaluation. The second page of appendix U is an actual self-, peer-, and teacher evaluation for the second pictured sculpture.

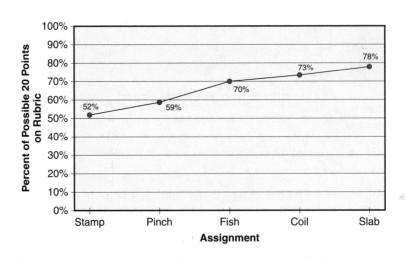

Figure 6.6   Dave Brown's Block 3 Ceramics and Pottery rubrics class run chart.

Figure 6.7   Example sculpture from Citrus County Schools, Florida.
Artist: Christina Neuman.

When arranging the table of contents for this book, I chose to place performance prior to essential information to communicate that performance is the ultimate goal of education. We know that norm-referenced tests almost always measure information. Nevertheless, it is performance that matters most. Essential information is important either: (1) as a prerequisite to deeper understanding, or (2) on its own merit. The next chapter describes in great detail continuous improvement with essential

Figure 6.8   Example sculpture from Citrus County Schools, Florida.
Artist: Shelly Baumeister.

information. I often advise teachers to begin the continuous improvement process with essential information. It is easier for most to begin with the simpler information than with performance. However, I sincerely hope that these teachers, once they have the process in place for information, move on to performance. The examples from the teachers listed in this chapter should make the journey much easier.

Figure 6.9   Example sculpture from Citrus County Schools, Florida.
Artist: Maggie Sharar.

7

Improving Learning of Essential Information

If there were no standardized exams measuring students' knowledge of facts, I would still be excited about this chapter. Every subject in every grade level contains essential information students should know. This information is so important, they should know it as an adult, not merely as a student to obtain the desired grade from a course.

Jonathan Zimmerman wrote in the June 19, 2002, edition of *Education Week* that "critics of national and state testing too blithely presume that a required body of facts will inhibit classroom inquiry. But facts and inquiry are like Siamese twins: You cannot have one without the other."[1]

Clearly one of the most discouraging aspects of schooling is memorizing trivia. To distinguish between types of facts, which include trivia and essential information, this chapter is entitled "Improving Learning of Essential Information." I have no interest in preparing students for TV game shows, but am quite interested in placing essential information in students' long-term memory.

Teachers will certainly tell stories containing trivia, as it makes up much of the intriguing details of any subject. However, the essence of this chapter is informing students during the first week of a course the essential information they are to know by the end of the course. An Oklahoma City high school student stated the benefit well. He said, "If they tell me the rules of the game, I'll play; it not, then I'm out of here." He was being interviewed regarding his teacher's practice of implementing the contents of this chapter. He saw providing the facts as telling him the rules of the game. Attempting to guess what will be on the test was a game he was no longer willing to play.

Some districts have brought together middle school teachers to agree on essential facts for science. Often they have decided to have 100 facts per grade. A major element of their endeavor is that the sixth-graders are responsible for the first 100 facts, the seventh-graders for the 100 from sixth plus the 100 from seventh, and the eighth-graders responsible for all 300. Ideally, students are provided the list from the current grade, prior grade (for review), and the next grade. They are not responsible for learning the next grade's information, but are quite curious. This curiosity creates some learning.

Certainly this decision impacts their state tests given in eighth grade. Sixth grade curriculum is often earth science, seventh grade is typically life science, and eighth grade is physical science. The state exam assesses all three of these sciences in the spring of eighth grade. Remembering sixth and seventh grade science in the spring of eighth grade is advantageous to the district and students. Even if there were no eighth-grade test, however, this decision is responsible education.

Another example, where the number 100 was used for essential facts, has a unique twist. It is from Shelly Carson, author of *Continuous Improvement in the History/Social Science Classroom.* She teaches 11th grade U.S. History in Palo Cedro, California. In her mind, she is teaching the third year of a three-year course in U.S. History; not a one-year course. The first history course came in fifth grade, which taught students content from the earliest times on the North American continent to the American Revolution. The second course, taught in eighth grade, teaches about the United States from the U.S. Constitution to 1900. Shelly's responsibility is to help students learn about the United States from 1900 to the present time. The unique twist is that, during the first week of 11th grade, students are provided the essential facts from all three courses, and every quiz, every quarterly exam, and the final include items from all three years. So, the process here is to randomly select 16 items from the 250 essential facts for the weekly quizzes. It is not unlike a sixth-grade teacher with 100 locations on a map from fourth grade, 100 more from fifth grade, and a new 100 from sixth grade, except Shelly's essential history facts cover a wider span of time. The structure in California of dividing up U.S. History into thirds is a wonderful concept; the problem is, students won't remember the content of prior grades unless a process like Shelly put in place is widely used.

The first responsibility of teachers is to as clearly as possible tell students what they are expected to know at the end of the course. "The *focus* of an earthquake is the point inside the earth where the earthquake begins; it is where the earth's plate shifts" is an example of an essential fact in sixth grade written by Debi Molina-Walters of Antioch, California. Not only did she write the facts as clearly as she could, but at the end of the school year her students edited the writing for next year's students. Everything possible is being done to take away the guessing game.

Often, teachers select vocabulary rather than essential facts. (See appendix I from Glenwood, Iowa). At other times, essential facts and vocabulary are combined. Debi Molina-Walters has decided to separate essential facts from vocabulary, but will give both quizzes in one sitting in order to save classroom time.

Once the essential facts are given to the students, the first quiz is administered. It is recommended that the number of quiz items be the approximate square root of the total for the year. When the teacher has 50 essential facts or vocabulary terms, for example, seven questions per week is an adequate size sample. For Debi, in the example above, since she has 100 essential science facts, her students have a 10-item quiz weekly.

WHY SQUARE ROOT?

The square root provides a large enough sample size to be accurate. The sample size is large enough if quizzing is done every week or every other week. Also, the square root works for both large and smaller numbers. For example, if a first-grade teacher has 25 math concepts to be learned during the year, five questions per week will work. Conversely, should a Spanish teacher expect students to know 900 vocabulary words, 30 words per week, randomly selected, gives accurate information to both the teacher and the students.

WHY SAMPLE?

The simple reason for sampling is there's not enough time to assess students continually on everything they need to know. The various curriculum projects across the United States that are working with data, and recommending that teachers assess their students on the complete body of knowledge three times a year, would do teachers a huge favor by recommending sampling. First of all, the beginning, middle, and end-of-the-year 100 percent assessment of all students is a grueling endeavor. However, the worst part of only assessing three times a year is that it doesn't give frequent enough information to inform the teachers' decisions. Sampling, when done weekly, or biweekly, takes the least amount of classroom time and provides the most up-to-date information.

WHY RANDOM?

It is accurate. Random, in literature, can mean mindless meandering. Obviously, this definition of random is not useful for this discussion. For mathematicians and scientists, random selection means accurate because no human biases are distorting the data. For educators, this means that students are no longer attempting to "psych-out" the instructor to determine what will be on the exam. They cannot "psych-out" the dice, so they might as well learn all the content. One of the ironies of continuous improvement is that the math and science teachers have been teaching probability and statistics in their classes for years but have talked about how the world outside of schooling works. Now these teachers have a way to use what they have been teaching in their world.

HOW DO TEACHERS SELECT THE RANDOM ITEMS?

There seems to be no favorite method of selecting random items and all seem to work equally well. Examples of how teachers with 300 facts might select random numbers are:

1. Two specialty dice: (1) six-sided—0, 1, 2, 0, 1, 2, and (2) 100-sided[2]

2. Three specialty dice: (1) six-sided—0, 1, 2, 0, 1, 2, (2) a 10-sided die—0, 10, 20, 30, 40, 50, 60, 70, 80, 90, and (3) another 10-sided die—0, 1, 2, 3, 4, 5, 6, 7, 8, 9

3. A fishbowl with 300 facts, each on an index card

4. Random number generators included with electronic spreadsheets programs, such as Excel

5. Random number generators included in graphing calculators

6. Resurrected bingo game with numbers revised to 1–300

7. www.random.org

8. Print questions, make transparency, cut questions into strips, place strips in bag, draw question at random. Place question on overhead projector.

Preparing Blank Graphs

Figures 7.1, 7.2, and 7.3 are the three basic blank graphs for a teacher with 300 essential facts and 25 students. She is quizzing the students on 17 of the 300 facts each week for 30 weeks. A perfect score is 425, which would

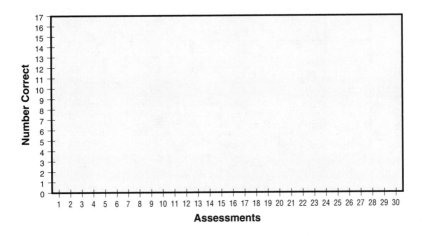

Figure 7.1 Blank student run chart.

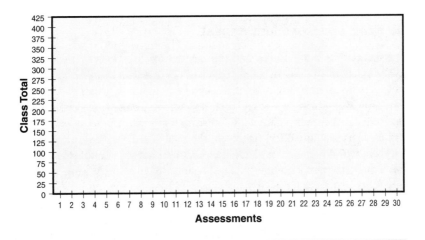

Figure 7.2 Blank class run chart.

mean that each of the 25 students answered all 17 questions correctly. Thus the *y* axis is 425 and the *x* axis is 30, for the 30 weeks. It matters not if the graphs are computer generated, as done for this book, or if they are hand-made by teachers or students. The blank graphs were made with Microsoft Excel. It was quite easy to type in the horizontal numbers and vertical numbers, and then use Word-Art to generate the labels on the top, bottom, and left side. Excel makes it easy to shrink columns and increase the size of rows, which is what I needed to do here to fill up the page. The only difficult part is knowing how to have Excel print the grid lines. The command is File, Page-Setup-Sheet, and then check Print Gridlines.

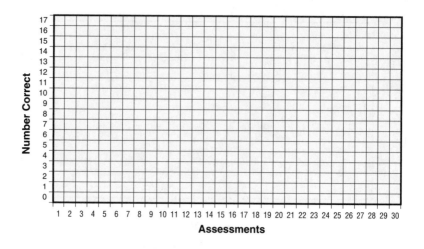

Figure 7.3   Blank scatter diagram.

Do Items and Questions Repeat?

The answer for items is yes and the answer for questions is sometimes. Every essential fact has an equal chance of being drawn from the total each and every week. It is possible for the same fact to occur several weeks in a row. However, during a weekly quiz, no repeats are used. In the fishbowl example above, when a fact is pulled from the bowl, it is set aside. When all the items are pulled for that week, the index cards are then put back in the fishbowl. When dice or electronic random number generators are used, and a duplicate number comes up, roll again. However, if the same number comes up next week, so be it.

The goal is not for students to know answers to questions, but to know the concepts and vocabulary. So, teachers usually ask the question in different ways each time a particular fact is chosen. Multiple choice, fill-in-the-blank, open-ended questions, and true–false are all used. However, sometimes teachers have good reasons for using the same exact question on different occasions.

GIVING THE FIRST QUIZ

The first time students and teachers experience this process they are both anxious. How will parents react to students being quizzed on items that have not yet been taught? Will this create stress? Will older students ignore it, because it "doesn't count on my grade?"

Some preparation is needed. First of all, the students need assurance that the quiz doesn't count for their grade and that the purpose is to show how they are learning individually and how they are learning collectively. They also need to be continually reminded that they will know the content at the end of the year. Appendix D is a letter from first-grade teachers Pat Fenneman and Marty Wurth in Harlan, Iowa, informing parents of their plan to quiz students weekly on a random selection of the Dolch sight words. They also included a complete list of the words. Either the letter worked, or their anxiety was higher than necessary. Anyway, no complaints arrived. Carolyn Ayres writes, "I make a big deal about thanking children for their mistakes, so we all can learn. Magically, as time goes on, the graph goes up and enthusiasm grows." Certainly this attitude from the teacher helps students communicate positive feelings at home and reduce parent frustration with a new process.

It has been my experience, since 1992, that some parents do question this random assessment of the end-of-the-year items. They are satisfied when they know: (1) their children are not graded on the quizzes, (2) a by-product of this process is that it takes away cramming (which they know is a waste of time), and (3) each quiz is really a practice for the end-of-the-year final, which will be graded.

Weeks One and Two Quizzes

Samples of the three basic graphs from week one are shown in Figures 7.4 through 7.6. Figure 7.4 shows a graph of a student who scored two of 17

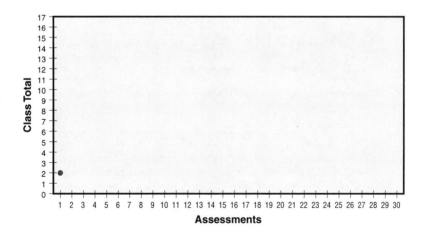

Figure 7.4   Week one student run chart.

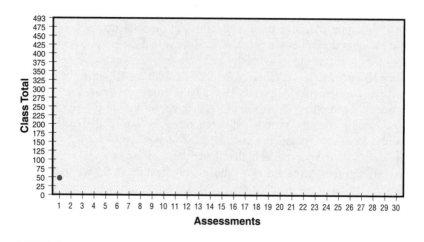

Figure 7.5   Week one class run chart.

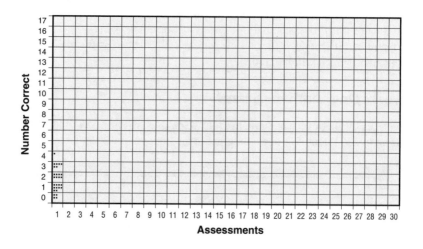

Figure 7.6   Week one scatter diagram.

correct the first week of school. On Figure 7.5, the dot is placed at "48" because, all together, the students answered 48 questions correctly out of a possible 493. Figure 7.6 is the accompanying scatter diagram with one dot for each of the 29 students. Four students answered none of the questions correctly, 10 had one correct, eight had two correct, six had three correct, and one had four correct. (The reader can count up the total to see precisely how the scatter diagram and class run chart are connected.)

Figures 7.7, 7.8, and 7.9 are from the same classroom on week two. Note that the score went down in spite of the fact that one student had eight correct. This example was selected because half of the time, week two will be worse than week one. The teacher's responsibility is to "hang in there" until the students see growth. Figures 7.10 and 7.11 are the class run chart and accompanying scatter diagram from one of Jeff Hoseley's economics classes in Meridian, Idaho. With teacher insistence, the students do witness

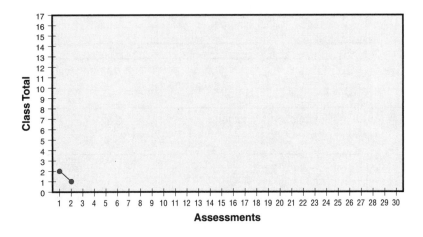

Figure 7.7   Week two student run chart.

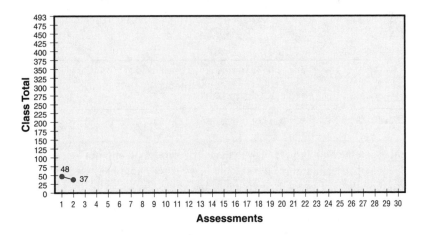

Figure 7.8   Week two class run chart.

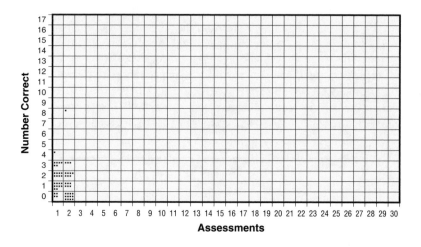

Figure 7.9   Week two scatter diagram.

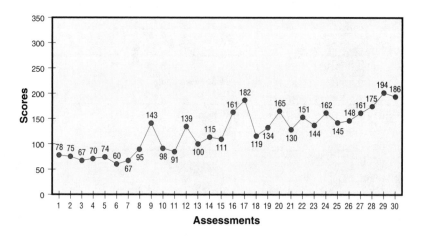

Figure 7.10   Third-period Economics spring class run chart.

their intellectual growth. Until then, the process continues because the leader of the classroom, the teacher, says it will continue. Once students capture the joy of both individual and collective growth, they beg for quizzes. An Iowa teacher returned from Christmas vacation on a Thursday, which was her normal quiz day. She thought she'd be nice and wouldn't quiz the students on the first day back from vacation. However, the students knew Thursday was her quiz day and they insisted on a quiz. At all ages the students capture the joy—it is intrinsic.

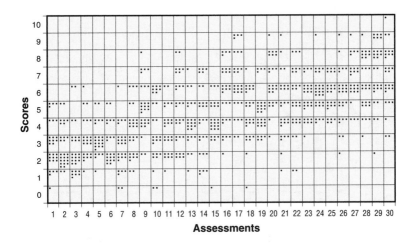

Figure 7.11   Third-period Economics spring class scatter diagram.

How Long Does This Take Each Week?

Giving the quiz, correcting the answers, giving 30- to 45-second explanations on items not yet taught, and recording results takes about 15 minutes per week after about five weeks of implementation. In the beginning of the year, it will take longer because the process is new and so many explanations need to be given on not-yet-taught items. Teachers experienced with continuous improvement say that most of the time is spent teaching—either review of prior content or preview of upcoming content. So, they don't see this as assessment time taking away from instruction; they see this as instruction. Barbara Nelson of Fremont County, Idaho, states it this way, "I often have experiences which lead me to believe I am actually teaching a lot of material during the quiz process and saving time later in the year." Barbara uses continuous improvement in her high school classes. Figures 7.12 through 7.14 are examples from her Physics, Chemistry, and Geometry classes. In the first edition of *Improving Student Learning,* there were no high school examples. Teachers like Barbara, Jeff, and many others have proven that the process suggested by Dr. Deming in 1992 works equally well with high school students. It is worth noting that secondary teachers find that adding up the total or percentage correct for all their like classes is quite valuable.

Karen Bueltel, of Glenwood, Iowa, expected to give up one guided reading lesson each week in order to give quizzes to her first graders. To her amazement, however, she tested them 1:1 as they finished math lessons or were reading silently. Time seems to be the biggest issue before teachers start continuous improvement, but, quickly, time issues are resolved.

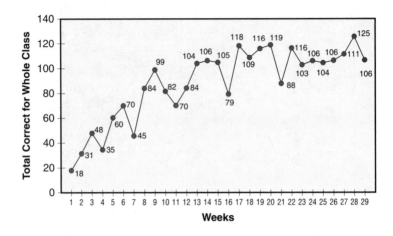

Figure 7.12   Period four Physics, Fremont County, Idaho.

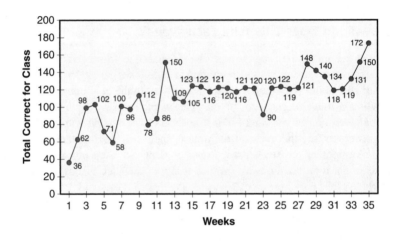

Figure 7.13   Period seven Chemistry, Fremont County, Idaho.

The biggest time saver may come in elementary and middle school mathematics. Most of the K–8 textbooks are about 33 percent review. Continuous improvement teachers are able to begin each year with the new content for their grade level, allowing the weekly quiz time to substitute for a majority of the needed review. Judy Flores, of Redding, California's Enterprise School District, prepared the *Enterprise Weekly* for this very purpose. The content for each grade level was clearly described by district teachers. Next, five items from the current grade, three from the prior grade,

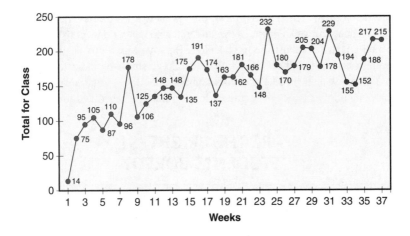

Figure 7.14   Period three Geometry, Fremont County, Idaho.

and two from two years past were randomly selected from their specific content. Quizzes were prepared and the masters sent to the teachers. Appendix Y contains example fifth-grade quizzes written by Judy. Even if 100 percent of one math period per week were taken up in review, this is far less review time than following the textbook and not coming to new content until Thanksgiving or Christmas time. Rochester, Indiana, has patterned their math quizzes on the *Enterprise*, but select seven from the current grade, two from the prior grade, and one from the earlier grade.

An interesting time saver comes from Iowa. The teacher has prepared answer sheets with the parts of speech listed after each number. When a word is randomly chosen, the students merely circle the correct part of speech. Obviously, teachers have the option of reading several sentences, each where the word is a different part of speech.

WHAT ABOUT THE IMPATIENT STUDENTS WHO WANT TO KNOW *RIGHT NOW?*

In every classroom there are a couple of students who want a complete answer *now*. Except for the last month of school, there is a strong probability that every quiz will contain some questions about content not yet taught. The process is for teachers to give a quick 30- to 45-second explanation and tell the students in which month they'll learn the specific content. However, a student or two are likely to protest. They want to know now. Cincinnati calculus teacher Steve Denny tells the students who really do want to know *now* which chapter contains the explanation. He says that a couple of students want to know so badly *right now* that they do go study the indicated chapter. Within a few days they have a fairly complete understanding. Steve also says the remainder of the class is content to wait until the scheduled time.

ARE THE BRIGHTEST STUDENTS BORED?

No, because an aspect of continuous improvement is being able to test out. Generally, teachers accept seven weeks in a row of perfect scores as evidence that the student has mastered the year's essential information. Of course, this does not mean they have met the performance standards, measured with and without rubrics. It only means they have met the expectation for essential information. The two choices available to teachers and students, once they have seven perfect weeks, are the same old two: acceleration and enrichment. This is entirely a value judgment. One student might receive content from the next grade level (acceleration), while another student has several assignments in informal geometry (enrichment), which is rarely an aspect of any grade's curriculum. An example of content from a different grade level comes from Rochester, Indiana. A fifth-grade student had seven weeks in a row perfect on North and South American locations. He was then given a map of Europe. When the rest of the class was taking their quiz on the Americas, he was taking a European quiz. The class received credit for his perfect score on North and South America, but he didn't actually take that quiz.

Figure 7.15 is a student run chart with seven weeks in a row perfect. Note that beyond the seven, perfect scores are credited, so the class graph doesn't go down, but the student is actually involved in either acceleration or enrichment.

The reason for seven quizzes in a row is probability theory. Once teachers reflect upon the theory they learned in middle school math and then apply it to their environment, they have some flexibility with the number of weeks. However, most stay with seven.

If a student scores 100 percent correct one week, what do the teacher and student know? They know there's a 50 percent chance the student knows all of the essential information for the year and a 50 percent chance the student was merely lucky that week. Items came up, by probability, that the student happened to know. What about two weeks in a row? This tells us there's a 25 percent chance the student was lucky and a 75 percent

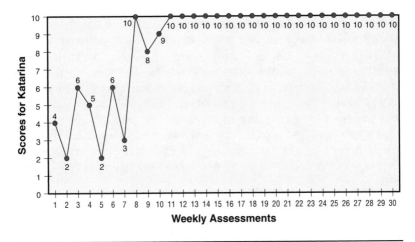

Figure 7.15 Seventh period 100 science facts student run chart for Katarina.

chance it is knowledge. Below are the percentages and probability up to seven weeks in a row with perfect scores:

Number of Weeks with Perfect Score	Probability Student Knows Year's Content
1	50%
2	75%
3	87.5%
4	93.75%
5	96.9%
6	98.4%
7	99.2%

Even though after seven weeks there's only a one percent chance that the student was lucky for seven weeks (the same probability as flipping seven coins and having all heads), some students elect to keep taking the quiz rather than have either enrichment or acceleration. Usually the teacher honors this request.

COUNTING UP THE TOTAL CORRECT

In order to expedite the process, and to not embarrass students, teachers have several ways of collecting numbers. Generally, students are in groups or can be grouped for the adding-up purpose. A monitor is assigned by the teacher to gather up the number correct for each student in their small group and hand it in to the teacher. It is then very easy to add up the totals of these subtotals to have a quick assessment of how the class scored. Jeff Burgard uses this as a mental math exercise with his students. They add up the total in their heads. The conversation might be, "This group has 28 correct, the next one has 17. Together, that's how many?" When he has the answer, he then asks for the total of 45 and whatever the third group scored. This continues until he has the total for the whole class. Afterward, he enters into the computer the individual score for each student in order to have a complete record.

Fifth grade teacher Catherine Blevins (Oklahoma City) has five monitors. The class sits in three groups, each with a monitor. Each monitor brings the total correct for their group to the front of the room, where monitor four writes down the three numbers and adds them up. The total is read off to monitor five, at the back of the room, where the graph is located, and this student places a new dot on the graph and draws a line to join it with the prior week's dot. This adding-up process takes less than a minute.

Kindergarten teacher Shannon Castle (Oklahoma City) takes a little more time in her class to add up the total. She assesses her students monthly on reading letters. After all have read letters to her, she sits the class in a circle while she adds up the total with Base Ten Blocks.[3] She says, "This student read 10 letters" and she picks up a 10-block. Then she reads off, one by one, the total number of letters read by students (without naming the student) and picking up the appropriate number of blocks. When there's a pile of ones, she asks, "Do you think we have 10 yet so we can trade for a 10-block?" They count up the ones and if there are 10, trade them for a 10-block. When they have 10 10-blocks, they trade them for a 100-block. So, even in kindergarten when students see the graph with the number correct, they know how the teacher arrived at the number.

CAN ALL STUDENTS MAKE RUN (LINE) GRAPHS?

No. Most teachers in the primary grades have students make a bar or column graph. In kindergarten, an adult often draws a light pencil line where the graph is to be colored. Then the students color over the line. In general, bar and column graphs are designed to show a moment in time, not movement over time. So the run chart is more accurate, but there's plenty of time to communicate this. Column graphs in primary grades are wonderful.

WHAT SHOULD BE THE GOAL?

Pine Island Middle School teacher Jenny Bushman used continuous improvement for her students to learn 50 essential grammar facts (appendix F) in seventh grade. Her run chart for sixth period is shown in Figure 7.16. If all of her sixth-period students were to answer correctly all seven weekly questions (seven being the approximate square root of 50), then the total correct for the class would be 105. A reasonable person might say to the class that the goal for the year is 90. Don't do it! Here's why:

The problem with most numerical goals is they are arbitrary. Why not a goal of 92? 100? Besides, the class's best week was 82, four better than their prior best week of 78. Should they celebrate their all-time best, or be sad because they didn't reach 90 or some other arbitrary number? It is far better, and this is an essential element of continuous improvement, to have the goal merely to score higher than we ever have before. In Jenny's example, the class had their all-time best in weeks 4, 5, 7, 8, 10, 13, and 14. So, seven times during the semester they were able to celebrate!

I asked a middle school student what happens when they have their best week and he responded, "Oh, our teacher is *really* happy."

When a teacher sets up a system to celebrate all-time highs there is a guarantee that celebrations will occur. When an arbitrary goal is set, two things can go wrong: (1) not meet the goal and be discouraged, or (2) meet the goal earlier in the year and then slow down. For example, if the goal in Jenny's class was 80, the class would have no reason to attempt to answer 105 correctly. They would overlook the fact that they missed 25 and still needed to improve.

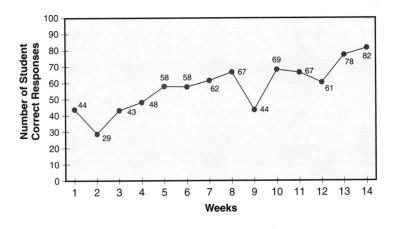

Figure 7.16   Jenny Bushman's sixth-period English class.

Teachers and students, however, do compare the number correct and the percentage of the year that is complete. For example, if the total possible correct for a class is 320, the students at the first quarter check to see if the class has at least 80 correct, then at semester if they have 160 correct, and at third quarter 240. Time will eventually win, but how long can students beat the clock? For example, it might be that when 90 percent of the year is used up, the students answered 88 percent of the questions. They should know that since 1992 I have no evidence of a perfect week on any quiz, so perfection is not the goal; the goal is having all-time bests.

WHAT ABOUT ABSENCES AND THE RESULTING DOWNTURNS ON THE GRAPHS?

Do absences discourage the students? Yes and no.

When people are absent, productivity goes down. This is true in all organizations, including schools. Students generally have no way of knowing that their absence hurt the class. But when learning is graphed, students see that their absence caused the graph to go down. Fifth-graders with 15 spelling words per week said, "When two students are absent, we know we're down 30 already. We need to try really hard to make this up."

Students at all ages admit they are absent sometimes for no good reason. However, on the day of the quiz they also admit they are less likely to be absent. This is somewhat true because classmates, upon their return, will say, "Where were you yesterday?! We needed you!"

Lloyd Roettger, professor at University of Central Oklahoma, taught the same class on both Monday and Tuesday nights during the spring semester of 2001–02. In prior years, students who were absent on Monday were just absent—they missed the class. However, when he introduced continuous improvement in his classes, quizzing them on 10 facts per week, randomly selected from 113 essential research methods facts, (appendix L) students made up the class. So even adult students feel the need to contribute to the success of the class. They don't want to be the cause of the decrease. (See Figure 7.17.)

So, a good argument can be made for graphing the total correct and having students know attendance is one variable. Another good argument can be made for computing percent correct alongside number correct. Figures 7.18 and 7.19 are two run charts of the same data from Jeff Hoseley's Meridian High School Government class. There were more absences at the end of the course, but those present scored a higher and

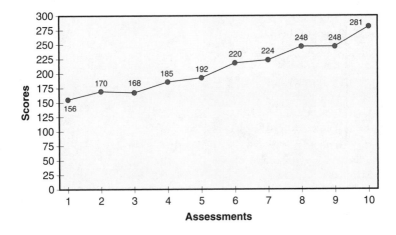

Figure 7.17   Graduate educational research Monday section class run chart.

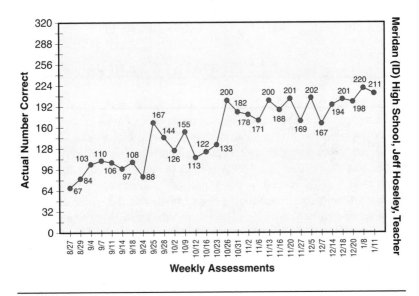

Figure 7.18   Second period American Government class run chart.

higher percent correct. Graphing the percent correct does not cause a problem; graphing the average correct does cause harm. (See chapter 17.)

When students see blanks on their own student run chart, it does remind them and their parents that they were absent. Debi Molina-Walters states, "This is powerful to show parents attendance patterns."

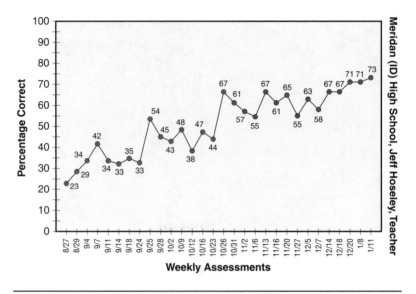

Figure 7.19   Second period American Government class run chart.

THE MULTIPLICATION TABLES

Duane Dober, a West Virginia principal, received an urgent call from one of his fourth grade classrooms. Fearing the worst, he rushed down to the room. However, to his surprise, the class wanted him to know that they answered 184 of a possible 189 multiplication facts. This was all-time high; the best of the year. Regularly, the teacher randomly selected certain multiplication facts, gave them a timed quiz, and counted up the total correct for the whole class. Duane took a digital picture of the whole class, with one student pointing on the graph to the all-time high. This photograph was then inserted into the PowerPoint presentation that showed continuously in the foyer of the school.

Regarding multiplication, some teachers have monitored speed rather than number correct. The time is recorded, with a time penalty of five seconds for incorrect answers. Obviously, as a class improves, this graph moves downward. A Minnesota teacher reported that when she changed from number correct to time to complete 100 percent of the worksheet, her slower students said, "Oh, boy! We get to finish." Within three days, the total time for the class had decreased and students who had previously given up on times tables had their hope restored. Sherri Soluri of Citrus County, Florida, told me that until she gave students time to finish a multiplication fact quiz, she did not know which students truly didn't know the facts and which students took longer to process the math.

I have known for years that triangle flash cards were an improvement over rectangular cards. The "flasher" covers up one number on the card. The "flashee" has to name the missing number. Depending upon which number is covered up, the "flashee" is presented with a division or a multiplication problem.

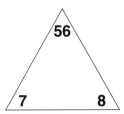

Iowa educator Kerry Newman took this idea and made the multiplication table quiz match the practice method. (See appendix G for three math quizzes ready to be copied and cut into thirds.) This is yet another example of how educators are adopting the principles of continuous improvement in their respective schools.

Elementary teachers Tim Sheppard and Nancy Hunter of Wenatchee, Washington, have another intriguing improvement upon the traditional multiplication test. Students are provided the 72 fact families for add, subtract, multiply, and divide (see appendix W). Eight facts are randomly selected from the 72 each week. One of the facts of each of the eight families are partially recorded for the quiz. For example, the teachers might write $3 \times 4 =$ ___. Students are to write the remainder of the fact family and complete the first sentence: $3 \times 4 = 12$, $4 \times 3 = 12$, $12 \div 4 = 3$, $12 \div 3 = 4$.

INSIGHTS FROM CINCINNATI

Steve Denny and Dave Bell of Cincinnati's Winton Woods High School summarize their observations regarding continuous improvement as "ah-ha's." My top 10 of their "ah-ha's" are:

1. Students have accepted responsibility for the learning goal.

2. Students are ready and anxious to help one another reach the learning goal.

3. Student ideas about how to reach the learning goal are plentiful.

4. Students have become active teachers of one another.

5. Intervention is much more successful now.

6. Teachers have a clearer picture of where they need to intervene.

7. Students have a much more accurate sense of their progress.

8. Parents with no background in our subjects (music and calculus, in this example), can walk into our rooms and immediately feel good about the progress being made.

9. Parents with continuous improvement background in industry are anxious to offer ideas and reflections. (In Cincinnati this often comes from Proctor and Gamble.)

10. Various aspects of continuous improvement motivate different students. Some are motivated by the class run chart (being a team player), some are more motivated by their own growth (student run chart) and some are more motivated by the competition of keeping up (scatter diagram).

The class run chart from Steve's Calculus class is shown in Figure 7.20. See appendix J for his list of essential calculus facts.

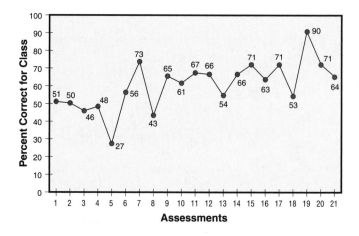

Figure 7.20   Pre-Calculus Honors class run chart.

CHARACTER EDUCATION

A very intriguing application of essential information learning comes from the Tipton, Iowa, Middle School. Principal Brian Krob quizzes students on character education definitions. Students have the definitions in their agenda books and teachers designed 65 questions on the vocabulary. Each week they are assessed on random questions and the totals for the school are posted. Five examples of character education definitions are:

1. Controlling one's actions is *self-control.*

2. Doing something without being asked is taking *initiative.*

3. Meeting deadlines is being *responsible.*

4. Taking pride in one's self is *self-respect.*

5. Sticking to a purpose or an aim is *perseverance.*

THE ENERGY

What is the energy that keeps this process moving from week to week in so many locales? It is student energy. As Oklahoma's Jay Troy writes, "They keep asking when are we going to have the next quiz. Students love seeing that they are growing." Christi Grossnickle of Rochester, Indiana, adds, "This just makes learning and teaching so much fun. It takes away so many behavior issues because all of our heads are together. Great energy comes from fun and heads together!"

Carolyn Ayres observes, "The motivation seems to come naturally with the process of testing, checking, learning from mistakes, improving, and being able to see the visible evidence of growth on the graphs."

REVIEW WITH SPELLING EXAMPLE

Because everyone growing up in the United States has experienced the Friday spelling test, I've chosen to retell the continuous improvement process with spelling as an example. (Figures 7.21, 7.22, and 7.23 are from Karen Fauss' second-grade classroom in Redding, California.)

During the first week of school, students are provided a list of the spelling words for the entire year. Students are told they will be quizzed each week on some of the words. They are not told ahead of time exactly

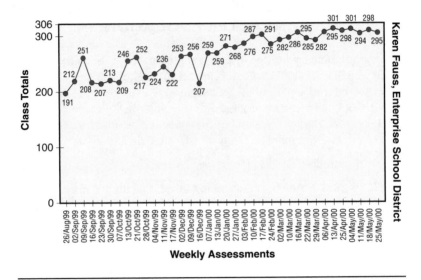

Figure 7.21 Spelling class run chart.

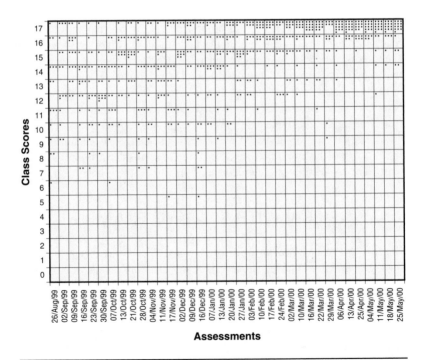

Figure 7.22 Spelling class scatter diagram.

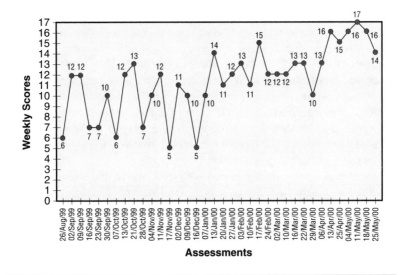

Figure 7.23 Spelling student run chart for one student.

which words, because this causes students to go home and memorize the words for the test. Teachers tell the students that the selected words are very important and should be known for life, not merely for a test. The spelling tests will not be graded, but at the very end of the year, all students are expected to know all the words.

The first week of school some words are randomly selected. (The sample size is the square root of the total words for the year). If an observer unfamiliar with continuous improvement walked into the classroom during the spelling test, it would look very familiar, except that the next spelling word is randomly chosen, rather than from a preset list. Everything else is the same: students have their pages numbered, they spell each word as it is dictated, and turn in the papers when done.

When students receive their corrected spelling test back, they retrieve their spelling graph and place a dot for the number correct and connect the dot with the prior week's dot. The teacher, or a designated student, then walks over to the class graph and records the class total. Some teachers print out a new graph each week from a computer and others add a dot to an existing graph. This is all individual teacher preference.

Teaching of the spelling is not random. The logical structure for teaching spelling that has worked before is used. It is the assessment that is random, not the teaching. The major difference is that the teacher knows which spelling words are in the students' long-term memory and which are easily forgotten.

Because of the constant review and preview, adjustments are made to lessons. Sometimes, teachers find no need to teach a particular pattern or word—students already know it. They also work and work to find a way for students to spell words that are particularly difficult. They experiment. For example, Arnoldburg, West Virginia, teacher Shirley Chenoweth hypothesized that it would be easier for her first-graders to learn their 100 spelling words if she organized them by number of letters, rather than in alphabetical order. So she took the list of words and retyped them by one-letter words, two-letter words, three-letter words, and so on. She was right; in about three weeks her graph shot up.

Another significant difference with continuous improvement is that teachers no longer find it necessary to offer rewards for high scores. The innate desire to do well and contribute to the class total is much more powerful than the stickers so often offered. The teacher does conduct class meetings to obtain student input regarding how to improve, and certainly the teacher is a cheerleader when scores go up and a counselor when scores go down.

MORE EXAMPLES

In chapter 6, Dave Brown's performance rubric for his ceramics class is shown as an example of using continuous improvement for performance. In this chapter, Figure 7.24 is the same class's record for essential information. Appendix V is the list of essential information the quizzes were based upon.

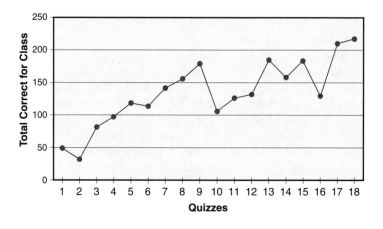

Figure 7.24   Block 3 Ceramics and Pottery I Concepts class run chart.

Much of chapter 14 consists of student comments from his classes regarding the quizzes and graphing. Dave says that the graphs accomplished at least two things in his classrooms: (1) improvement, because learning became more important than grades, and (2) the students were able to process and use information in useful ways. It is very heartening to see the arts teachers accept their responsibility for teaching essential information. I'd never want to see their focus move from performance to information, but their responsibility is not 100 percent performance. See appendix M for an example of Hope Showley's work in Rochester, Indiana. She excitedly told me about the day the students came to her and said, "We've been studying. Somebody in class knows everything on the list (and thus we can learn from them), but nobody knows these five items; you'll have to teach them." Think about it—Hope prepared the list and the students requested to learn what she wanted them to learn in the first place.

Dee Lovejoy in Glenwood, Iowa, gave her students a blank world map at the beginning of fifth grade and asked students to label anything they knew. Most students labeled five or less locations. At the end of the year the least anyone labeled was 50 and most were 75 or higher. Appendix X is the list of locations she gave the students. Each student also had a world map with 100 locations numbered. For each quiz, 10 locations were randomly selected and the students wrote down the name of the number on the map. Each of the four columns on the list were color coded on the map, so that if number 30 was randomly selected, they would know they were looking for a country and countries are all labeled with the same color. At Dee's school, the fourth-grade students have U.S. map locations, fifth-graders have world locations, and sixth-graders focus upon Roman history. However, each successive grade level is responsible for the prior grade's information plus the current grade's information.

John Bueltel is an art teacher in Glenwood, Iowa. His list of art concepts is similar to Dave Brown's in Appendix V, although since he's in middle school and Dave teaches high school, it's not quite as complex. John faces the problem of having a two-year curriculum that rotates. Often the music, art, technology, and health teachers have this situation. John's solution, which makes great sense, is to give the students the essential facts he wants them to know over a two-year period and his graphs extend for two years, unlike the one-year graphs shown in every other example in this book.

Woody Wilson of Parkersburg, West Virginia, assesses his students on geography locations, American history essential (he calls them fabulous) facts, and world history facts. His graphs and lists are quite similar to the other examples in this chapter. However, Woody has one of the most unique adaptations of continuous improvement I've seen. His students all have a laminated set of 20th-century presidents and five markers, labeled one through five. Every week they have a five-item quiz. When the randomly selected statement is read, the students must place the marker for the statement on top of the person who was president when that event occurred. Five sample statements are:

1. The United States goes to war with Spain, seizes the Philippines, and annexes Hawaii.

2. Congress passes the Interstate Highway Act—the president signs it.

3. Martin Luther King is dead.

4. The Soviet Union launches Sputnik.

5. The Iranian hostage crisis dominates the news.

PERFORMANCE VERSUS ESSENTIAL INFORMATION

Dr. Deming's theories were largely rejected by U.S. business leaders from 1950 to 1980 because he insisted that it was possible to have higher quality and lower prices at the same time. Business leaders knew for sure that lower prices (and lower quality) were available from Japan, average prices (and average quality) were available in the United States, and that higher prices (with higher quality) came from Europe. The notion of high quality/ low prices was a completely unfathomable idea. Not until Japanese manufacturers, working with Dr. Deming, proved this was possible, did American business leaders need to listen.

Education has a similar problem. Educators believe that if the public wants more information learning, then time has to be taken from performance learning. Likewise, if America wants more performance, time is taken from learning information. This is a false dichotomy. We can have more information and better performance at the same time. New Mexico's Kevin Baker is joined by many others using continuous improvement when he says, "Performance goes up because I'm not spending so much time on review." Jean Wilson and her colleagues, of Parkersburg, West Virginia, have written an essential information list about the writing process. This is yet another powerful example of how teachers see learning information assisting performance. Their work is included in appendix Z. Jean states that now her feedback, in regards to student performance, is understood by the students because of the continual review/preview of concepts in appendix Z. How can business have higher quality and lower costs? By spending less money on rework, warranty repair, and returned items. How can education have more time for performance assignments and increased learning of essential facts? By not having to waste so much time on review—by not giving permission to forget and thus saving considerable time.

ENDNOTES

1. "Don't Know Much About History, Why Not?" *Education Week* (June 19, 2002): 37.
2. Game Science, 228-392-4177, 7604 Newton Drive, North Biloxi, MS 39532.
3. Base Ten Blocks are used by students to compute, prior to computing abstractly. There are four blocks: one is represented by a 1 cm cube; 10 is 1 cm × 1 cm × 10 cm; hundred is 1 cm × 10 cm × 10 cm; and thousand is a 10 cm cube.

8

Special Education and English Language Learners

SPECIAL EDUCATION

The initial work with continuous improvement in special education was done with reading fluency. The process for special education reading fluency is exactly the same as described in chapter 5, with two modifications. The first is the need to assess fluency weekly, rather than monthly. The purpose of the weekly fluency assessment is encouragement; students and adults must know that their hard work is paying off. Figures 8.1 through 8.4

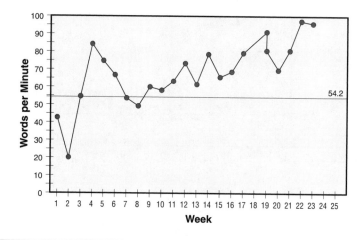

Figure 8.1 Special education reading, student one.

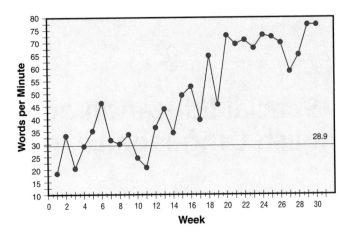

Figure 8.2   Special education reading, student two.

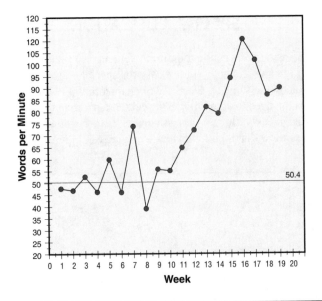

Figure 8.3   Special education reading, student three.

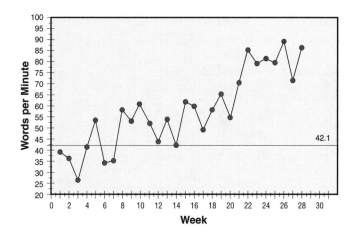

Figure 8.4 Special education reading, student four.

are early examples of special education reading fluency. After a period of time, all four show improvement in fluency. The graph is a visual that says, "I can do this." Compliments are OK, praise is fine, but proof that I'm reading is stupendous.

A second special education change is a baseline drawn across the graph showing the average for the first seven assessments. The student whose results are shown in Figure 8.5 was assessed 21 times during the 2000–01 school year on 10 Dolch sight words, randomly selected from 100. The average number of words she read the first seven weeks was 4.8.

The baseline is needed when educators encounter the most difficult of reading situations. Figure 8.5 is from Marilyn Evans' Las Cruces, New Mexico, classroom. Without the line, observers would draw the false conclusion that no improvement occurred. If no improvement occurs in weeks eight to 21, then half of the weeks would be below the average of 4.8 and half above the average. However, in this example all but three data points, after the first seven for the baseline, are above the average. Thus, the student did improve her ability to read sight words during the year, even though the improvement was ever so slight.

This minor improvement was so encouraging to the student and her parents that hope was restored. The next year she was quizzed 32 times on 15 Dolch sight words randomly selected from 220. Figure 8.6 documents the second year of reading. No baseline is needed; any observer can see the improvement!

Marilyn and her colleagues at Mesilla Park Elementary School provided the insight regarding how to have a class run chart when all of the

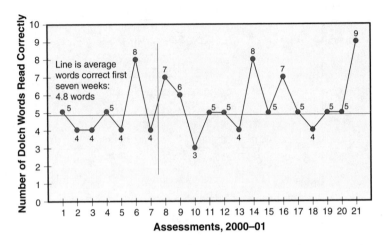

After seven weeks, student's record is 11 assessments above the average and four below the average. If no improvement had occured, then student would have had 7, or the remaining 14 assessments, above the average and 7 below the average.

Almost all improvement can be seen at a glance; but the most difficult of special education students need the average line drawn after seven assessments.

Figure 8.5   One special education student's run chart.

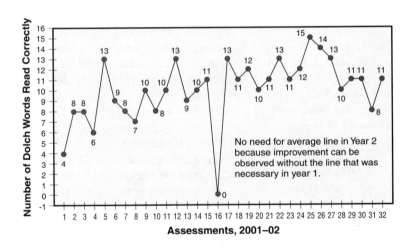

Figure 8.6   One special education student's run chart: year two.

various individual education plans (IEPs) are diverse. They devised a rubric: one means the student did not meet his or her IEP goals, two means the student met the goals, and three means the student exceeded the goals. Thus a special education class can now have a class run chart. A class of 10 special education students, for example, is working to achieve a total of 30 on their graph.

Many topics are taught in special education that might not be on anybody's IEP. For example, one California teacher determined that her students had little idea regarding where the 50 U.S. states were located. Her graph for the states was no different than any other graph from general education described in chapter 7.

Another use of continuous improvement in the special education classroom is vocabulary development. Appendix I is a special education vocabulary list from Glenwood, Iowa. The teacher was particularly amused and happy when she was having a stressful time and a student said, "It looks like you are befuddled today."

Marilyn Evans states that it is so powerful when special education teachers have the same IEP objectives as the general education teacher. The students in special education need extra help to learn what others are learning in the general classes, but do not necessarily need different objectives. On one of my speaking tours, I was addressing approximately 50 special education teachers. I asked them to check out an observation for me. I said, "It seems like secondary special education teachers, and some elementary special education teachers, have become homework clerks. Their number one job is to help students with the homework assigned by general education. This is a shame; you have all of this extra education to help our most difficult students and you have been reduced to being a homework tutor. Is my observation correct?" They replied with a loud, "Yes!"

So what is the solution to the homework clerk problem? It is what Marilyn stated above: Teachers in special education and general education need the same objectives. When general education teachers are very specific about what is to be learned (essential information and performance standards), then the job of the special education teachers is to help their students meet the objectives set by general education. When the special education student receives the expectations for the year, that is the moment the special education teachers receive their expectations. The special education teachers are no longer homework clerks, but partners in increasing success and decreasing failure on year-long expectations.

One of the most extensive uses of continuous improvement in special education is at James Marshall High School in Oklahoma City. The 12 special education teachers all start their classes with lists of 100 essential facts for the class. In this large high school, the special education department is able to have its own teachers for each subject, so these students are experiencing continuous improvement in all subjects. Clearly, leadership from the department chair, Shelly Campbell, has been a major aspect of this implementation. She reported that the staff reviewed each other's lists to assure they were appropriate and the facts from all teachers were printed and placed in a booklet for the students. It was seeing all of the content from history to English to civics to geography to math in one bound booklet that captured the spirit of togetherness. Shelly said that this process gives special education students and staff a real, concrete goal. They have a purpose and are working together. Even students unable to learn the standard curriculum have their expectations listed, such as knowing their home address, and so on.

Special education is about the individual student, so when special education teachers talk about continuous improvement implementation they give examples of student success. Marilyn Evans tells of a student who had the same IEP goals for five years and finally mastered them during his first year of continuous improvement. In language composition, on the New Mexico standardized test he went from the 17th percentile in fourth grade, to the 55th in fifth grade, to the 64th percentile in sixth grade. All students need regular feedback to know they are learning, but it is even more important in special education because many students have given up. Why else would a student have the same IEP goals for five years?

The best tool for individual growth in speech articulation is the web. appendix S is a blank articulation web chart. (Some call this a radar chart; the terms are interchangeable.) With the help of Marlane Parra, Las Cruces, New Mexico, the web has been fine-tuned.

There are 32 spokes on the web, one per sound that an articulation student may need to master. The zero to six is the articulation rubric. A zero means the student cannot pronounce the phoneme; a one means the student can imitate the phoneme; a two means the student can produce the phoneme in isolation; a three indicates the student can produce the phoneme in a word; a four means the student can produce the phoneme in a sentence; a five means the student can produce the phoneme in a conversation during therapy; and a six means the student can produce the phoneme in spontaneous conversation. Each time an assessment is given, a different colored pen is used to connect the dots. The legend is made using the pen color to write the date of the assessment. Students normally come to speech for help with only a few phonemes. The web documents the prior successes by putting so many dots at "6," and also by showing improvement when dots move up to the "6."

It is healthy to say to students: There are 32 English phonemes on this chart. Of the 32, we are working on three. Pretty good—29 down and three to go. Your chart shows you know 29 of the 32 troublesome phonemes and

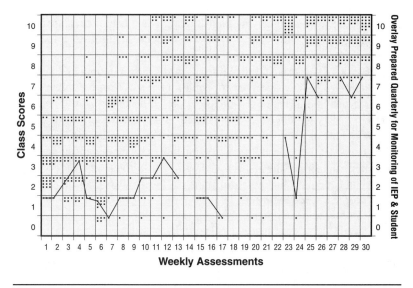

Figure 8.7   Science facts—seventh period class scatter diagram with overlay.

we are working on three. Together, we'll move all of the dots to the outside of the web chart.

Physical therapy can use the same web format. The spokes are the various tasks to be accomplished and the zero to four is the rubric from cannot perform, can perform with help, can perform when being observed, and performs always.

The final use of continuous improvement in special education, which is somewhat varied from the applications in general education, is writing into monitoring IEP's that student overlays are to be produced and observed quarterly. Somewhere between forgetting about monitoring students and constant inspection is a happy monitoring experience. The quarterly study of a scatter diagram, with the special education overlay as shown in Figure 8.7, should take little time and yet meet both the spirit of the law and actual monitoring requirements. The gaps in the graph are due to absences.

ENGLISH LANGUAGE LEARNERS

English language learners have benefited greatly from the use of continuous improvement strategies. For some, such as students in Natalie Olague's Albuquerque dual language classroom, all graphs look the same except that there are Spanish reading graphs and English reading graphs. The beauty of the cooperation developed through continuous improvement is that a student who is higher in Spanish reading can help a student who is lower in Spanish reading. These same two students might reverse the help when they are working on English reading.

Ontario, California's Mary Miller uses all of the continuous improvement strategies reviewed earlier. Appendix Q is the list of English commands, terms, and directions she expects her students to know. There are always a variety of languages represented in her classroom, so all of the quizzes and the answers are given in English. For example, she might say, "What does stand up mean?" and the students draw a person standing up. She then demonstrates the answer when going over the quiz. Mary has her students not only graph their own progress but to also graph the whole class's progress. (See Figure 8.8.)

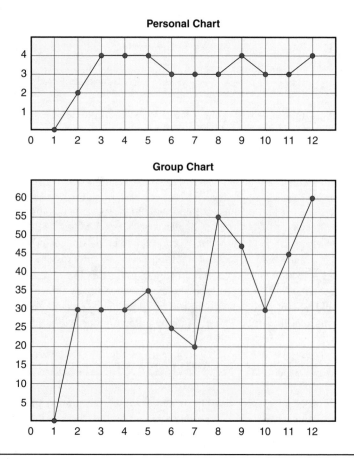

Figure 8.8 English language learner's key concepts.

Jan Lopez, also from Ontario, California, teaches sixth grade. Even though she is a general education teacher, most of her students speak Spanish as their home language. Her students moved from 23 percent at grade level to 67 percent with continuous improvement. Her students have infrared remotes to answer all questions on the weekly quizzes. They receive immediate feedback on their answers and all data is recorded on the teacher's computer.

Sometimes, the ELL teacher is using vocabulary rather than phrases. When vocabulary is the choice for continuous improvement, teachers have been very careful to select enough vocabulary for the year. Clearly, 100 vocabulary words for a student new to the United States is not enough for a year. Different teachers have chosen various numbers of words, but the expectations are high and reasonable.

A FINAL NOTE

Continuous improvement for special education and English language learners is almost the same as in general education. In fact, the implementation of continuous improvement is so similar that I almost didn't write a separate chapter. However, the adaptations developed by special education and ELL teachers were so ingenious that this chapter had to be included. My hope is that special education teachers will be inspired by the contributions of the great teachers referenced in this chapter, and invent even more improvements for continuous improvement. I also hope that general education teachers will not skip this chapter because the insights provided here can help all increase success and decrease failure.

9

Monitoring Discipline, Attendance, Late Buses, and Other Time Wasters

ontinuous improvement philosophy and tools can be used for monitoring and improving everything, including eliminating irritants and time wasters. Consistently people ask, when an irritant has virtually disappeared, "How did you accomplish that? Do you know people in high places? This has been a problem for years and you solved it in no time." The answer is always the same—"a dot on the wall."

Jean Jaworski of Citrus County, Florida, and Scott Mills of Rochester, Indiana, tell almost identical stories regarding school buses. For years, nobody was able to solve the problem. Often, it seems the people with the power to solve the problem don't think there's a problem. A simple graph communicates that there is a problem. In Jean's case, one bus always left later than the other buses. In Scott's case, one morning bus always arrived 10 to 15 minutes before anyone was on duty to supervise. Can you imagine how middle grade students reacted to being on the bus an additional 10 minutes, just sitting in front of the school?

The graphing and posting of the data caused people responsible for bus schedules to figure out what was causing the problem. Figure 9.1 shows bus departure times, with the tardy bus visible on most days. This compares to all other buses that left at the exact same time. First of all, the graph communicated that there was a problem. It was a scheduling problem, not a bus driver problem, that was causing the frustration. Figure 9.2 shows bus departure times in February; the scheduling problem was solved. Scott's results in Rochester were identical; once the graph was placed in the school foyer, the schedulers were able to fix the problem. Somehow the graph communicates the facts to all parties, whereas prior to the graphs, the people who could

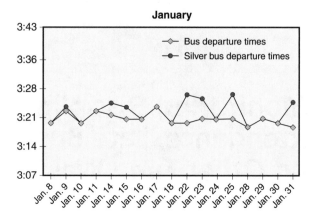

Figure 9.1   Bus departure times for January.

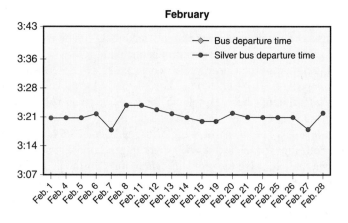

Figure 9.2   Bus departure times for February: all buses left at same time.

solve the problem thought there was merely a difference of opinion regarding buses.

Office personnel don't know how many interruptions a classroom has because there may be up to 10 people doing the interrupting. One teacher had their students graph the number of interruptions each day and deliver the updated graph to the office. All involved in the interruptions immediately worked together to reduce them. Colleagues of this teacher at first thought she had an "in" with the principal. There was no "in"; the office staff, for the first time ever, truly saw the magnitude of the problem.

School personnel all over the United States have tried many different carrots and sticks to improve attendance. Catherine Blevins in Oklahoma City merely had the students graph the number present each day. Figure 9.3 displays daily attendance for a portion of 2001–02. The simple act of having a student graph the attendance brought about improvement. Students in the classroom admitted that the graph improved their attendance. Questionable absences were reduced because they knew their absence would affect the classroom. She began this process because she had some chronic attendance problems. In general, attendance went from approximately 16 present per day to 20 per day, with 24 being perfect. The bus, classroom interruption, and attendance problems are quite similar. In all three examples, the people who could solve the problems didn't think there were problems—until they saw the graphs.

Continuous improvement is marvelous for discipline in all grades. It shares the responsibility for behavior with all involved. Chapter 2 describes schoolwide discipline problem solving; the classroom is quite similar. Charles Thomas, of Arnoldsburg, West Virginia, began monitoring behavior in January of 2002. Christmas vacation gave him the time to devise a most unique system. He used many of the quality tools described in chapter 16 to study misbehaviors and causes. The students said there were six misbehaviors: (1) talking or interrupting, (2) out of seat, (3) playing around in desk, (4) hurting others, (5) pencil sharpener at wrong time, and (6) not paying attention. Each of the six were color coded, the color choice having no significance. The students were all provided a sheet of one-inch graph paper for January. They wrote the dates they were in school that month along the bottom of the graph paper. When students misbehaved, Charles merely said to

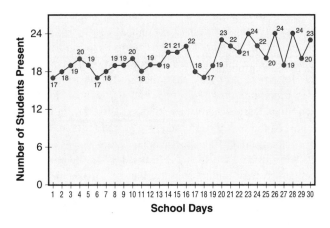

Figure 9.3   Catherine Blevins' classroom attendance.

the student, "That's a green" and made a tally mark. The involved student took out his/her graph and colored in a green above the correct date. At the end of the day Charles recorded the total number of infractions on the classroom graph. (See Figure 9.4.) The only concern the students have, when "good" on a graph shows them going "down," is that all visitors must understand that this graph is *supposed to* go down. They are not becoming "stupider" in some subject. (I have added the control chart upper control limit (UCL), central line (CL), and lower control limit (LCL) to separate special from common cause variation, as described in chapter 23 on control charts. These extra three lines were not present in the classroom.)

It is amazing to me that the stories from different parts of the United States are so similar. Karen Bueltel also started tracking discipline, after Christmas vacation, with her first graders. She put a tally mark down every time "any behavior interrupted my teaching or any other child." Karen states that, "every time the principal came in the classroom, some girls would take him over and explain that going down is a good thing."

Shelly Carson describes in *Continuous Improvement in the History/ Social Science Classroom* how she developed a rubric for behavior with the substitute teacher. When she returned to the classroom, each student wrote down a number. She calculated the average, and had an almost perfect picture of behavior when she was absent. She also had the rubric score from the substitute to see if perceptions matched.

Marilyn Evans from Las Cruces, New Mexico, was assigned a special education student for five hours per week of instruction in reading. This student was well known for his repeated misbehaviors and it seemed nobody could control him. Marilyn and the student agreed on his four most irritating misbehaviors. Marilyn explained that she was going to graph his misbehavior and they were going to work on reducing the number of these four incidents. However, she couldn't sit around all day and count him. There were other students at the same time, so she divided up the five hours into 20 15-minute segments and numbered them, then each week she randomly picked five of the time slots and wrote them in her planning book. The student saw her randomly pick the times and write them down, but didn't know which times were selected. She then counted during these randomly selected times. At the end of each hour, she brought him up to her desk and they recorded the number of misbehaviors during the times she counted. Some hours she didn't count and some hours she counted more than one 15-minute segment. It was random with no pattern for him to figure out. He seemed immune to punishment and there were no new bribes that would make him behave, but he *really disliked* the graph going up. He wanted the graph down. The person with the ability to solve the problem (the student, in this case) for the first time really saw the problem.

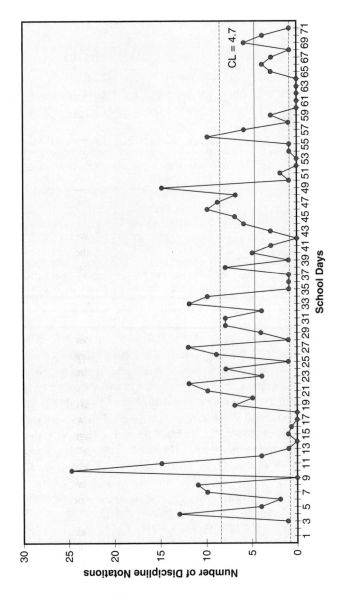

Figure 9.4 Number of discipline notations. Charles Thomas, Arnoldsburg, West Virginia.

Christi Grossnickle of Rochester, Indiana, had her students make a rubric of bathroom behavior. Each day, one boy and one girl were randomly selected to state how the behavior of the class was in the bathroom. The rubric the students wrote is below:

Restroom Rubric

	Great	So-So	Bad
Voice and Feet	I whisper only when needed. I walk.	I talk out loud. I run or jump around.	I yell and talk in my loud voice.
Wash Hands	I use one pull of soap. I use three pulls of towels.	I use more than one pull of soap. I use more than three pulls of towels.	I use way too much soap. I use many pulls of towels. I throw towels on the floor or ceiling.
Toilet Use	I am careful while using the toilet. I remember to flush. I report accidents to my teacher.	I am not always careful in using the toilet. I sometimes forget to flush. I don't always report accidents.	I am not careful when using the toilet. I never flush. I never report accidents to my teacher.

There are numerous instances available of continuous improvement for monitoring irritants: trash on the grounds, dirty facilities, and poorly written IEP's. The only change needed is random selection, graphing of results, and the generation of hypotheses for improvement. There's not time to count all the trash in the campus, but one location can be randomly selected each day, the trash counted, and improvement theories attempted. The principal does not have time to inspect the building each day to see if the night custodians are completing their work. However, one random location can be inspected. Why should the "IEP Police" inspect all IEPs at once? Select the square root of the total IEPs every other week and inspect them. The lessons learned can help improve the whole system, instead of causing harried staff to feel spied upon.

All of the topics of this chapter are time wasters; they detract from the central mission of schools. Time wasted on bus duty detracts from time to tutor and plan. Time wasted picking up trash detracts from preventive cleaning and maintenance, which takes money from library books when a huge maintenance problem occurs. Interruptions detract from learning, but we need not merely cope; educators can use "dots on the wall" to improve the workplace.

10

What Students Have to Say

"Help me with this problem," I asked eighth grade math students. "You have been telling me for 15 minutes how much you like the weekly quizzes and graphing. Now I need your help when talking with other math teachers. Many math teachers tell me it is a waste of time to quiz students on topics not yet taught. And yet you love it. What do I say to other teachers?"

The response was, "Tell the math teachers we love it because it is fun to try and figure out the answer on our own. Then, when the teacher explains how to do the problem, we are listening to see if we got it right." The key word from the quote is "listening." It seems like the preview questions are a hook; they cause the students to want to know.

Jay Troy, an Oklahoma educator, has interviewed many students regarding continuous improvement. Often the students are in programs for learning and/or behavior problems. A student who had been removed from her regular school and almost removed from the alternative programs was asked about quizzing and graphing. She said, "We like the quizzes because we can see that we are learning."

Students in Rochester, Indiana, wrote their superintendent, Bob Poffenbarger, regarding their thoughts on continuous improvement. One of them said, "Thank you for coming and interviewing us. We really appreciated all the comments. We all liked how you videotaped us and our graphs. If you hadn't met Lee Jenkins, there wouldn't be any graphs."

Dave Brown's high school art classes, regarding the graphing of weekly quizzes, said:

"It's been a lot of the same answers and you remember after awhile."

"I liked them because you are quizzed without a grade, which doesn't put pressure on the student to learn them on their own. They were taught to a group over a period of time, not just one day."

"It was easy (kinda) for me to do this test."

"This is much better than using the books."

"This is better because some students do not enjoy reading."

"This was better than book work!!"

"Every day you learn more and more, which is like studying."

"I didn't even have to study the night before the exam and I didn't have any trouble on the final."

"Ten out of 10! The class quizzes have everyone learn it better."

"The quizzes did help me learn more about pottery. It helped me learn more because we did quizzes every day, rather than trying to study all of the information in one night."

"Yes, yes, yes! This is a lot easier because you don't have to cram the night before."

"Now it is stuck in my head."

"I think the quizzes helped me out a lot."

"I did the final like it was nothing."

"The quizzes were easier and more fun to do."

"We will never forget."

"This was great because we reviewed for the final all year."

Middle school students seem to always have profound insights. This topic is no different. Three comments are:

"When I have homework, I get out of chores. With this list, I always have homework."

"We can memorize a short list, but this is too long; we have to *know* it."

"Since there's no school on Friday, you'll have to give us the quiz on Thursday."

Here are comments from Ann Miller's Science classes in Rochester, Minnesota:

"I think it is fun because of not having to cram it all in your head; this way it is easier to remember."

"I think it is working because sometimes we get the same ones. You could also get different ones too. It's fun too because you don't know what's going to come up. We also get chances to roll the dice."

"I think random sampling is fun because you get to roll dice and it can be any number."

"I think that you could learn more if you use random sampling. But a disadvantage is that sometimes the same numbers come up. I think if you don't know what's coming next, you learn them faster and better. So, I think random sampling is a good thing."

"I think what we are doing is a good way to learn the words that will be on the final test, so I think we should keep doing it."

"I think random sampling is a good idea because then the kids can't study just the ones that we are going to do. It makes them study the whole study sheet."

Debi Molina-Walters' sixth grade students write:

"I like it. It identifies what we need to learn, so I can focus on those things and not waste time since I know what I need to do."

"(The quizzes) help me track my progress and they tell me what I need to review and study."

"The Life Journal (collection of all standards and graphs) has taught me how to set goals and make a plan of action to reach them. I also learned how to study."

"Give me a seventh-grade Life Journal and tell the seventh-grade teachers about continuous improvement."

"We should have a journal and get to do this every year."

In a Tyler County, West Virginia, eighth-grade middle school classroom, I was interviewing students on continuous improvement. They told me that at about four weeks into the year they were answering about 45 percent of the math questions correctly. I explained we had a big problem—what if the students finished the eighth grade math by March? What should the teacher do in April and May? They replied, "Teach us the ninth-grade math." I said that it wouldn't help their grades, they were graded on eighth-grade math, not ninth grade. The reply was, "We don't care; give us a head start on ninth grade."

It is truly amazing what graphic proof of learning does for attitudes.

Kerry Newman sums up this chapter by stating that she doesn't think she's ever seen anything that makes parents as happy as continuous improvement. Why? It's because the natural outcome of excited students is parent joy.

11

How to "Mess Up" Continuous Improvement

Over the years, I have observed several ways educators have lessened the impact of continuous improvement or even completely destroyed the implementation. Hopefully readers can learn from these unnamed, well-intentioned people.

Mess-Up #1: "This Doesn't Work." These teachers, so accustomed to attending staff development to hear a new method, mistakenly classify continuous improvement as yet another method. They believe that continuous improvement means that all they have to do is give quizzes and graph; learning will then automatically occur. They show me a graph, such as in Figure 11.1 and say, "See, this doesn't work."

Sorry, continuous improvement is not a teaching method. The graphs inform the students and their teachers if the methods being used are working. For example, Jeff Burgard once analyzed errors in his students' writing and found that the largest number of conventions errors were with commas. He then assigned comma worksheets, but the students' performance with commas did not improve. The graph showed that the selected method did not work; other methods must be used until one is found that works. It is so healthy for teachers to be able to say to students, "I had a hypothesis that these worksheets would solve the comma problem. Well, as you know, not all hypotheses are correct; please help me establish a new hypothesis." Jeff and his students understand that the graphs do not teach; they tell us if our selected teaching methods are working.

Mess-Up #2: "We Need a Goal." Yes, a goal is needed, but the continuous improvement goal is to perform better on the next assessment than we

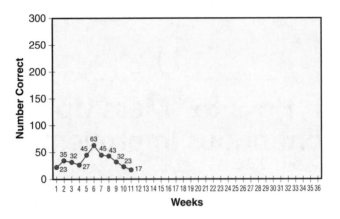

Figure 11.1 Class run chart: giving up.

have ever performed. There is no need to set any other goal. When an artificial goal is set, one of three negatives occur. The first is that the students never reach the goal and are discouraged. They will always have some weeks better than ever before, but might not meet some arbitrary goal. Figure 11.2 is such an example. Assume the class set a goal of 260. The students would leave the year feeling like failures, when their learning progress is remarkable. The second negative is the students do reach the goal, but only once. They only have one celebration, whereas when the goal is to beat the prior best record, students have numerous happy celebrations. Figure 11.2 also shows, in bold, the 14 classroom celebrations of all-time highs over the course of the year. The third problem is that students meet their goal with several weeks left in the year and see no reason to continue working; they have met their goal.

Mess-Up #3: "Compute the Average Correct." In a culture that is so used to seeing the average for everything, it makes sense to compute the average. I can best explain the problem with computing the average by using an example. If a second grade teacher has 200 spelling words for the year, gives 14 spelling word quizzes each week, and then graphs the average correct, half of the students must be below average. When the average correct is on the wall, and the students have their own student run chart, what they see when they look at the class progress is they are above or below average. When the class total is displayed they see how they contributed to the success of the class. In the spelling example, it is not uncommon for a student to begin a school year spelling three to five of the words correct for a number of weeks and then to end the year consistently spelling 13 of the 14 correct. Most would say, "Great growth." However, when the

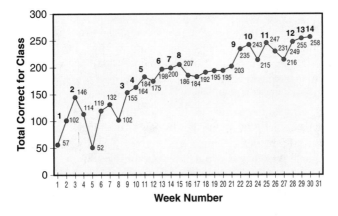

Figure 11.2   Fourteen celebrations during the year.

average is plotted on the wall, 13 is still below average. Educators know that on any given topic half of the students are below average, but in many instances, the logic of 50/50 escapes the thinking and "below average" becomes a synonym for "not very smart." We cannot accept a plan that systematically communicates to 50 percent of our students that they don't quite have what it takes to be successful.

Mess-Up #4: "Offering a Reward for Gains on the Graphs." The students don't need the teachers' money; they need the teachers' ears. When a teacher says, "I'll give you popcorn if the math graph goes up," the students' motivation has changed from learning the math to having popcorn. But when teachers give their ears instead of their money, the conversation is not about popcorn. It is, "Well, our math graph has not gone up for three weeks. What do you kids think we should do? What are your hypotheses regarding our improvement in learning?" Teachers often have established time slots to listen to individual students, but rarely have set aside class time to receive student input regarding how to improve the classroom learning.

Mess-Up #5: "Completing Half of the Graphs." For some reason, there are teachers who only have student run charts or only the class run charts. Almost always they are disappointed in the results. It seems that the power of continuous improvement for students is to have documentation both that they are learning as individuals and that the class as a whole is improving. Continuous improvement is not about group totals versus individual effort; it is about both combined. There is a great sense of accomplishment in knowing that the class "team" celebrated their success and that I contributed. Completing both the student and class run charts is essential for continuous improvement to succeed. Another way of analyzing this is realizing that completing 50 percent of the graphs does not deliver 50 percent of the benefit. This is an example of one plus one not equaling two, but much more than two.

Mess-Up #6: "Not Being a Cheerleader." Nobody can imagine the coach of a sports team being interviewed regarding a winning season saying, "Oh, it was nothing; I expect to always win—no further comment." We've all watched the gymnast sitting down next to the coach after a performance. Together they watch the display of the judges scores and, when the scores are high, they celebrate together. So Mess-Up #6 is recording the results, maybe posting them, but saying nothing to the students about how proud you are of their efforts. One of education's frustrations is the inability to tap the coach's expertise in the classroom. Many teachers are more successful in athletics than in teaching. Why? One reason is that on the playing field these coaches are masters at bringing the team together to focus upon the team goal. The team works in a synchronized manner. However, in the traditional classroom, there's no team effort. At least there wasn't before continuous improvement. Now, these teacher-coaches can bring their coaching ability into the classroom and will feel much better about all of their professional life.

Mess-Up #7: "The Standards Are Too Low." The expectations are so low that students begin the year with their run chart showing 70 to 80 percent correct already. There's not much room for improvement when this occurs. I see this most often with spelling, but Mess-Up #7 can occur with any subject.

Mess-Up #8: "No Preview." These teachers cannot bring themselves to quiz students on content that has not yet been covered. So they teach chapter 1 and give a chapter quiz. Then they teach chapter 2 and quiz on chapter 1 plus chapter 2, and so forth. They picked up the review aspect of continuous improvement and this is certainly better than mere chapter tests, but the preview aspect of continuous improvement is every bit as powerful as the review component. I need to say, however, that there are a number of teachers who make Mess-Up #8 in order to begin continuous improvement quickly, and then switch over to the review–preview process.

Mess-Up #9: "Attempt to Implement Continuous Improvement without Dropping Some Routines." Time and energy are not available for all the good ideas. Something has to be dropped. One example of a frequently dropped activity in "continuous improvement" classrooms is chapter tests. They measure short-term memory and add no value to all of the other data the teacher is collecting.

Mess-Up # 10: "Not Thinking Systems and Long-Term for All Routines." Since the goal is a "J" curve at year's end, the quarterly exam needs revision. Instead of an exam on the contents of the first nine weeks, students should receive a version of the year-end final at the end of the nine weeks. This exam is graded, but since only 25 percent of the year's content has been taught, students are expected to only answer 25 percent of the questions. The grading scale is 22 percent, or higher, for an "A." At semester, another final is administered; the grading scale is 45 percent, or higher, for an "A." At the end of the third quarter, the grading scale is 68 percent, or higher, for the "A," and at the year's end the students are ready for the 90–100 percent for the "A." The weekly nongraded quizzes and the graded quarterly assessments are to keep the "end in mind," to use Stephen Covey's words.

Both Jenny Bushman and Debi Molina-Walters are implementing this in their classrooms for 2002–03. At the time of this writing, they both have over 90 percent A's (including all special education students) from the first quarterly "final."

Mess-Up #11: "Grading the Weekly Quizzes." It is not fair to grade students on content that has not yet been taught. The plan described in "Mess-Up #10" is fair because students are only accountable for the percentage of the content that has been taught. But, some protest, "Students won't try to raise their quiz score if I don't grade them." Yes, they will. It takes students awhile to see the value of the graph and feel the joy of witnessing both their individual and collective learning. Nevertheless, the intrinsic motivation does "kick in" and students do not need the extrinsic motivation of a grade to want the graphs to increase. Students need extrinsic motivation to cram, but only need intrinsic motivation to learn.

Section IV

Enthusiasm Maintained

12

Maintaining (or Restoring) Enthusiasm for Learning

Children are born motivated to learn. Children enter kindergarten still possessing this enthusiasm for learning. Educators need not motivate children to learn; this was accomplished at birth.

The responsibility of educators is to eliminate the loss of innate enthusiasm. I have never heard anybody debate whether children are born motivated to learn. Furthermore, kindergarten teachers don't tell me that children generally lose their yearning for learning prior to beginning school.

I press with the question, "You mean that year after year, every student still has innate enthusiasm for learning at kindergarten's commencement?"

Teachers reply, "Well, it's rare for a kindergartner not to be enthusiastic."

So I probe further. "Maybe one or two students a year start kindergarten with their natural joy for learning gone?"

"Oh no," kindergarten teachers reply. "Maybe one child every five years has had the yearning for learning driven out."

Enthusiasm is not officially considered an asset by educators. Five-year-olds in kindergarten are looked upon as people who have much to learn in the next 13 years. Their educational ledger has many empty pages.

If enthusiasm were considered an asset, educators and other adults would see five-year-olds as having a second ledger completely filled. The children have much knowledge and information to gain, but they have all the enthusiasm they'll ever need. Educators and parents must use all of their collective wisdom to protect this invaluable asset, which is carried around by every kindergartner.

When a new business starts, there are also two sets of assets: one is the ideas of the entrepreneur and one is the finances. No matter how great the ideas, when the finances run dry, the business is in serious trouble. In education, one start-up asset is the enthusiasm of the students entering our schools. No matter how great the educational opportunities, it is difficult to successfully educate students who have had pages ripped from their enthusiasm ledger.

Dennis Fox describes, from the perspective of a parent, the process of enthusiasm loss.

"What would you like your daughter to get out of being here in school?"

The guidance counselor looked at us expectantly. I responded that our five-year-old, who had flourished in preschool, had always been excited about learning and was interested in reading. Our main hope as we registered her for kindergarten was that public school would not dampen her curiosity about her expanding world.

The counselor's response, "I know exactly what you mean!" encouraged us. The town, after all, had a reputation for good schools. That's why we moved here. We were off to a good start.

As it turned out, though, our experience since that optimistic beginning three years ago has been mixed. The school has many creative, caring teachers. But the educational journey hasn't been as idyllic as we had hoped . . .

By January of her kindergarten year, with the pressure to produce strings of letters and numbers out of sync with her own priorities, our rebellious daughter decided reading was no longer fun.

In first and second grades, the excitement came back, though only intermittently. Recess remained her favorite time of the day, the only time she could do as she pleased. We discovered that even a good school has difficulty building on the many interests every child has when those interests don't match more narrow academic demands.

I would be less surprised by this—and maybe wouldn't have expressed my initial concern about the school's excitement-destroying potential—if I hadn't twice experienced something similar two decades earlier." [1]

Enthusiasm can be measured; one needs only to ask the students. Figure 12.1 is a sample questionnaire used by students to communicate enthusiasm. Younger children obviously need more explanation and examples, but they readily give opinions. Figure 12.2 charts the loss of enthusiasm collected in the Enterprise School District (Redding, California). The data was collected over a three-year period. The percentage of happy faces was compiled for each of nine grades, from kindergarten to grade eight. The Carlisle (Pennsylvania) Area School District has continued the practice begun in the Enterprise School District and found that the loss of enthusiasm levels off after grade eight, continuing at about 40 percent happy faces in high school. This is such good news, as I had predicted the decline continued.

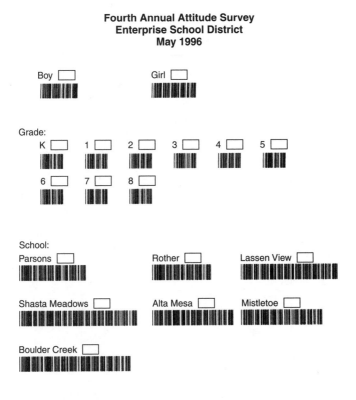

Fourth Annual Attitude Survey
Enterprise School District
May 1996

Figure 12.1   Enterprise School District annual attitude survey.

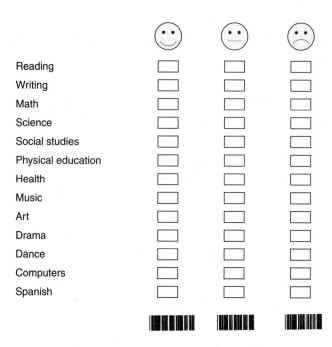

Figure 12.1 *Continued.*

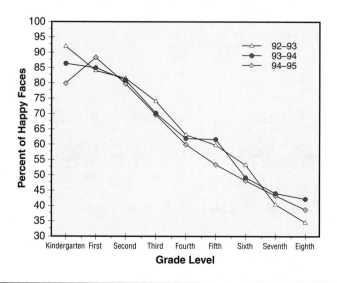

Figure 12.2 Enterprise School District 1992–1995 attitude survey results.

Educators and the public know that students lose their enthusiasm as they grow older. With no data on when this enthusiasm is lost, it is easy for educators to incorrectly assume when the loss occurs. For example, elementary teachers often assume that they keep enthusiasm high and believe secondary educators cause the loss.

The data clearly show that each grade level contributed to the loss of enthusiasm. The loss is gradual, slow, and continual. It is a myth that elementary teachers are able to keep enthusiasm high and secondary teachers are unable to match this accomplishment. Dr. Deming must have known about the happy faces when he wrote that Western society continually destroys its people, creating shortages of good people.

A common reaction from educators is, "What are we responsible for—learning or enthusiasm?" The answer is both. Because educators are responsible for both learning and enthusiasm, having talented, dedicated, creative teachers in the classroom is crucial. It would be much easier to staff classrooms with teachers who have the attitude of, "You're going to learn whether you like it or not" or "Learning will take care of itself; just have fun."

Orchestrating classrooms so that all students progress in learning *and* maintain their enthusiasm for learning is an incredible challenge. It is, however, the responsibility of educators to maintain enthusiasm while increasing learning. We must not allow ourselves to stray from this path.

After seeing the happy face data for three years, hearing many discussions on the need for an aim, reviewing Dr. Deming's aim for education, and seeing the kind of learning growth I have described throughout this book, staff of the Enterprise School District wrote and accepted the aim, "Maintain enthusiasm while increasing learning." When the aim was adopted, however, the staff did not know how to accomplish it; but three years of losses in student enthusiasm convinced them that the future would be no different unless changes were made.

Two Enterprise teachers, Shelly Carson and Jeff Burgard, took the theory of Dr. Deming and my frustration and provided a solution. They describe the process in detail in their books, *Continuous Improvement in the History/Social Science Classroom* and *Continuous Improvement in the Science Classroom.*

Essentially, they established a simple rubric for enthusiasm and measured it monthly. Students reported each month how they felt about the prior month. A five stands for "I loved it," a four is "I liked the class," three means the class was OK, two communicates "I disliked it," and a one means "I hated this class." The students graphed their progress individually and plotted it on a class scatter diagram.

Each month the students gave written suggestions regarding how to make next month better and all of the suggestions were discussed with the class.

Some suggestions were always implemented. Classroom joy improved when the students were given the opportunity to establish hypotheses regarding what would improve enthusiasm. The students all want to know if the suggested changes show up as improvement on next month's enthusiasm run chart.

This chapter does not purport to explain all of the details developed by Carson and Burgard, but to give enough information so that educators know that Dr. Deming's profound knowledge is correct and they can do something about the loss of enthusiasm in which they are immersed.

Carson and Burgard told their students they were not going to motivate them, but were going to listen very carefully regarding: (1) practices that demotivated, and (2) the students' hypotheses regarding improved enthusiasm. Jeff Burgard relates that one class believed that if the students established the seating chart and room arrangement, enthusiasm would improve. It was quite perplexing for students to learn that their hypothesis was wrong, but equally exciting that they had a teacher who would allow this type of an experiment. I asked one of Shelly Carson's 11th graders, who was filling out the monthly Plus/Delta, "Is this a waste of your time?" The student replied that each month Mrs. Carson makes at least one change based upon what we say. The pluses make us feel good, but the Deltas, suggestions for change, are what increase student enthusiasm.

Figures 12.3 through 12.5 are from Carolyn Ayres' second grade in the Enterprise School District (Redding, California). Learning from Carson and Burgard, she implemented the exact same process in grade two mathematics. Even in second grade, enthusiasm has to be restored.

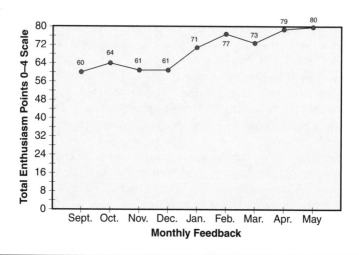

Figure 12.3   Mrs. Ayres' enthusiasm class run chart.

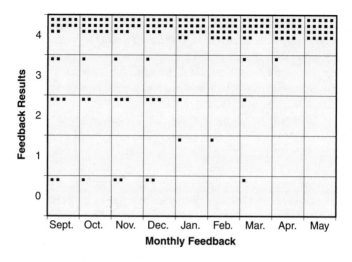

Figure 12.4   Mrs. Ayres' enthusiasm class scatter diagram.

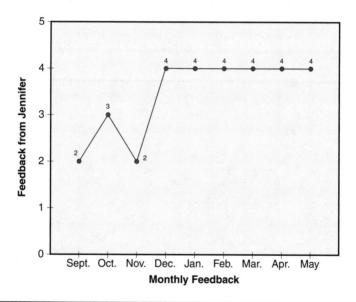

Figure 12.5   Math enthusiasm student run chart for Jennifer.

Sixth-grade teacher Craig Jaworski of Citrus County, Florida, took Carson and Burgard's advice also. He tracked enthusiasm and found, to his consternation, that enthusiasm dropped after the beginning of the year. However, he didn't stop there. He listened to the students, monitored attitude regularly, and was able to turn around the slide in enthusiasm. We, as adults, are in charge of enthusiasm.

The following is a quote from *Six Sigma*, written by Harry and Schroeder,[2] "When there is no system of measurements in place to gauge customer satisfaction, can an organization genuinely say that its customers are a top priority?" Here's my rewrite of their question: When there is no system of measurements in place to gauge student satisfaction, can a school district genuinely say that its students are a top priority? The work of various educators, described in this chapter, provides other educators a method of implementing what they truly believe: the students are top priority. Probably the very first U.S. school district to purchase multiple copies of the first edition of this book was the Palatine, Illinois, school district. Robert Ewy, the director of planning, collected "happy face" data from 1998 to 2001 with almost identical results to the Enterprise School District in California. He then asked the staff if they were merely going to collect data, or was enthusiasm important enough to attempt to stop the loss. The staff decided enthusiasm was really important, but they didn't know what to do. They were provided Carson and Burgard's books and implemented their processes. The jump for the 2002 school year is most impressive; Bob is overjoyed. He states, "We can expect both learning and joy in learning at the same time." Figures 12.6 through 12.10 document their 2002 results. One line on each graph is an average percent of happy faces from 1998 to

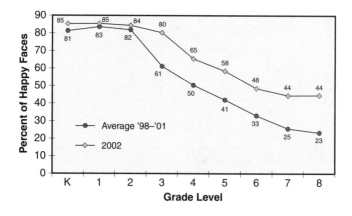

Figure 12.6 Palatine, Illinois, reading enthusiasm.

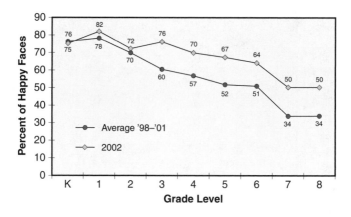

Figure 12.7 Palatine, Illinois, math enthusiasm.

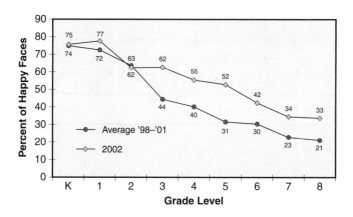

Figure 12.8 Palatine, Illinois, writing enthusiasm.

2001. The numbers from 1998–2001 are almost exactly the same each year even though different students come into the new grade each year. The second line on each graph is the 2002 results.

Counselors can also garner students' perspective of their prior schooling using Carson and Burgard's enthusiasm concept. Figure 12.11 is an enthusiasm graph from one student who had recently completed ninth grade. He most willingly told me his perceptions of every grade and every subject. All I needed was two ears and a set of colored pencils to keep the information from becoming too confusing.

Eric told me, on a scale of "loved it" to "hated it," how he felt about every subject in every grade. I added school itself as one of the categories.

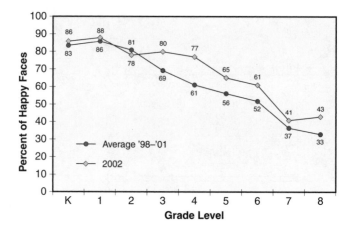

Figure 12.9   Palatine, Illinois, science enthusiasm.

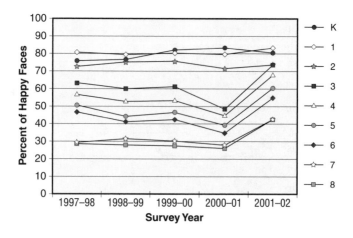

Figure 12.10   Schoolwide enthusiasm by grade for Palatine, Illinois.

"School" was not on the original research recorded in the beginning of this chapter and should be added to the student questionnaire. Ninth-grade Reading/English is very encouraging. After years of feeling like a failure, his middle and high school teachers excelled with him in this subject. Educators are in charge of enthusiasm much more than we may know; we cannot allow ourselves to think the students are in charge of attitude.

When counselors have the completed graph, they can question students for further insights. For example, I asked Eric how it was possible to love

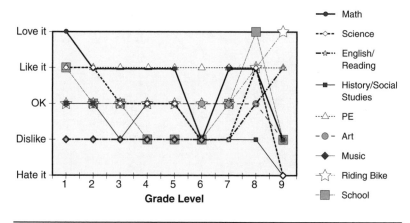

Figure 12.11 Eric's school history.

school in eighth grade and to dislike history. He replied, "I can take one bad teacher; beyond that, it's too much to take."

Other questions Eric can answer are:

1. What did your eighth- and ninth-grade English teachers do to change your attitude toward English?

2. What caused the slump in science? Name the specifics.

3. How can your 10th-grade teachers restore or maintain your enthusiasm?

Dr. Deming's psychology, plus my happy faces questionnaire and frustration, plus Burgard/Carson's solutions, plus Palatine's success, equals great hope. The loss of enthusiasm we all know about is not in the genes nor the hormones.

ENDNOTES

1. D. Fox, "Square Pegs in Round Holes," *Education Week* (June 5, 2002): 31.
2. M. Harry and R. Schroeder, *Six Sigma* (New York: Doubleday, 2000): 4.

13

Celebrations versus Rewards and Incentives

At first it might seem that celebrations and rewards/incentives are synonyms. Or if they are not synonyms, they are so nearly the same thing, that for all practical purposes, they are the same. In fact the two are completely different.

The sales manager offers a trip to Antigua to the top salesperson. This is the offering of an incentive, pure and simple. The contest is held, several compete, most figure they have no chance of winning the trip, and one salesperson enjoys the sites, food, and culture of beautiful Guatemala.

A second sales manager has posted on the wall, for everyone to see, the total sales for the organization. They are posted weekly. She sees that a particular week was exceptionally great and spends an amount equal to an Antigua trip celebrating with all of the sales staff and their families. Even the lowest-performing salesperson feels honored, because if his/her sales were taken away, the month might not have been so successful. Or if this salesperson had no sales, he/she contributed in many other ways to make the organization work. Everyone contributes and everyone celebrates. Some will dislike this example, feeling that in the cruel world of competitive business, Antigua is better.

No matter what the opinion of readers regarding the business example, no parents send their children to school to continually be the losers. Parents have a right to expect that their child will be a winner. Schools, however, are normally organized with incentives and rewards handed out at assemblies. We must ask ourselves if it is realistic for 85 percent of the students to come to assemblies every month and be really happy for the 15 percent who are continually being honored? How do adults feel when they are supposed to applaud the same 15 percent every month? The kids feel the same.

Bob Thomas said it best in the *Springfield (Missouri) News-Leader* on Sunday, May 27, 2001. He wrote, "This morning, I took time off from work to attend the first-grade awards ceremony at my grandson's school. I did this because I am a good grandparent and because I feel some responsibility as a fellow teacher. Of some 100 shiny-faced, freshly scrubbed soon-to-be second-graders, about 15 were invited onstage time and time again to be presented with awards in art, spelling, PE, reading, and so on. After the awards were presented in each area, the small group of winning students lined up in front of the stage to face the audience and bask briefly in the cheers and applause.

"By the end of the presentations, I had seen those children and heard their names so often that I felt as if I knew them.

"After the awards were given out, all the remaining first-graders were marched briskly across the stage to accept their completion certificated and return to their seats with no time for any recognition from the audience. This was done without fanfare. As the lady next to me said of her daughter, 'They are breaking her heart.' The man on the other side replied, 'We send them here to learn so early that they are not valuable.'

"Next year, I will take my grandson fishing on awards day. His teacher will say, 'That family just doesn't care,' or 'No wonder he is not doing any better.'

"We do care. I just don't want to watch him hurt again."[1]

The teachers and principals conducting the awards assembly are not intentionally trying to hurt 85 percent of the students. When they went into teaching and were asked, "Why do you want to become a teacher?" they did not say, "So that I can hurt 85 percent of the next generation." They sincerely believe the awards assembly is motivating to children. Sad.

Instead of awards, we need celebrations and the best synonym for celebration is "thank you." A group of teachers asked their fifth graders what would be a good way for them to say "thank you" for all their hard work and high graphs. The students said, "Give us 15 minutes in the gym to talk with our friends." Another celebration was one student calling up the principal on the classroom phone and telling him the class had their best week of the year. Everyone applauded and the students went back to work. Some classrooms have a routine, including chart, movement, clapping, and a yell. They experience this routine after every all-time high.

Some celebrations are spontaneous. Jana Vance wrote about her English class's spontaneous celebration. When the class realized how well they had done, "At first it was complete silence in the room and then they were suddenly yelling and jumping and I found myself yelling and jumping too. What a good feeling, what a way to end the week and what a way to end the year—knowing they have learned what we set out to do in the beginning!"

Jean Wilson states that the biggest surprise to her, in regards to continuous improvement, was how much her 10th-graders enjoy the process. This is especially true for students who have experienced failure in the past. The simple statement, "I know this," is a celebration all by itself. She goes on to say how continuous improvement develops character in that there are always setbacks (low scoring weeks) that must be overcome. The overcoming is a higher week punctuated with a feeling of pride and celebration.

A principal told me that the change from rewards to celebrations is very touching. Students stand up for applause, because their class or grade level has exceeded their prior all-time best. Celebrations inspire child, teacher, and administrator because they include in the recognition the other 85 percent. We must recognize that awards assemblies produce dropouts—first in the heart and mind, next with the body.

ENDNOTE

1. B. Thomas, *Springfield (Missouri) News-Leader,* 27 May 2001.

Section V

Beyond the Three Basic Graphs

14

The Histogram: High Standards to High Success

The fourth graph is the histogram. Whereas the three basic graphs—the class run chart, the scatter diagram, and the student run chart—show movement over time, histograms display a moment in time. Figure 14.1 is one week's data from one quiz. The graph shows how many students answered correctly none of the five questions up to all five questions in Debi Molina-Walters' Antioch, California, sixth-grade science classroom.

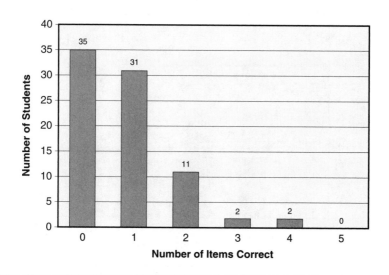

Figure 14.1 Essential science vocabulary—first week of school.

Because the "bell-shaped" curve is such a significant aspect of American schooling, a chapter devoted to two more important curves is essential. The "L" and the "J" curves are present only by hard work and devotion of educators; the "bell curve" merely is evidence of existence.

In the first week of the school year, when students have barely been provided the essential information to be learned and the performance standards to be demonstrated, the curve of the students' assessments should be in the shape of an "L." This shape indicates that the standards are probably appropriate; the students have much to learn. The hard work mentioned in the prior paragraph refers to the difficulty of setting the standards just right. The standards need not be so hard that great failure occurs, but not so easy that a sizeable portion already know the content. So, the histogram constructed from week one's data is very important to gauge the appropriateness of the expectations; it's the evidence of high standards.

Figures 14.2 through 14.5 are also from Debi's classroom. They show the progress of all three of her classrooms with the learning of science vocabulary. Figure 14.2 shows progress at the end of the first quarter, Figure 14.3 was made at semester, and Figure 14.4 documents progress at the third quarter. One of the saddest aspects of American education is the pressure upon teachers to end the year with a "bell-shaped" curve. What this means in practice is: don't give too many A's, and be sure the A's you do give are balanced by an equal number of F's. "Bell-shaped" curves are for the middle of the school year; yes, some students do learn faster than other students.

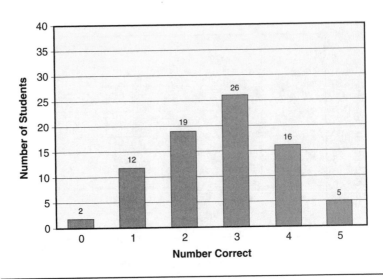

Figure 14.2 Essential science vocabulary—end of first quarter.

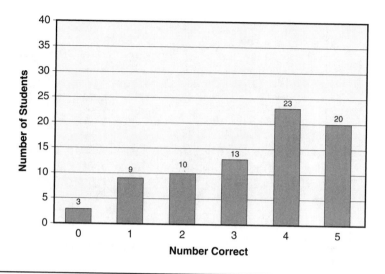

Figure 14.3 Essential science vocabulary—end of first semester.

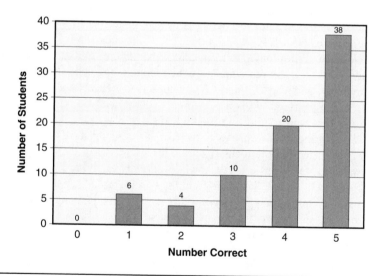

Figure 14.4 Essential science vocabulary—end of third quarter.

The "J" curve shown in Figure 14.5 is Debi's last week of the 2001–02 school year. Readers can see that almost all students met the year's expectations, a lot of growth since the "L-shaped" graph was produced nine months earlier. The "J" curve is the evidence of high success.

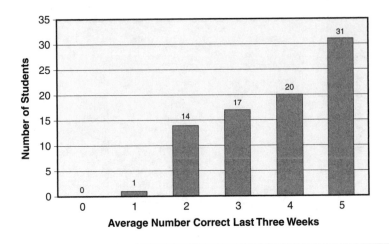

Figure 14.5 Essential science vocabulary—end of year.

At the end of the school year, most teachers using continuous improvement do grade the final weeks of the quizzes and/or construct finals based upon the total content. The grading is now fair because all of the content has been taught. So, if Figure 14.5 represented the vocabulary portion of the total science grades for her students, many would object because there are far more A's than any other grade. In the second paragraph of this chapter, I wrote that both the "L" and "J" are the result of teachers' hard work. Obtaining a year-end "J" is not luck; everybody involved—students, parents, teachers, and administrators—all had a part.

There are many downsides to the fear surrounding standardized tests. One of them is that the focus is on the tests rather than the learning. So when the tests are over (often in April), everybody can now relax. Sad. The real work to bring the classroom from the bell to the "J" happens between standardized testing and the end of the year. It's bringing along the last few that requires us to have the most talented teachers possible!

Critics will not attribute the "J" to hard work, however. They will throw around a most powerful term at these teachers: *grade inflation*. This term causes the most dedicated teachers to question themselves. Are they really too easy? Do they expect too little? Should more failure occur? To help answer these questions, we need to first define both inflation and grade inflation.

It is generally accepted that *inflation* means that a particular item, with no improvement in quality, now costs more. The exact same McDonald's hamburger that used to cost 15 cents now costs 79 cents. That's inflation. *Grade inflation* means that students learned no more, but were given higher grades anyway. Certainly grade inflation, as described here, is not being advocated.

What *is* being advocated is high standards (both performance and essential information) that are communicated clearly to all students during the first week of school. Next comes the continuous improvement process and Dr. Deming's management principles, as outlined in this book and implemented by numerous teachers since 1992. The results are that far more students meet the "A" expectations than before. This is not inflation; it is improvement in quality.

On every faculty I've ever seen, there are teachers who see themselves as primarily sorters of young people. They say, "Take that kid out of my class," or "These students all have ADHD," or "If I take the graduate, classes in helping English language learners, I'll get them in my room," and so on. The other teachers see themselves as developers of young people. Those who see themselves primarily as sorters will yell "foul" when their developer colleagues end up with a "J" curve and give the "A's" the students deserve. Administrative support and understanding are crucial here, not only for the developers, but in hiring more teachers who see their job as developers.

Jana Vance's Rochester, Indiana, high school writing class, on a one to four scale, also ended up in the curve of a "J." This is especially important because the students with learning disabilities are assigned to her sections of English. (See Figure 14.6.) The science writing in Jeff Burgard's Redding,

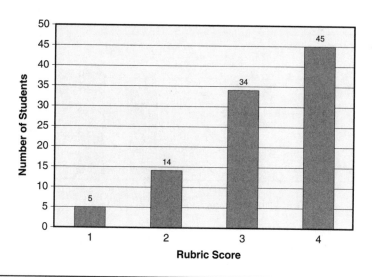

Figure 14.6   End-of-year writing assessment: ninth grade. Rochester, Indiana.

California, class has the same "J." He uses a six-point rubric (appendix T), but the results are identical (see Figure 14.7). For some teachers, the histogram is not really the fourth graph, but the most important graph. At a recent workshop, a teacher wrote, "Moving from 'L' to 'J' is one of the most effective ways for students to see that they are improving. When students can see that they are moving together toward improvement as a team, they will feel more confident about themselves and their abilities."

Three other "L" to "bell" to "J" curves from elementary, high school, and graduate school classrooms supplement Debi's middle school "J" curve. The process is the same. The reading example is from Debbye Welch's Oklahoma City third grade (Figure 14.8), the high school example is from Dave Bell of Cincinnati (Figure 14.9), and the graduate example is from Lloyd Roettger at the University of Central Oklahoma (Figure 14.10).

The "L" to "J" happens to be my initials; the coincidence seems nice, so my e-mail address is LtoJ@earthlink.net. While it would be nice for readers to remember my name and my e-mail address, of far greater importance is implementation of the "L" to "J" in classrooms. The futures of many students literally depend upon their teachers' understanding of the content of this chapter and unwillingness to submit to the intense pressure for a "bell."

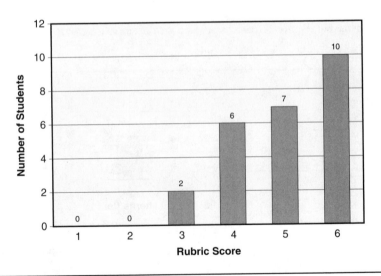

Figure 14.7   "J" curve for middle school science writing.

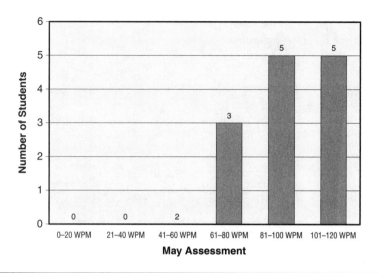

Figure 14.8   "J" curve for third grade reading fluency.

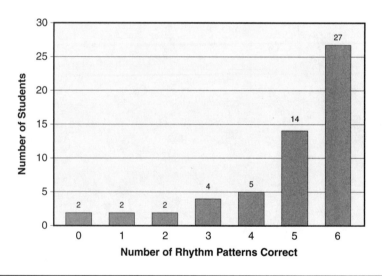

Figure 14.9   "J" curve for high school music rhythm patterns.

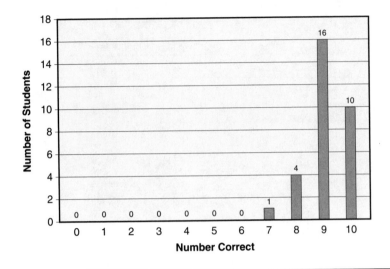

Figure 14.10 "J" curve for Lloyd Roettger's graduate educational research class.

15

Disaggregating the Data

Why do educators need disaggregated data? It is to gain further insight. The class run chart and scatter diagram can be disaggregated. This breaking down of the data into subsets can be of considerable value to teachers. For example, in one school district the girls outperformed the boys on 40 of the 43 subtests of their state's norm-referenced exam. The only tests where the boys outperformed the girls were mathematics in three elementary grades. Obviously the district had a gender achievement gap. Providing teachers this data six months after the exams are completed is of limited value. However, providing teachers a means of producing disaggregated run charts and disaggregated scatter diagrams as the year progresses is of significant value.

The class run chart in Figure 15.1 and scatter diagram in Figure 15.2 are from Steve Denny's Calculus class (see appendix J) at Cincinnati's Winton Woods High School. He was very surprised to find that the girls had lower scores on weekly quizzes, because they had higher grades. So he asked the girls why this might be happening.

After gender, the second most common way to disaggregate the data is by ethnicity. The four ethnic groups in Figure 15.3 almost end the year at the same point; only one white student separated the groups. The exciting news about this class is that the achievement gaps, so prevalent during the school year, are virtually nonexistent at year's end. Wherever educators are concerned about achievement gaps, but don't have a continuous improvement process, they are usually unable to close the gaps in spite of best efforts.

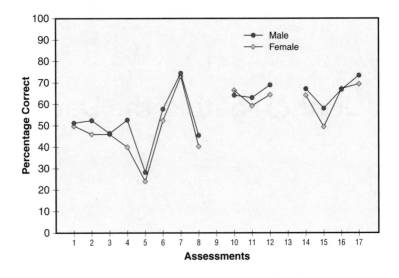

Figure 15.1   Fifth period Mathematics (MUP Pre-Calculus Honors) class run chart.

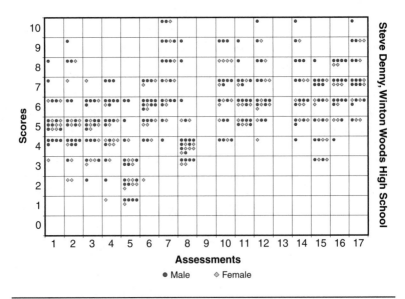

Figure 15.2   Fifth period Mathematics (MUP Pre-Calculus Honors) class scatter diagram.

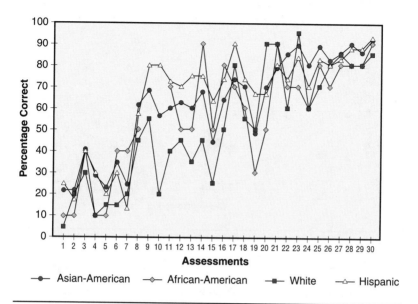

Figure 15.3　Class run chart by ethnicity.

Winton Wood's Dave Bell completed a most intriguing disaggregation of data. He has eight vocal groups in his choirs and needs to know if each of the groups are learning the rhythm patterns in appendix B. Figure 15.4 is his class run chart; Figure 15.5 is a similar run chart, but only for tenors. Dave needs each division of his choirs to pull their own weight in order to have peak performances. The disaggregated data gives him insight previously unavailable.

When one hears people laud the benefits of disaggregated data, it almost seems as if the proponent believes the data gives answers to learning problems. The data does not give answers. The sequence is as follows:

1. Gather the numbers and disaggregate the data.

2. Graph the data.

3. Study the graphs for insight.

4. Use the insight to establish hypotheses (ask students for help).

5. Carry out the hypothesis in order to gain knowledge.

The point that is so powerful is not that Steve Denny had information showing that the girls were performing less well on the weekly quizzes than the boys. It is that he asked the girls for insight, they helped him establish a hypothesis for improvement, and he carried out an experiment.

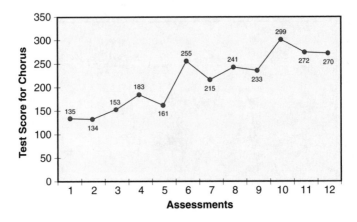

Figure 15.4   Chorus rhythm patterns.

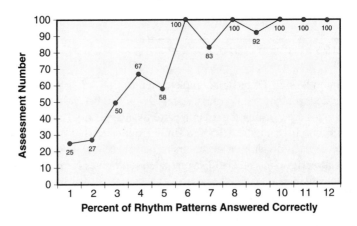

Figure 15.5   Run chart for tenors.

In this chapter, I have shown three ways to disaggregate data: gender, ethnicity, and voice part. There are hundreds of ways to disaggregate data—by years attending your school, birth date in a kindergarten, attendance percentages, disability, reading level (in a class other than reading), prior school, or poverty. The caution is to disaggregate the data only if it has a potential to give insight for future improvement.

Some will want to disaggregate the data based upon multiple intelligences or learning styles. The first question to ask in any disaggregation is whether or not there is any significant difference between the various groups. For example, if a teacher finds that all of the students with preferences for different learning styles are progressing at the same rate, then learning styles are being honored and there's no further need to monitor according to learning styles. The aim here is not to disaggregate data for fun, but to determine where the learning gaps are and address them.

A technical note: The run charts in this chapter are all percentage correct run charts. It would do no good, for example, to use actual numbers in classes of 15 boys and 10 girls. The progress of boys versus girls cannot be compared unless there are equal numbers of boys and girls or percentages are used. The percent correct for boys can be accurately compared to percent correct for girls in the previous example.

16

Item Analysis

Whater classes have the totals described in chapters 4 to 8, item analysis is next. Without the totals, educators have no way of knowing if the time spent on item analysis is worth the effort. Without item analysis, educators have less direction in their attempt to improve learning. The run charts show if learning is being produced at an acceptable rate and if it is likely year-end standards will be met. The "J" shaped histogram documents year-end success. Disaggregated run charts and all scatter diagrams give insight to assist educators in increasing learning as shown on the run charts and histograms.

All methods of item analysis described in this chapter are for the same purpose—giving insight that can be used to increase learning. Item analysis is for both the individual student and the classroom as a whole. Spelling can serve as an example. With continuous improvement, students are provided a list of the year's spelling words the first week of school. The list is kept in students' data folders. When spelling tests are returned to the students, they highlight the words they spelled correctly. Words that are not highlighted have either not been randomly selected or were misspelled.

The three tools for collecting the whole class errors are tally marks, histograms, and Pareto charts. Students should use the tools to gain and report their insights. First, they use tally marks to determine how many times each error was made. Second, they make a histogram, graphically showing the numbers of each type of error (see Figure 16.1 for writing error example).

Kerry Newman of Glenwood, Iowa, prepares the math assessments for teachers in her school district. Included with each assessment are check boxes for teachers to list the number of times each question was missed. For

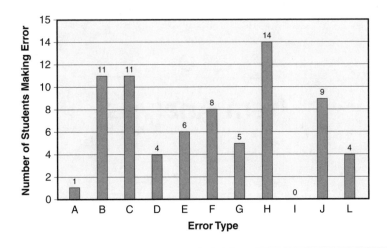

Figure 16.1   Writing errors: total for class.

example, if this week's quiz assessed standards 35, 42, 15, 6, 80, 4, 45, 71, 96, 45, and 67, she has a sheet of paper with blanks for each teacher to fill in the number of errors.

☐ ☐ ☐ ☐ ☐ ☐ ☐ ☐ ☐ ☐ ☐
35 42 15 6 80 4 45 71 96 45 67

The errors per item can easily be added up in order to inform instruction on an ongoing basis.

Young children, given a calculator, can produce a Pareto chart, the most informative tool for item analysis. If a teacher assigns three students to produce Pareto charts for six weeks, and rotates them like senators, little further direction will need to be given during the year. For example, Pareto monitors are assigned to their committee for six weeks. At the end of week two, one "senator" is replaced. At the end of week four a second "senator" is replaced. After this the rotation continues with a new senator each two weeks and terms are six weeks long. The Pareto committee, after four weeks, will always have one senior member, one mid-term member, and one freshman member.

Actually, students don't need to construct the histogram, but the first time through it might help them see the connection between the Pareto chart and the histogram. The next step is to take the histogram and organize it in descending order. Figure 16.2 is the same as Figure 16.1, except in descending order. Note that the top of each column displays the total errors for the whole class.

The next step in producing a Pareto chart is to compute a running percentage. Students are to determine what percent of the total class errors were contributed by each error. These percentages are recorded on the Pareto chart because it is a running total.

Figure 16.3 is a completed Pareto chart of the data compiled for the two prior graphs, which come from Tim Sheppard and Nancy Hunter of Wenatchee, Washington. The value of the Pareto chart is that it helps classes

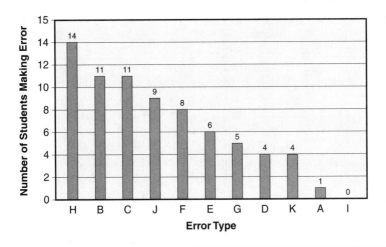

Figure 16.2   Writing errors in rank order.

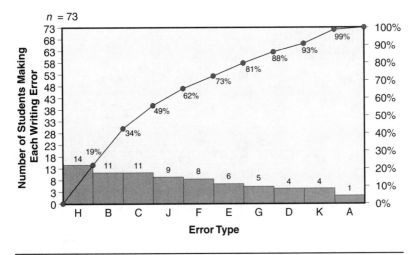

Figure 16.3   October Wacky Writing Pareto chart, Wenatchee, Washington.

focus upon the few errors that are contributing the most to student difficulty. Not every error can be given equal attention, so the Pareto chart moves from simple item analysis to priority setting.

The Pareto chart is equally useful for analysis of the learning of essential information and performance. The number at the top of each column reflects the number of students, out of 15, who lacked a particular writing skill or trait in their paper. Fourteen of the 15, for example, did not organize their writing into paragraphs, 11 did not vary sentence length, and 11 did not edit for spelling. On the Pareto chart it can easily be seen that these three writing skills accounted for 49 percent of the errors on one writing assignment. Focus is obvious. (Note the short sentence I wrote to give variety in my sentence lengths.) The complete list of their writing categories is listed on pages 62–63. By comparison, Jean Wilson of Parkersburg High School, West Virginia, uses nine categories for her writing item analysis: capitalization, diction, apostrophe, specific details, transitions, sentence combining, consistency in number, inference symbol, and beg/mid/end.

A second "senator" committee could be organized in the classroom to compute the mean, median, mode, and range. This committee also reports their statistics to the classroom. It is not that reporting the mean, median, mode, and range is an essential aspect of continuous improvement, but students need real data, on an ongoing basis, to internalize these basic statistical terms.

On a wall adjacent to where the Pareto charts are posted, the learning steps should be displayed. They are:

1. Collect the data.

2. Graph the data.

3. Gain insight from the graphs.

4. Generate hypotheses from the study of the graphs.

5. Test hypotheses to gain knowledge regarding how to improve our learning.

Students should experience regularly how people move from mere information to knowledge. They first have raw data, the information, in the form of tally marks. The combined graphs (run charts, scatter diagrams, histograms, Pareto charts, and statistics report) are combined to give insight. Either the teacher or student committees can record insights for decision making.

Three other examples of Pareto charts are included in this chapter: error analysis on a high school business class writing assignment (Figure 16.4), letters missed by kindergartners (Figure 16.5), and types of discipline referrals

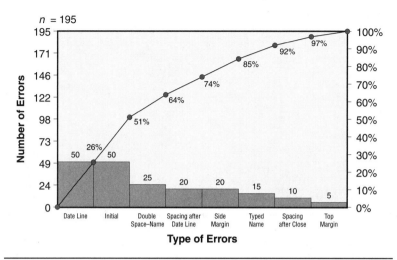

Figure 16.4 Formatting errors—high school business class writing assignment.

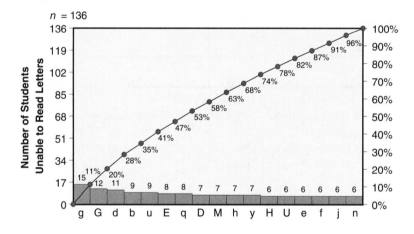

Figure 16.5 Letters missed by more than five students.

to the office (Figure 16.6). If a school provides a copy of QI Macros to their business teacher, the business students can provide Pareto charts for the whole faculty. Some teachers will prefer the student involvement with the "senator" committees, others will be very content to place tally marks in the box of the business teacher and receive a completed Pareto chart the next day. It matters not how the data analysis is accomplished, only that it is done.

Certainly there are other ways to perform item analysis. Sometimes students write each essential fact on an index card. When the fact is

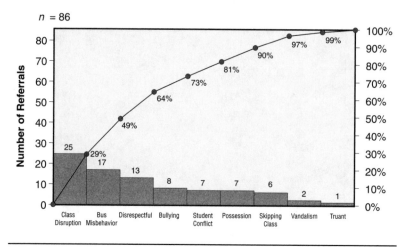

Figure 16.6   Middle school discipline referrals.

correctly answered on a quiz, a mark is placed on the card. The second time it is answered correctly, the card is thrown away. These cards are kept on metal rings and students enjoy carrying around rings with fewer and fewer index cards.

One final note: Often I see teachers, who have been convinced of the need for data collection, focus upon item analysis as the major data activity. The problem, like so many other educational changes, is that these teachers don't know if the hours spent on item analysis resulted in instructional improvement. It's the three basic graphs, plus the "L" to "J" on the histogram, that inform teachers whether or not the item analysis effort is actually resulting in improved learning.

17
Quality Tools

When students learn to use quality tools, there is clear value for them in the present and their future. Students knowing how to use affinity diagrams, fishbones (cause-and-effect diagrams), and Plus/Deltas to solve issues before them is quite impressive. Students wrestle with long cafeteria lines and other annoyances when then are learning about quality tools. Two books, *Tools and Techniques to Inspire Classroom Learning* by Barbara A. Cleary and Sally J. Duncan and *Future Force: Kids That Want To, Can, and Do! A Teacher's Handbook for Using TQM in the Classroom* by Carolyn Wick and Elaine McClanahan are written specifically to help teachers teach and use these tools in their classrooms. In addition, Susan Leddick et al., wrote *Quality Tools for Educators*, which is a very complete description and collection of quality tools.

Improving Student Learning will not duplicate the fine work from these three books, but will describe, in my opinion, the ultimate use of the tools—to improve learning of academic content. The best time for quality tools to be used, in conjunction with continuous improvement, is when the plateaus occur on the class run chart. For example, when writing has not improved during the last three assessments or when the math concepts run chart has flatlined, then these quality tools come into use.

Using students to help with analysis of learning problems sounds foreign to many. If it were not unusual, *Education Week* would not have published an article describing one project. In the May 29, 2002 edition, Lynn Olson wrote an article entitled "Students to Investigate Causes for Achievement Gaps." In her article she states, "Researchers have proposed numerous causes for the achievement gaps between minority and nonminority students and those from rich and poor families. Now, students will have a chance to seek and provide their own views.

"In the first phase of an unusual project, researchers at the City University of New York have trained 32 youth researchers between the ages of 14 and 21 to conduct a detailed study of how their peers view the achievement gap, its causes, its consequences, and its potential remedies."[1]

The fishbone is the tool that communicates the common aim of all of us working together, going the same direction. If the class writing run chart has formed a plateau, the first step in using a fishbone is to make the blank fishbone with only the aim. In this case, the aim is to improve writing as measured by rubrics and shown on the class run chart.

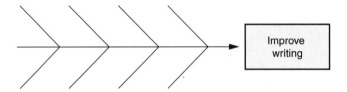

Secondly, the affinity diagram is used by students to brainstorm ways to improve their writing. Each student and the teacher are to write one idea per sticky note. The notes are categorized and given headings. The headings become the names of the bones, and ideas under the heading become sub-bones. As this is being built, other ideas will come to mind for insertion as the sub-bones of the fish.

Often fishbone developers use the five terms *equipment, people, material, methods,* and *environment* to help with brainstorming. These generic headings can be posted to help students with their thinking while using the sticky notes.

With brainstorming finished and recorded, the next step is to agree upon which hypotheses have the best chance of helping. The students are reminded that all of the ideas recorded on the fishbone are hypotheses to be tested; nobody knows for sure what will help. If the correct hypotheses are selected, the class run chart will improve. Voting is certainly one way to determine which hypothesis should be tested first. A class might vote on the main bone headings first, before voting on the specific sub-bone ideas. Students could be given three index cards to write their top three ideas down. The top idea is given three points, the second idea is given two points, and the third idea is given one point. If points are written in the lower right corner and the idea on the face of the card, it will be easy to collect the data. A more detailed description of this tool, nominal group technique (NGT), is described in Susan Leddick's *Total Quality Tools for Education.*[2]

Students can continually refine and refer back to the fishbone and NGT for second, third, and so on, hypotheses. Even if a hypothesis is correct, and the graph climbs upward, it is unlikely the graph will move on to perfection. More hypotheses will be needed at a point in time. When this occurs, new ideas can be added to the fishbone and votes can occur again.

Natalie Olague, Valle Vista Elementary teacher in Albuquerque, New Mexico, used quality tools most effectively to involve all her students in learning. She teaches in a dual-language classroom (Spanish and English). Students have a half day in English with her and a half day in Spanish with a colleague. Her students made histograms of their results from prior assessments in both English and Spanish. Figures 17.1 and 17.2 are her two histograms.

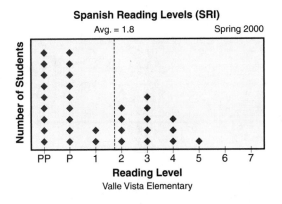

Figure 17.1   Spanish reading levels histogram.

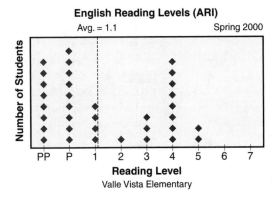

Figure 17.2   English reading levels histogram.

The students then made a fishbone (Figure 17.3) regarding causes for their low scores and developed action plans together. The scatter diagram (Figure 17.4) documents their results in English reading over a three-year period. Similar results were accomplished in Spanish reading, mathematics, and writing.

At the end of the year, teachers from the second grade up have found the priority matrix to be an excellent tool for students to tell their teacher(s) which teaching techniques worked the best. The priority matrix ranks opinion.

The priority matrix is a tool designed to help leaders better listen to their customers. Figure 17.5 is a blank priority matrix designed for learning the relative importance of up to eight items. The priority matrix can be

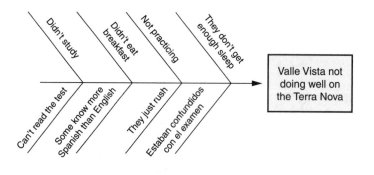

Figure 17.3   Example cause-and-effect diagram.

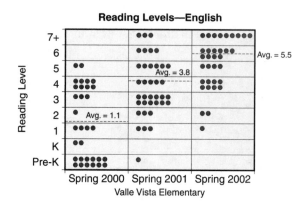

Figure 17.4   Scatter diagram over three years.

Name: _____   Topic: _____

Option	Item	Voting matrix							Totals	
1		1/2	1/3	1/4	1/5	1/6	1/7	1/8	1	
2		2/3	2/4	2/5	2/6	2/7	2/8		2	
3		3/4	3/5	3/6	3/7	3/8			3	
4		4/5	4/6	4/7	4/8				4	
									5	
5		5/6	5/7	5/8					6	
6		6/7	6/8						7	
7		7/8							8	
8									Total	28

Figure 17.5   Blank priority matrix.

made for any number of items, but this sample shows eight. After the items are brainstormed, they are placed in any order on the blank priority matrix. Participants then compare each item to the others. If item 1 is more important than item 2, then a 1 is circled. Next, item 1 is contrasted with item 3, item 4, item 5, and so on. Each of the eight items is contrasted to the other seven items.

After describing the many ills of ranking, it seems contradictory to include the priority matrix, which ranks concepts and opinions. It is not harmful, however, to rank *opinions* during the decision-making process. It is the ranking of people and their achievements that is harmful to the improvement process.

After all of the rows are completed, the number of times each item was selected is tabulated and recorded at the far right. The totals from each participant are then added up for a grand total; if the sum is not 28, an error in counting or addition has been made. The results communicate the most important to least important aspects of a topic for which opinion, rather than results, is needed.

The priority matrix is a superb tool in helping educators make complex decisions, such as what can be done to slow the loss of enthusiasm for learning or ways to improve learning. It is helpful for a teacher to rank from high to low the relative importance of students' ideas, but ranking the students themselves is harmful. For example, seventh graders, as shown in Figure 17.6, said that homework was the number one reason why students lose enthusiasm for learning. This is a ranking that teachers should listen to and explore in depth. Good can come from ranking opinions, whereas no good can come from ranking people.

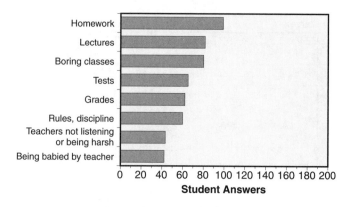

Figure 17.6　Why do students lose their enthusiasm for learning?

Quality tools are designed to give all a voice in the decision making instead of making the decisions based upon popularity or whoever yells the loudest. Isn't it ironic that a principal can return from an administrative meeting irritated that a decision was made in administrative cabinet based upon who yelled the loudest, enter a faculty meeting, and not see that decisions are made in the same manner? An upset teacher, seeing how "yell-loud" decisions are made, can return to the classroom and fall, unwittingly, into the same trap. Quality tools are for all levels of the organization.

Technically, the Life Journal cannot be called a quality tool, but in the lives of many teachers implementing quality improvement, the Life Journal has become a quality tool for improvement of learning. Shelly Carson and Jeff Burgard first used this term and wrote about the Life Journal in their books. Shelly wrote, "The Life Journal is a student handbook designed to record student data and monitor continuous improvement in three areas throughout the school year. It is a living document that represents the individual student's journey on the road to success."[3]

The journal is approximately 50 to 60 pages and includes the aim, Keys to Success, quality tools, charts, information lists, instructions and procedures, journal paper for reflection, and sections to record progress in the areas of information, performance, and enthusiasm. When students need a place to address a question, interpret a quote, write important facts, or brainstorm ideas for continuous improvement, they will utilize the Life Journal as the place to record such information. The use of the Life Journal simplifies data collection.

The continuous improvement journal was named the "Life Journal" by an eighth grade student, who realized the importance of the journal. He said, "This book is our *life*. If we lose this thing, we're really going to be lost."

Debi Molina-Walters learned about the Life Journal from Burgard and Carson and implemented it at her school. She writes that the Life Journal:

- Increases awareness of the expectations and standards. What are we doing and why are we doing it?

- Is used as a guide to manage and monitor learning. What do I know and what do I need to study/practice?

- Increases communication between home and school.

- Increases students' accountability for their own learning.

One student told Debi, "I can no longer lie to my mom. I have to study and know what's expected of me."

So what is the Life Journal? It is merely the organization of all expectations and blank graphs for a year into a booklet. Teachers reading this book will begin with one subject. Students will have one student run chart and the classroom will have one class run chart, one scatter diagram, and hopefully histograms moving from "L" to "J." However, as these teachers progress in their ability and knowledge of continuous improvement, they add more and more. So, the Life Journal has lists of all essential information for the grade, all rubrics for all subjects, blank student run charts for all subjects (information and performance), blank graphs for monthly recording of enthusiasm, and a method of item analysis. A student interest questionnaire can be added as well as a description of learning styles and multiple intelligences. When teachers at a school cooperate, then all students are provided a Life Journal outlining expectations for all classes. (Again the LJ for Life Journal is coincidence).

Increasingly, teachers are not only providing students the content for their grade level and prior grades, but for future grade levels also. Even though students are not responsible for next year's content, they like reading it.

Debi Molina-Walters shares that one of the outcomes of parents seeing the Life Journal is they remark that the students of today are learning more than they did when they were in school. Today's educators need parents to come to this realization, because so much is in the press stating the opposite.

ENDNOTES

1. L. Olson, "Students to Investigate Causes for Achievement Gaps," *Education Week* (May 29, 2002).
2. S. Leddick, *Total Quality Tools™ for Education* (Dayton, OH: PQ Systems, 1998).
3. S. Carson, *Continuous Improvement in the History and Social Science Classroom* (Milwaukee: ASQ Quality Press, 2000).

Section VI

Reflection

18

A Reflection upon Profound Knowledge

I had to decide whether to place the theory of profound knowledge at the front of this book or at the end. Convincing arguments can be made for practical first, then theory. Or one can argue that theory first sets the stage for better understanding of practical. In actuality, theory is the bread of the sandwich to hold the good stuff in place.

So, one of the best treats readers can give themselves is to now reread chapter 3 on profound knowledge. By reading theory again, the practical essence of this book can be held more firmly in place by two slices of theory. Take the opportunity to reflect upon the theory now that you have read the practical. If you think I'd enjoy hearing about your reflections, the e-mail address is LtoJ@earthlink.net . Label the subject as reflections.

Section VII

Accountability

19

Results on Standardized Tests

The recent history of California's standardized, norm-referenced tests includes the California Assessment Program (each student is administered $\frac{1}{30}$ of the test; valid for schools, but no individual scores), the California Learning Assessment System (focus upon performance rather than information), nothing for five years, each school district selects own exam and state pays the bill (only lasted one year), the Stanford Achievement Test, version 9, with the Educational Testing Service now holding the contract. Teachers and administrators within the Enterprise School District of Redding, California, where I served as school district superintendent, developed the continuous improvement strategies presented in this book. The period of time was the "nothing" listed above. One could argue that this is unfortunate (because hard to prove improvement) or fortunate (time was available to develop a completely different view of classroom data). I shared results from Enterprise District's criterion-referenced exams in the first edition of *Improving Student Learning*, but in 2003 norm-referenced data are available from many locales.

I was not surprised at all by the review of research literature reported by Russell Gersten of the University of Oregon. He reported, in mathematics education, "only two practices that boost student achievement—peer tutoring and giving students regular feedback on their progress."[1] Continuous improvement is based upon feedback and making adjustments because of feedback. Further, when students are involved in the planning regarding a plateau on the class run chart, the first idea they always have is "we could help each other."

Nevertheless, this book is not written to improve test scores, but to improve learning. Improved test scores are a by-product of improved learning. In the preface, I described the strategies being used to improve test scores. Except for alignment and continuous improvement, these approaches all come from the same theoretical position: the system is fine; the people are a problem. Continuous improvement is founded upon Dr. Deming's observation that 96 percent of the problems are caused by the system and 4 percent by the people. The first three methods for improving test scores, discussed previously, assume that the problems are the students and the second three assume the problems are the staff. Below is a restating of the strategies in use today:

1. Teach only subjects being tested, which allows triple the time for reading and double for mathematics.

   Theory 1: Our students are not smart enough to learn all subjects.

2. Teach test-taking skills.

   Theory 2: Our students really know the content, but need significant practice and help with multiple-choice tests.

3. Provide students incentives for high scores.

   Theory 3: Our students are lazy and uncaring; only incentives will bring out the best on the tests.

4. Provide staff incentives for high scores.

   Theory 4: Our staffs are lazy and uncaring; only incentives will bring out the best on the tests.

5. Threaten staff with loss of jobs.

   Theory 5: Our staff will only work hard if they think they will be unemployed. They really do know what to do to improve learning and just need a threat to make them do what they already know is best.

6. Buy scripted programs.

   Theory 6: Our staff are not very smart; we'll tell them what to say.

It is no wonder newspapers across the United States are quoting educators that the joy is gone from school and learning. Test scores must go *up!*

I should add here that some school districts have been very successful improving student learning, with resulting improved test scores, by aligning curriculum. Clearly, continuous improvement applied to aligned curriculum will be much more successful than applying continuous improvement to nonaligned curriculum. Alignment efforts assume the problem is the system, not the people.

So, when schools use continuous improvement, as described in this book, and see an increase on norm-referenced tests, it is quite exciting. The teachers and administrators are not devalued, the students have not had their joy in learning removed, they have not had the curriculum devastated for only reading and mathematics, and they have proven they learned more anyway. The essence of this book is that student joy can be increased, staff joy can be increased, learning can improve, and test scores can rise—all at the same time. *Improving Student Learning* is a how-to book describing how such results can be achieved.

Even though I do not know all of the applications and results from the first edition of this book, I have been informed of significant norm-referenced results from various states. Of particular interest is the Enterprise School District in Redding, California. All of the examples from the first edition of *Improving Student Learning* are from this district where I served as superintendent from 1986 to 1999. The subject where continuous improvement has had the most impact is mathematics, with the use of the "Enterprise Weekly" (see appendix Y for examples). Math is the consistent high performer at Enterprise. Figure 19.1 shows five years of improvement on the SAT-9.

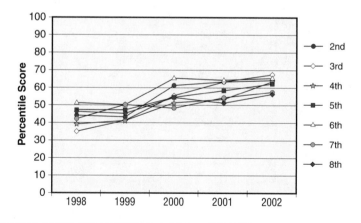

Figure 19.1   Enterprise SAT-9 math results.

Carlisle, Pennsylvania, has begun the same trend. In the first year after mathematics continuous improvement became a district focus, their benchmark comparisons improved as shown below:

Grade 1   78 to 84 percent successful

Grade 2   84 to 86 percent successful

Grade 3   82 to 85 percent successful

Grade 4   61 to 68 percent successful

Grade 5   57 to 59 percent successful

In Rochester, Indiana, five years of increased test scores have occurred on their third-grade state tests. (See Figure 19.2.) The first, and most concentrated efforts were in grades K–2, which were reflected in the third-grade fall exams.

Of great interest to me, and a topic for further research, is the connection between the shape of the curve from weekly quizzes and the results on standardized, norm-referenced exams. Figures 19.3 shows is the quiz results for the three weeks prior to the standardized tests for science vocabulary, and Figure 19.4 shows the results for the same three weeks from the essential science information. Debi Molina-Walters' vocabulary quiz is five questions per week (thus a total of 15 questions for the three weeks) and her essential information quiz is 10 questions per week (thus a total of 30 questions for the three weeks). When districts have aligned curriculum and when continuous improvement is in place, can educators have a reasonable

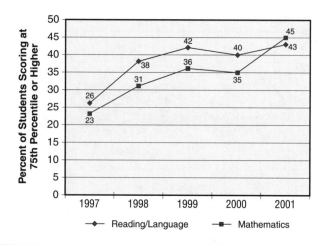

Figure 19.2 Rochester, Indiana, third grade.

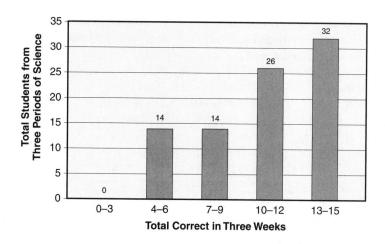

Figure 19.3   Science vocabulary: three weeks prior to standardized tests.

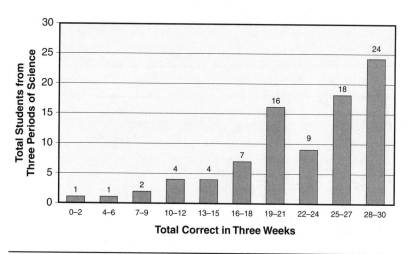

Figure 19.4   Science essential facts: three weeks prior to standardized tests.

assurance of acceptable scores on standardized exams? Can teachers concentrate on creating as much of a "J" curve as possible prior to the exams and forget about all of the other gimmicks designed to raise test scores? If educators could have the assurance that putting the content of the essential information into students' long-term memory would result in increased test scores, then much stress could be reduced in schools. By the way, the students scored an average of 93 percent correct on the district's science exam.

There are several EdD and PhD dissertations now being written regarding Dr. Deming's quality principles applied in schools. Some reader will grab onto this question and research it for the good of education.

In Oklahoma City, the press recognized the improvement brought about through continuous improvement in Britton and Wheeler Elementary Schools in 2002. Students at Wheeler Elementary were able to explain all of their graphs to the television crews. Continuous improvement works in our high-poverty environments also.

Another testing success is from Virginia Beach's Corporate Landing Middle School. Prior to implementation of continuous improvement in eighth-grade social studies, their school average score on Virginia State History Tests was 40.8 percent. With two of the six eighth-grade social studies teachers implementing continuous improvement, the scores rose to 46.7 percent. The year after, with all six teachers participating, the scores rose to 78.4 percent. This 2002 increase in performance was publicly noted at an October 2002 board meeting.

Figures 19.5 and 19.6 clearly display improvement from no continuous improvement to partial implementation to 100 percent participation. Note how much better the "pioneer" teachers did the second year of implementation.

This latest example follows two common patterns. Continuous improvement begins with teacher leaders (Shawn Hirano, in this example)

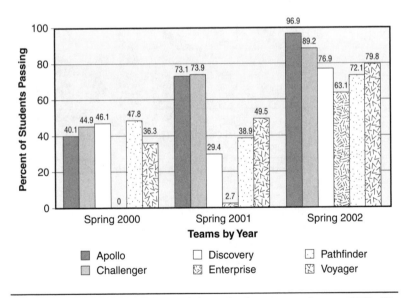

Figure 19.5 Corporate Landing eighth-grade History scores by year 2000–02.

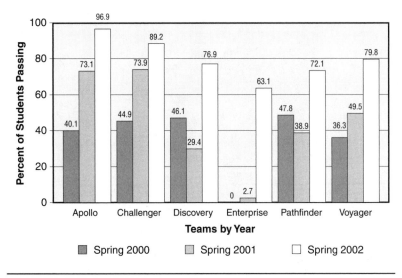

Figure 19.6 Corporate Landing eighth-grade History scores by individual team 2000–02.

with significant support from administrators (Ron Nash in the central office). Secondly, gains on standardized tests are not widely noticed until all of the teachers at a grade level or department are actively participating.

ENDNOTE

1. D. Viadero and E. W. Robelen, review of research literature by Russell Gersten, *Education Week* (February 13, 2002): 30.

Chapter 20
School-Wide Improvement

School-wide improvement is the result of two simultaneous efforts: continuous improvement and alignment. Often when the term *alignment* is used, it means aligning curriculum with what the developers of norm-referenced exams deem important. Such alignment may or may not be important; it depends upon the environment of local educators. In this chapter, alignment refers to the work of each educator, each grade level, and each major division (elementary, middle, and high) being aligned with each other.

Richard Elmore wrote in *Unwarranted Intrusion* that "school personnel must share a coherent, explicit set of norms and expectations about what a good school looks like before they can use signals from the outside to improve student learning. . . . Low-performing schools aren't coherent enough to respond to external demands for accountability."[1] Chapter 20, through the discussion of alignment, is designed to give faculties the foundation necessary to agree upon their norms and expectations.

ALIGNMENT

Examples of aligned performance expectations follow.

Writing, for a school that uses a one to four rubric: write an aligned rubric that spirals. Levels three and four from first grade become levels one and two for second grade, while new levels three and four are added. Then in third grade, levels one and two are the second grade levels three and four, while new levels three and four are added. This process continues up through the grades.

The writing power points from Mary Bohr in Rochester, Indiana, is an excellent example for creating such a set of rubrics. (See appendix R.)

Reading fluency has been aligned in several locations. Students are expected to read not only more difficult text as they progress through the grades, but at a faster pace. Aligned fluency rates could be as described in the Table 20.1. The fluency rate is for grade-level text, preferably nonfiction.

Beginning reading levels have been aligned using Marie Clay's Reading Recovery Book Levels. Kindergarten is expected to read level four books, first grade level 18, and second grade level 36.

Essential information needs to be aligned also. Basically, students have a right to know what content is new for the current grade level and educators have a responsibility to not give students permission to forget content from prior grades.

Spelling expectations could be actual words or the listed words and other words that use the same spelling pattern. (See Table 20.2.) I recommend using high-frequency word lists and lists of most frequent spelling patterns when aligning spelling.

Table 20.1 Aligned fluency rates.

Grade Level	Fluency Expectation
First	60 words per minute
Second	100 words per minute
Third	120 words per minute
Fourth	130 words per minute
Fifth	140 words per minute
Sixth	160 words per minute
Seventh	180 words per minute
Eighth	200 words per minute

Table 20.2 Spelling expectations.

Grade Level	Possible Expectation
Kindergarten	30 words
First	30 kindergarten words plus 70 first-grade words
Second	100 prior words plus 100 new words
Third	150 new words plus 150 of the 200 prior words Drop 50 words known by all or almost all third graders
Fourth	200 new words plus 200 of K–3 words
Fifth	300 new words, plus 300 of K–4 words

A wonderful pattern for aligning *mathematics* has been developed by Judy Flores of the Enterprise School District in Redding, California. Students are provided the new expectations for their grade level and review copies of the prior two grades. Each grade level has specific new content that is not repeated at other grade levels. The review process is implemented by building each weekly quiz 50 percent from the current grade, 30 percent from the prior grade, and 20 percent from two grades prior. (See appendix Y.)

The only concern I've heard expressed regarding the alignment of U.S. *history* (appendix R) expectations is the lack of connectivity between U.S. and world history. My response has been that schools need to first align U.S. history and two or three years of world history. Then educators can build one aligned history sequence, if desired. As students, most of today's current educators experienced an unaligned U.S. history; our elementary, middle, and high school teachers all attempted to teach all of U.S. history to us. The school year always ended about the time of the Civil War, however. A suggested U.S. History alignment is: fifth grade up to the War for American Independence, eighth grade from the Constitution to 1900, and eleventh from 1900 to the current time.

Geography locations and terminology are both alignment candidates. Terminology doesn't seem to be an issue; teachers can agree which grade level is responsible for *delta, peninsula,* and so on. It should be equally easy to agree upon which locations on a map should be known at each grade level. It is not. Fifth grade teachers have to give up their historic fascination with memorization of the state capitals and fourth grade (or whatever grade teaches a particular state) will have to back off on their state geography expectations.

The problem with specific state expectations is that other grade-level teachers seem to not care about these locations, so alignment does not occur.

SCHOOL-WIDE DATA

The second aspect of school-wide implementation of continuous improvement is the gathering of school-wide data. Teachers in their own classrooms do not need an aligned curriculum in order to become experts in continuous improvement. In fact, school-wide implementation of continuous improvement depends upon the expertise of teacher leaders. However, when a principal desires to use continuous improvement as a major process for improving student learning, the expectations must be aligned. If one teacher assesses reading with Reading Recovery Book Levels, one with Accelerated Reading Levels, and one with fluency, there are no common denominators to add up.

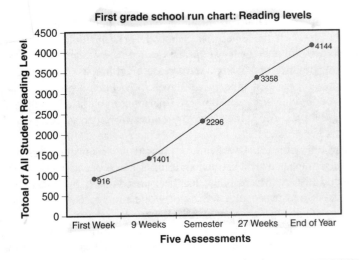

First grade school run chart: Reading levels

Figure 20.1 First grade school run chart: reading levels.

I am not advocating that all teachers use the same teaching strategies, but the grade-level expectations and feedback system have to be uniform for school-wide implementation of continuous improvement. Figure 20.1 is an example of reading levels added up for all of Columbia Elementary's (Rochester, Indiana) seven classes of first-graders. This grade-level graph complements the class run charts and student run charts kept in the classroom. The grade-level chart is posted in the hallway.

Science will serve as an example for school-wide implementation of both alignment and continuous improvement. Assume there are 100 essential facts for each of the three grade levels. The enrollment for the hypothetical school is 250 students per grade level. The agreed-upon quizzing of students is as follows:

Grade Level	Expectations	Weekly Quiz	Total for Grade Level
Sixth	100 essential facts	10	2500
Seventh	200 essential facts (100 sixth plus 100 seventh)	14	3500
Eighth	300 essential facts (100 sixth plus 100 seventh plus 100 eighth)	17	4250

The total possible correct for the whole school is 10,250 (2500 + 3500 + 4250).

Teachers are not expected to teach the same content in the same manner, although they are expected to learn teaching methods from each other. The principal is not to compare class to class or grade to grade, but every week note four data points: total for sixth grade, total for seventh grade, total for eighth grade, and total for whole school. First comes alignment and development of teacher expertise with continuous improvement, then school-wide improvement is available.

Just as it is the teacher's job to cheer on their students, it is the principal's job to cheer on both students and teachers. The principal is to look for the weeks when a particular grade level or the whole school improves and find as many ways as possible to say, "Thank you." Bill Eich, a Glenwood, Iowa principal, has teachers share good news about student learning at his faculty meetings. Teachers like the chance to say things like, "This is the fourth time this year my class scored their all-time high in science. They were so excited!" Cheryl Downs, principal of Columbia School in Rochester, Indiana, has a "powwow" with each grade level to discuss regularly their grade-level totals. Because of this, the staff reports that students study the grade-level charts just like the class and individual ones. When a grade level or the whole school improves by the smallest of margins, even by one, the principal should find a struggling student and thank him or her. For example, if an eighth-grader has three correct on his most recent quiz and the whole school improves by one, the principal has an opportunity for a private thank you. "If it were not for you, the school would not have improved this week. Thanks, and keep on improving. I know your score is not the highest in the room, but I also know you are improving and that is what we are here for."

All of the traditional energies principals put into honoring the student of the week, and other failed methods of motivating, can now be utilized for honoring the whole student body for their continuous improvement. The job is to devise methods for everyone to know how smart the students are becoming.

Communicating progress for grade levels and the whole school is done by placing graphs in the hallways. The graphs can be on chart paper or on a TV monitor. When a TV monitor is chosen, the school needs a dedicated computer connected to the monitor that is placed in the foyer. Each week's data is entered into Excel and connected to PowerPoint, using the linked Paste Special command. Then an automatically rolling PowerPoint presentation continually displays graphs, announcements, and digital photographs of school events.

The principal has four responsibilities for continuous improvement implementation—two are hard, one is easy, and one is pure joy. The hard work for the principal is helping teachers implement continuous improvement in their classroom and organizing time for teachers to reach consensus on aligned expectations. The easy part is adding up the totals each week for essential information and every other week or monthly for performance expectations. The pure joy is celebrating how well the students are doing.

Many U.S. principals are under intense pressure to raise test scores. They would rather improve learning, but have gone from program to program to program with no improvement. So now they are passing the pressure on to the teachers. The teachers have gone from program to program to program with no improvement, so now they are passing the pressure on to the students.

Continuous improvement is a completely opposite approach; the principal is not the provider of fear and tension, but is a team member helping everybody, each and every week, to learn information and meet performance expectations that were outlined the first week of school.

Both state laws and tradition expect principals to be inspectors. Continuous improvement is suggesting that far less time be spent on inspecting, whether this be formal evaluations, checking lesson plans, or other inspection devices. The time is to be used aligning school expectations, regularly gathering feedback on student learning, celebrating, and brainstorming ways student learning can be increased.

ENDNOTE

1. R. Elmore, *Unwarranted Intrusion*, www.educationnext.org/20021/30.html .

21
District-Wide Improvement

D
istrict-wide improvement, using continuous improvement, is a process encompassing several years of effort. The two districts with which I am most familiar that are implementing continuous improvement district-wide are Rochester, Indiana, and the Carlisle Area School District in Pennsylvania. Their superintendents, Bob Poffenbarger and Jerry Fowler, have taken the lead; everyone in the system knows their focus. While each of these two superintendents has his own personality and their stories are different, great similarities exist. In this chapter, I am sharing the insights I've learned from them.

INSIGHT #1: REFORM RELIES SIGNIFICANTLY UPON TEACHER LEADERSHIP

The demands on educators today are complex and far-reaching. The days when top-down models were effective and efficient approaches in dealing with these demands are gone. To be successful now and in the future, school districts must develop collaborative styles where as many people as possible hold leadership responsibilities. Today's classroom is just too complex. To accomplish this goal, both superintendents rely heavily upon teacher leaders. The development of these leaders is essential. There is a need for staff development for all, but the need for development of teacher leaders is even more important. Some of these teacher leaders might eventually become administrators, but most will remain in the classroom. Working hand-in-glove with principals and department heads, these teacher leaders can have far-reaching influences on improvement and change. In many respects, they view themselves as colleagues with principals and supervisors, as opposed to subordinates in the instructional process.

Jerry, with assistance from Pennsylvania's Digital School District Grant (one of only three in a state of 501 school districts), was able to release some of his teacher leaders part-time to assist other teachers. Kelly Brent, for example, teaches two periods a day of high school algebra and assists other teachers throughout the district for the remainder of the day. Carlisle has about 130 teachers working on a variety of instructional activities to improve learning. All have a say and a stake in the outcome of the district-wide implications of their efforts. At the same time, all are gaining valuable skills in how to influence and get commitment from others without the negative baggage that often comes through traditional authority channels.

INSIGHT #2: BEGIN WITH VOLUNTEERS, BUT DO MOVE TO MANDATORY

I often recommend that with any new initiative there be a three-year plan. Teachers can sign up to be year one, year two, or year three implementers. The members of the staff who are either uninterested, or have seen very few initiatives last for three years, sign up for year three. If the new idea goes away before year three, they won't be bothered. Other teachers are not willing to be the pioneers, but don't want to wait until all the decisions have been formalized. Year two is best for them. In this way, administrators can work with the teachers who, with this concept, are the pioneers.

The work with the pioneers has significant advantages because these volunteers work out the rough spots, learn, develop their leadership ability, and are not involved in philosophical fights; the effort is voluntary. Jerry began with a group of three teachers and their administrators. This was his total group for a year. The next year he moved to 18 teachers and their principals. In year three, his group was 50 teachers and any principals not formerly involved. The effort was still voluntary.

In year four, Carlisle had involvement of 84 teachers, but selected elementary schools and all math teachers from grades 6–10 were mandated to implement continuous improvement. All of his mandated efforts are in mathematics.

Bob, as of this writing, is involved in year five of continuous improvement. He is now mandating continuous improvement in grades K–9 for all core subjects. He has voluntary participation with teachers outside core subjects and in grades 10–12. Grades 10–12 are implementing one year at a time until all grade levels K–12 have continuous improvement.

INSIGHT #3: REMOVING BARRIERS WORKS BEST FOR STAFF BUY-IN

The central leadership question to staffs is, "What are the barriers to implementing continuous improvement?" Both superintendents listen directly to staffs and also have others listen and relay information. Sometimes the intermediaries garner more honest feedback than would be shared directly. When superintendents act quickly to remove the barriers listed by staff, not only are the staffs appreciative, but then they use their energy to be creative instead of bemoaning their situation. For example, Jerry found out that first-grade teachers believed that 10 math questions per assessment was too many for first-grade students, the middle school teachers wanted less multiple choice, the pre-algebra was too easy, and the sixth- and seventh-grade standards were almost exactly the same. Teachers also said it would be easier to revise exams if an extra exam was provided for their notes. All suggestions were implemented.

INSIGHT #4: THE SUPERINTENDENTS TAKE THE "HITS"

Both superintendents are out in front of this effort; staffs have the comfort of knowing their superintendent will help out if there are any significant complaints. In such change environments, everyone must understand his/her role. For example, teacher leaders see and work with their colleagues every day. Superintendents and other administrators do not. On the occasions when mandates are delivered or directives must be given, it is important that teacher leaders are not caught in the middle. In some cases, the teacher leader can use a directive to actually achieve higher credibility with his/her colleagues. After all, he/she must comply with the directive as well! When parent meetings are held on continuous improvement, Bob is an active participant. Yes, teachers and principals give a great deal of the details, but Bob is not a passive observer.

INSIGHT #5: SUPERINTENDENTS PARTICIPATE IN CELEBRATIONS

Both Bob and Jerry are actively involved in celebrations. It is not possible, nor desirable, for these two to participate every time a class, school, or grade level has an all-time high, but this does not mean they are never invited to a celebration. Bob's administrators forward voice mails to him on a regular basis. Sometimes, his involvement is a voice mail from students describing their all-time best. He then forwards this to board members, other administrators, and interested parties. In this way the celebration involves more than one classroom with one teacher. Crucial to this insight is the fact that staffs and students know how much joy the superintendent receives from their learning.

INSIGHT # 6: COMMUNICATING DIRECTLY WITH TEACHERS

Both superintendents communicate directly with teachers. Most formal communication to teachers comes through the principals, but this does not mean superintendents cannot talk to teachers. When superintendents lead continuous improvement, they must have the 1:1 and small group conversations with teachers to inform their decision making. If they don't have these details, decisions cannot be as well constructed. Jerry uses teacher committees and his staff development council to get direct feedback. He also occasionally sits in on curriculum council discussions. The curriculum council is made up of department heads, principals, and assistant principals. He has found that attending conferences with small groups of teachers can be very effective in opening thoughtful channels of communication that otherwise would not have existed.

INSIGHT #7: SUPERINTENDENTS ARE PROACTIVE WITH THE PRESS

These superintendents do their best to inform the press of their continuous improvement efforts. While working in Rochester, for example, the press was in the room while teachers were asking detailed questions regarding implementation. Some questions could have been considered a criticism, but Bob wanted the press to know all of the ups and downs of implementing continuous improvement. Jerry's staff has a totally decentralized approach to media contact on instructional issues. Everyone is encouraged to invite the press, both print and television, to observe programs and activities. In addition, a central office contact meets with reporters each Thursday to answer questions and discuss what is happening in the district.

INSIGHT #8: SUPERINTENDENTS MUST BE WELL READ

How many books does a person have to read on a particular topic in order to become an expert on the subject? When I was teaching fifth grade, a student read 50 books that year on the Civil War and had completed 200 by the end of seventh grade. He was an expert. I don't know the answer to my question, but the number is significant. Teachers know if their superintendent attended one session on a topic, read an article, listened to a tape, or is truly an expert. They will follow a well-informed educator. Superintendents can also demonstrate their knowledge and commitment by making presentations. Both Jerry and Bob usually speak several times a year at local and regional conferences on continuous improvement and other topics. They often copresent with a teacher, principal, or other members of their staffs.

INSIGHT #9: INVITE VISITORS

When visitors from other school districts come to Rochester and Carlisle, it is very encouraging for educators. I recently had the privilege of sharing successes in Oklahoma City with educators in Jenks, Oklahoma. I was so proud of the Jenks educators, from a highly esteemed suburban district, that they would spend a day learning from urban educators. Great joy emanated from the Oklahoma City educators as they shared their stories, successes, and tribulations. Jerry and Bob know this about their staffs and actively recruit visitors as one way to compliment their staffs. Jerry's district has run its own conference the last two summers. It is organized by a committee of teachers and principals. With the exception of the keynote speakers, just about every presenter is a teacher from the region. About 100 educators have attended each year.

INSIGHT #10: PRINCIPAL EVALUATIONS CHANGE

Principals are overloaded with laws to enforce. Several years ago, while at a meeting in Washington D.C., the speaker shared a list of almost 100 federal programs designed to accomplish the same thing. Why so many laws? He reported that legislators need to campaign that they authored new legislation, not that they made the system work better. All of these laws are dumped on educators at the local level. I know that principals could be evaluated solely on one premise: Did you do what the superintendent, assistant superintendents, board members, state legislators, state superintendent, governor, and the president told you? However, these two superintendents have made a major focus of their evaluations based upon barrier removal. Are the principals removing the barriers that are keeping their staffs from doing their best, and more specific to the text of this book, are they removing barriers keeping staffs from implementing continuous improvement?

INSIGHT #11: PROVIDE TIME FOR STAFFS TO REACH AGREEMENTS

When educators believe every teacher is to perform in isolation, all planning time is in the evening, home alone. However, systemwide improvement will not occur with all-alone planning. Bob and Jerry provide time for staffs to reach agreements. Appendix C is an example of Carlisle agreements in second grade mathematics and sample questions for each concept. This is much more time-consuming than it might seem because each grade level needs new content; no duplication from prior grades. The built-in preview–review process of continuous improvement takes care of the review. Kelly Brent, of Carlisle, reports how exciting a new school year is for her students. And what do textbooks and tradition do with this excitement? She says, "At a time when students are the most excited about school, we give them review." For many, boredom results because they simply don't need the review. With continuous improvement, we can start the new school year with the new content for the year; quizzes take care of the review.

The teachers in Carlisle and Rochester have been provided the time to reach the necessary agreements regarding content. They cannot merely copy state standards or textbook objectives because they do not clearly specify the new content for each grade level. In Rochester, leadership for these connections is provided by Mary Bohr, a classroom connections coordinator. Her job is to facilitate grade-level to grade-level articulation of essential information and performance standards. This is the reason why the report card of the future (chapter 16) could be developed by the Columbia faculty. Mary is also responsible for coaching teachers in continuous improvement implementation in their classrooms.

INSIGHT #12: HYPOTHESES TESTING IS THE NORM

Not every new idea works. Much less fear is present among staff when they know they are continually testing out ideas instead of being accountable for "doing what they are told." This is as much a cultural phenomenon as it is anything else. The Carlisle Area School District is committed to creating a culture where exploration is valued and encouraged. Jerry suggests that you can get a sense of your progress in changing the cultural context in which you launch your improvement model by the variety of approaches that evolve at the classroom level. Continuous improvement is not a recipe to be followed but a process to be adopted. As such, each teacher should be able to interpret and demonstrate how it looks in his/her classroom once a conceptual understanding is achieved.

INSIGHT #13: STAFFS ARE UNIFIED ACROSS THE DISTRICT

From kindergarten to grade 12, teachers can have a common experience with continuous improvement. They all see that they can learn from each other. For example, teachers at all grade levels can discuss the power of review–preview or their class's response to the class total. They can talk about the record keeping process and ways to have the students accept more of the responsibility. Teachers at different schools can discuss their student's mastery of dissimilar content, because they are unified by continuous improvement. Often, administrators attempt to achieve this unification through program adoption and are frustrated. Continuous improvement is a process, not a program, so it helps unify teachers—for example, art and mathematics—who would not otherwise be unified.

INSIGHT #14: CONTINUOUS IMPROVEMENT HELPS TEACHERS WITH PACING

Every administrator and teacher know that sometimes the year ends with some content untaught. The "solution" used by some is to monitor lesson plans or insist that teachers complete chapters by specific times. Of course, teacher resentment of such mandates is high. Continuous improvement gives teachers a means of pacing themselves. They have data to support taking longer with certain concepts and also data to support spending one day on a topic or even skipping it. For example, teachers using continuous improvement usually find the math chapter on statistics can be quickly reviewed or skipped. An assignment from a teacher could be, "Look over the chapter on statistics with a friend or two, and determine if there is anything included in the chapter that we don't already know." By skipping known content, pacing is much easier to accomplish. Also, there are times when pacing does not work—the year ends and logarithms are not taught. However, because they are on the list of essential information, they have come up all year; mini-lessons have been taught, so the students are not leaving the year totally uninformed. (True story from Carlisle.)

INSIGHT #15: STAFFS ARE MORE JOYFUL

One of Dr. Deming's admonitions for leaders is to create joy in the workplace. Superintendents are to accomplish this proactively, not merely by a "hands-off" approach. Yes, teachers like compliments like everyone else, but a greater joy comes from students being so excited.

INSIGHT #16: MORE PROBLEMS ARE SOLVED AT SCHOOL LEVEL USING DATA, INSTEAD OF POWER, IN THE SUPERINTENDENT'S OFFICE

A Rochester parent insisted that her child qualified for the gifted program. However, when she saw the class scatter diagram with an overlay for her son, she knew he was not performing above many other students. Having served 14 years as a superintendent, I know that, typically, these issues become power struggles to be settled in the superintendent's office or become the start of a campaign for school board. Continuous improvement and its data help to make the conversations reasoned. Another example is a Carlisle student convincing his father that nobody was learning algebra. Again, the scatter diagram with overlay came to the rescue. The father saw that the class, as a whole, was learning, but his son was not. An attitude changed, a conversation took place at home, and the fibbing student learned algebra. The superintendent was not involved; data took the place of a power struggle.

INSIGHT #17: DATA DOES THE TEACHER-CONVINCING

Just as data convinced the two parents in the previous examples, data convinces teachers rather than this being left up to the administrators. Teachers will change when they see accurate data from their classroom. An Iowa teacher, for example, realized the power of continuous improvement when she started continuous improvement in October. Through random selection of the whole year's content, questions came up on area and perimeter. Great, she thought; we completed area and perimeter in September. To her amazement, the students did not remember area and perimeter. She immediately realized the need for review–preview. The power of continual review and continual preview came from the data, not from the administrators. Both Bob and Jerry recount many stories of hesitant teachers who later stated how much the data convinced them of the value of continuous improvement. They discovered that teachers were much more responsive when data drove their observations rather than authority figures. A number of teachers even volunteered to make the changes. This data-convincing then puts the teachers and the administrators on the same side—how can we make this process the most valuable in the least amount of time?

INSIGHT #18: FORMAL TEACHER SELECTION COMPLEMENTS CONTINUOUS IMPROVEMENT

Bob writes that, without formal selection of the best available staff and development of current staff, the continuous improvement cycle is less sustainable. He considers the teacher selection process of Dr. Vic Cottrell, president of Ventures of Excellence in Lincoln, Nebraska, and continuous improvement to be most compatible.

CONCLUSION

In conclusion to this chapter, I've listed below the steps for implementing continuous improvement that I observe in school districts, including Rochester, Indiana, and Carlisle Area, Pennsylvania:

1. Develop teacher leaders.

2. Principals use continuous improvement for some aspect of the job for which he/she is personally responsible.

3. Calculate and graph grade level, department, and school totals.

4. Conduct celebrations for *all,* instead of awards assemblies.

5. Employ continuous improvement in planning and reporting documents. This means that the culture of education is changing. Continuous improvement is not an add-on; it's the way we think and operate.

6. Use continuous improvement in finance, operations, and personnel. There's no reason that continuous improvement cannot begin here; but a superefficient district warehouse, using continuous improvement, will not be seen by teachers and principals as something that can be modeled for improved learning.

22

Control Charts versus Ranking

One of the more difficult tasks for first graders is to put numbers in order from smallest to largest. The assignment, "Put the numbers 60, 14, 52, 6, 41, and 25 in order from smallest to largest" is not so easy for six-year-olds. In fact, many six-year-olds need Base Ten Blocks to accomplish the task so they can see that 14 and 41 are not equal. Nevertheless, this is first-grade math.

The test scores have just arrived. What do educators from the principal's office to the state departments of education to the U.S. Department of Education do to communicate the results? They fall back upon their knowledge of first grade mathematics; they rank the numbers from largest to smallest.

Ranking always creates more problems than it ever solves. Not only does a school's rank depend a great deal upon luck, it is not helpful. Under the guiding principles of continuous improvement, educators are always attempting to improve. With ranking, no improvement can occur unless somebody else does less well or doesn't improve as much as another. If I'm in third place, in order for me to be in first place, somebody else has to lose his or her spot.

Besides the win/lose issue, ranking causes people to come to false conclusions. In chapter 3, under the profound knowledge discussion on variation, I explained Dr. Deming's two types of variation: special and common cause. Ranked data causes people to believe that all data is special and there's no common cause variation. The top school is special by virtue of its place and the lowest-rank school is also special. Further, people infer that the teachers at the top school are better than other teachers and the teachers at the bottom-ranked schools are despicable. Poor psychology from ill-informed leaders causes them to give awards to the teachers at the top-ranked schools and threaten the bottom-ranked faculties with termination. As an example, I've placed the ranked scores from 60 elementary schools.

School	Percent of Students Scoring "Successful" on State Exam	School	Percent of Students Scoring "Successful" on State Exam
1	100	31	67
2	100	32	66
3	100	33	65
4	97	34	65
5	95	35	64
6	87	36	63
7	86	37	63
8	85	38	61
9	83	39	60
10	82	40	60
11	81	41	58
12	79	42	57
13	79	43	56
14	79	44	56
15	79	45	54
16	79	46	54
17	78	47	51
18	78	48	51
19	77	49	51
20	76	50	49
21	76	51	48
22	76	52	46
23	74	53	46
24	74	54	45
25	73	55	43
26	73	56	37
27	73	57	35
28	72	58	32
29	71	59	31
30	69	60	31

Figure 22.1 is a control chart produced from the ranked data. There are two important lines on the chart: the upper control limit (UCL) and the lower control limit (LCL). These lines are neither goals nor specifications; they are measurements derived from the data itself. The UCL is approximately three standard deviations above the mean and the LCL is approximately three standard deviations below the mean. It is a given that there will be variation among the 60 schools. The control chart, however, answers the question, "Which variation is special and which is common?" In Figure 22.1 there are 11 special schools above the UCL and 13 special schools below the LCL. Some schools are special-positive and some are special-negative. All other variation between the two lines is common variation. If the school board and superintendent are unhappy with the performance of schools scoring between the upper control limit and lower control limit, they need to blame themselves. The schools between the lines are "in the system of the district." The solution to the unhappiness is to improve the whole system, and no principal is in charge of the whole system.

What about schools that scored above the system? Unless the scores are the result of higher than normal wealth for the district, the schools are candidates for study. What can we learn from these schools to help improve the whole system? And what about those schools that are below the system? They need to be studied to determine what can be done to help them. Often, people begin by blaming the staff, but that is the last choice to be used. First, leaders must study how to help. They must look for root causes of the

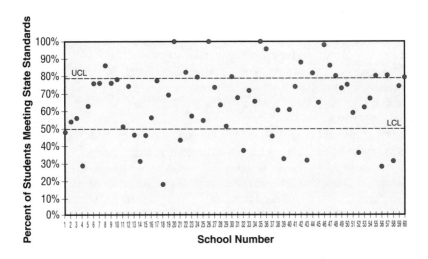

Figure 22.1   Control chart for 60 schools.

poor assessment results. Perhaps the school has had four different principals in the past five years, a fact over which the faculty has little control. They cannot be held accountable for this turmoil.

The control chart provides superb direction for district curriculum staff. Job one is to improve the whole district. The schools within the system, between the UCL and LCL, will most likely rise with an improved system. The lessons learned from the schools above the UCL will most certainly help. The next job is to spend dedicated time with the schools below the LCL. Unless a district is flush with money, there are a limited number of educators in the curriculum department; they cannot spend much time at each school. In fact, if they do spend an equal amount of time at each school, it is so little time that they are ineffective. The control chart guides them regarding where to invest significant time.

Control charts like the one in Figure 22.1 can also be constructed with data from each teacher rather than from each school. In one district, when administrators studied the results, they found one teacher's math scores above the UCL. This was especially interesting since he taught in the school with the most poverty. They asked the teacher why he thought the scores were so high. He replied that he skipped the first third of the textbook, which was review of the prior year's content. He started the year with the new content for his grade level. Other teachers followed the textbook and started teaching the new content for their grade about 10 weeks prior to the exam. Without the control chart, the administrators would have never gained this insight that was used to help improve the whole district. It is worth noting here that the control chart compares the results of each classroom to the system as a whole and does not compare teacher to teacher.

Figure 22.2 displays standardized reading results for 75 second-graders in one school. All the typical test publisher states is that the average score is 57 percent. The control chart tells so much more. It shows that the instructional system in place produces students who score from the 41st to the 71st percentile. However, the system is out of statistical control because so many students are not within the system. Parents enrolling their child in second grade could easily be fooled; the newspaper said the school scored above average, but there is no indication that parents should have confidence their child will be above average. One has to reach the uncomfortable conclusion that school ended with a "bell" curve, not a "J" curve.

Figure 22.3 displays the number of referrals per teacher for a school. It was done to determine whether or not teacher "B" was in the system of referrals present in the school. When ranked data (11, 5, 2, 2, 2, 2, 2, 2, 2, 1, 1, 1, 1) is presented, it looks like a special cause, but it is wise to drop the numbers into a computer program and check it out to be sure. Often, we believe some event is special when it is not. For example, if the teacher

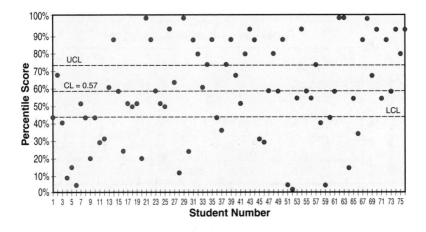

Figure 22.2   Second-grade reading.

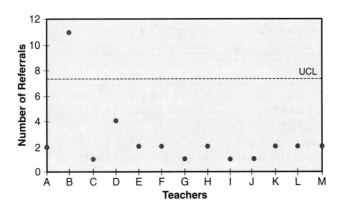

Figure 22.3   Referrals by teacher.

with 11 referrals had sent seven students to the office instead of 11, this teacher would be in the system—no special cause.

The resources used to produce the control charts include *Total Quality Tools for Educators (K–12)* by Susan Leddick et al.[1] There are eight different control charts, all used with specific types of data. Computers can compute the control limits, but human beings need to tell the computer which of the eight charts to use. *Total Quality Tools for Educators* provides precise directions for making this determination.

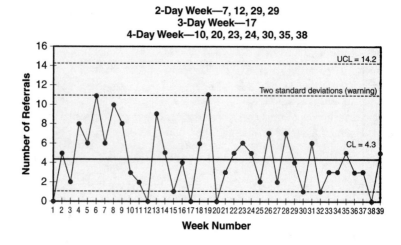

2-Day Week—7, 12, 29, 29
3-Day Week—17
4-Day Week—10, 20, 23, 24, 30, 35, 38

Figure 22.4 Number of discipline referrals each week.

Figures 22.1 through 22.4 were produced by *QI Macros for Excel.*[2] As the title indicates, these macros written for Excel are an add-on to Excel. The lines between the dots were removed (an option with the macro) to show that these control charts do not show movement over time. Figure 22.4 is a discipline graph showing movement from week to week. The dots remain to indicate movement of time. Not only are control charts available, but most of the quality tools described in Susan Leddick's book can be constructed with this software.

Teachers and administrators following the learning processes described in this book will find that the control chart can be of great assistance. Below is a comparison of ranking and control chart leadership:

Ranking	Control Charts
1. Raw numbers	1. Raw numbers
2. Rank numbers	2. Determine which control chart to use
3. Deliver rewards and punishments	3. Construct control chart
4. Keep pressure off self by blaming others	4. Study results
5. Gain no knowledge	5. Use insights to establish hypotheses for improvement
6. Count days until retirement	6. Gain knowledge from testing hypotheses

Administrators with control charts still have personnel issues to solve. The difference is that the "ranking" administrator sees everything as personnel issues and thus they apply the carrot and stick to all issues. As Peter Scholtes tells us in *The Leadership Book*, the donkey is between the carrot and the stick; that's what ranking administrators think of those to whom the carrot and stick are applied. Administrators who use the control chart rather than ranking know that personnel issues cause approximately three to five percent of their problems. They put most of their energy into solving system issues, communicate to the 95 to 97 percent how much they are appreciated, and work on personnel issues in a manner that doesn't destroy the system.

ENDNOTES

1. S. Leddick et al., *Total Quality Tools for Educators (K–12)* (Dayton, OH: PQ Systems, 1998).
2. J. Arthur, *The QI Macros* (Denver: LifeStar Publishers, 2002).
3. P. Scholtes, *The Leadership Book* (New York: McGraw-Hill, 1998).

23

Gaining Insight from Norm-Referenced Tests

Whereas classroom and schoolwide learning is monitored weekly, biweekly, or monthly, the assessment of a school district is annual. Some school districts have quarterly assessments, but these are really efforts to improve the annual results; the real district-wide measures are annual.

Regarding norm-referenced assessments, there's nothing wrong with an annual audit. The state annual exam is an audit. It might be a poorly written audit, children may experience multiple choice too soon, and a host of other problems can occur. Nevertheless it is reasonable for education to have an annual audit.

The problem with norm-referenced assessments is the terrible statistics, awful psychology, and horrendous "leadership" used in conjunction with these audits. If people responsible for norm-referenced assessments used Dr. Deming's profound knowledge, the audit would not be nearly as controversial.

Great management of these audits begins with defining improvement. Most U.S. governors have set five percent increase in average scores over last year as improvement. Some have said improvement is a five percent increase for every ethnic group. Continuous improvement theory defines improvement differently. Step one is agreement upon a definition of success and failure. Often, districts agree upon "above the 50th percentile" as their definition of success and "below the 20th percentile" as their definition of failure. The second step is goal setting. What number is needed to show improvement? The answer is, "better than ever before," not five percent, three percent, or 2.8452 percent—merely improvement.

After the above two tasks are completed, the definition of improvement becomes "more students experiencing success" than ever before and "fewer students experiencing failure" than ever before. The superintendent can publish a letter to parents stating that this is the best-prepared class of fifth graders they have ever sent on to the middle school. How can superintendents say this? They have the documentation to know that more students met the district's criteria for success and fewer met the criteria for failure.

RUN CHART

The first question many school board members ask when test scores are returned is, "Did we improve?" When administrators describe the results from many different assessments, the board members (and people who live with the data daily) can become overwhelmed with so many different numbers. If each grade level has assessments in language, reading, spelling, and mathematics, and seven grades are assessed, that's 28 numbers to keep in mind. Too much. The solution in some states has been to construct a complicated (often secret) formula that leaves school personnel confused.

Adding up the percent of students meeting the district's criteria for success and the percent meeting the criteria for failure is much easier and understood by all. Figure 23.1 is an example district run chart. It clearly shows that the district has a pattern of more students scoring above the 50th percentile and fewer students scoring below the 20th percentile. This graph

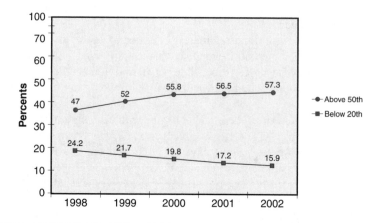

Figure 23.1   District run chart.

gives no insight regarding which grade levels improved, which subjects, which schools, which ethnic groups, and provides no useful planning information. It only answers the question, "Did we improve?"

Figure 23.2 begins to provide some of the insight necessary for improvement. It has six lines and is the first disaggretation of the data. It has three success lines and three failure lines; two lines are for elementary schools, two for middle schools, and two for high schools. The insights needed to generate hypotheses for future improvement come from disaggregated data. For example, Figure 23.1 shows that the district is improving, but Figure 23.2 communicates that this is occurring in spite of high school scores.

There are probably as many ways to disaggregate the data as there are questions. Run charts are generally disaggregated by gender, ethnicity, grade level, subtests, and so forth. It is possible to build into software a mechanism for educators to create any group desired and assign students, classes, or schools to the group. The computer could then produce any graph described in this chapter (and more) for the new group. When modern technology takes care of the labor, imaginations run wild with the possible run charts. Examples are ninth-grade language scores for students enrolled in vocal music, third-grade math for African-American girls, all fifth graders who have been enrolled in a school since kindergarten or first grade, and so forth. Obviously, run charts can even be constructed for individual students.

Run charts are so valuable because they give a view over time. What are the patterns and trends? They help people resist the temptation to merely compare this year to last year. When scores slip for a year, viewers

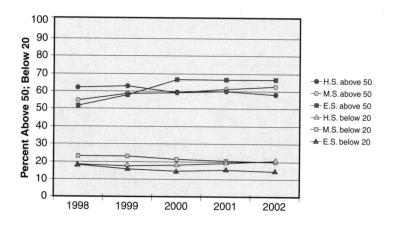

Figure 23.2   District run chart disaggregated by high, middle, and elementary schools.

can see if there's a downward trend or if the one year is an anomaly. A fifth-grader explained to me, while explaining his class's run chart, that their downs were not nearly as deep now as they were in the beginning of the year. One could only hope for this type of sophistication from adults studying district-wide data.

SCATTER DIAGRAM

The progression of this chapter is from the most overall graph to the most precise item analysis for an individual student. The second chart discussed is the scatter diagram. Figure 23.3 is a district scatter diagram, with each dot representing a school. The chart shows the percent of students above the 50th percentile. The schools can be color-coded by elementary, middle, and high school or all left black, as in the example. As with the scatter diagram for classroom use, administrators can connect the dots for any particular school to compare their school to the district as a whole. (See Figure 23.4.) When administrators responsible for district improvement can have the run chart and the scatter diagram side by side, great insight is present. A view of the district as a whole is obtained that cannot be garnered from studying one sheet of paper of the district and one sheet of paper per school.

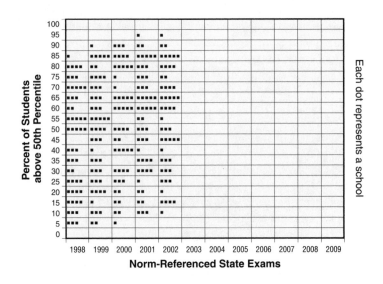

Figure 23.3   Math above the 50th percentile: district scatter diagram.

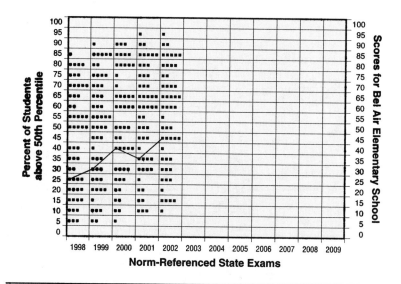

Figure 23.4   Math above the 50th percentile: overlay for Bel Air School.

WEB CHART

Leadership within a school district can come from central office curriculum specialists or site-based educators. The third graph looks at the district from a curriculum basis, while the fourth will study improvement by school. The curriculum graph is the web or radar chart. It allows a district to see the results from every assessment for up to five years. It only takes two sheets of paper (sometimes better that the sheets be 11 × 17, however). Figure 23.5 is a success web chart displayed for all norm-referenced exams for a district. Each line from the center of the graph to the outer edge represents zero percent to 100 percent success. The dot on the line indicates the percent of students who met the district's criteria for success—50th percentile or higher, in this example.

On the success web, the goal is to move each and every dot closer and closer to the 100 percent represented by the outer edge of the biggest circle. The failure web, Figure 23.6, is the opposite; the goal is to move the dots closer to the center at zero percent failure. This example, from the same district as the success web, displays all of the same subjects except that it shows the percentage below the 20th percentile. When the dots are all jumbled together near zero percent, they are hard to see, but they don't really need to be seen. This represents all the subjects/grade levels where failure is almost gone. It is when the dots and lines can clearly be seen that there's a problem.

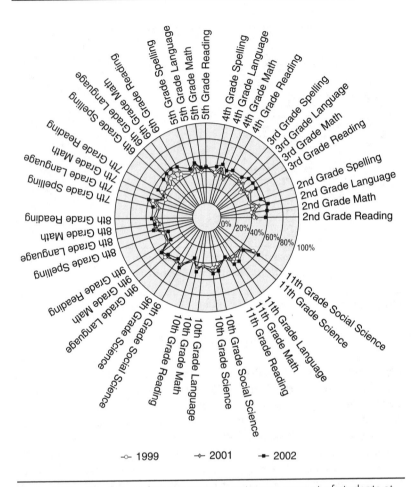

Figure 23.5 Continuous improvement: year-to-year percent of students at or above the 50th percentile.

The web meets several needs for educators. It does not answer the overall "school board" question of the run chart, but answers specific questions for grade levels and subjects. The data displayed on the two web charts would traditionally come from 120 sheets of test publisher reports: one sheet of paper per subject, per grade, per year (four subjects times 10 grades times three years). The problem with 120 pages of test results is brain overload; it is almost impossible to organize all of this in one's mind to gain insight. The two web charts accomplish the organization task for educators. So even though readers might at first struggle with

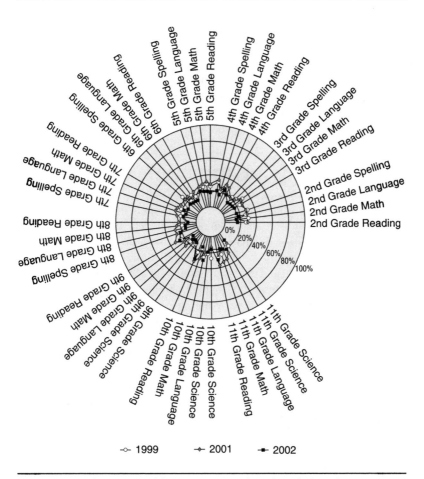

Figure 23.6   Elimination of failure: percent of students below the 20th percentile.

the web chart, they should remember it contains 120 pages of data on two sheets of paper.

A significant aspect of the web chart is the constant reminder to educators that they are responsible for increasing success and decreasing failure—both at the same time. Within any school community there are certain educators more responsible for increasing success and others more responsible for decreasing failure. The webs honor both of their efforts.

The webs do not display averages because averages cloud both successes and failures.

CONTROL CHART

The next graph in progression from synthesis to analysis is the control chart. It views improvement by site rather than by subject, as with the web. Because the control chart is America's answer to its obsession with ranking, I have written it as a separate chapter. If control charts were not in a separate chapter, they would have been described here.

HISTOGRAM

After control charts, when there is a need for even more in-depth data for a particular grade or subject, the histogram is the perfect graph to begin the analysis. Figure 23.7 is a district's spread of data from the same line on the two prior webs. The run chart gives the overall view, the web gives a more detailed overall picture, and the histogram is very specific. It provides three pictures of grade and subject data that are obscured by reporting averages. First, the histogram communicates to all schools with high levels of poverty that they also have students scoring between the 90th and 99th percentile, and to schools with high levels of wealth that they have students who are failing. Averages hide both truths. Secondly, histograms give a much more complete visual of the school district than averages. Figures 23.8, 23.9, and 23.10 are from three different school districts with the same average scores. Clearly, each of the three districts have different profiles and may have different hypotheses for bringing about improvement.

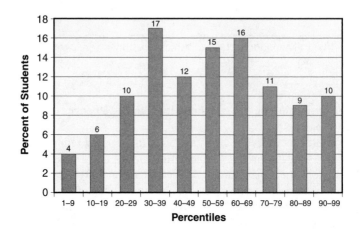

Figure 23.7   11th-grade Social Studies in 2002.

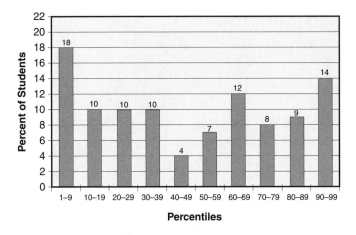

Figure 23.8   Mathematics by deciles: District A.

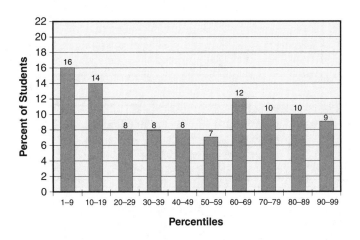

Figure 23.9   Mathematics by deciles: District B.

The third advantage of histograms is that they restore hope. Educators studying histograms believe they can move students from one decile to the next higher decile. Also, they can point to their results the following year. Increasing an average score, on the other hand, is quite abstract and difficult to conceptualize. I realize that the publication of the second edition of *Improving Student Learning* is not going to cause policy makers to substitute continuous improvement graphs for averages. However, if every school moved one decile higher, the average score for a district would increase.

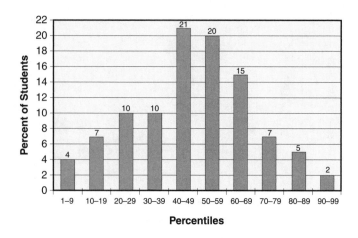

Figure 23.10   Mathematics by deciles: District C.

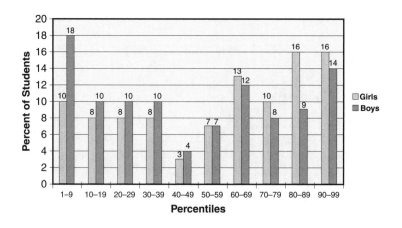

Figure 23.11   Male/female by deciles: reading.

When administrators provide their staffs with the insights provided by these continuous improvement graphs, the newspaper-published numbers are more likely to improve than when staffs have mere average scores.

Histograms can also be disaggregated by gender, ethnicity, or any other variable. Figure 23.11 is a gender-disaggregated histogram showing two years of data for each decile. If a district had data from five ethnic groups over three years, that would be 15 columns per decile for a total of 150 for the whole histogram. That's certainly too much information, except for the convenience of modern technology. Software can mute all 150 columns in the background and allow the user to click on the data of interest. For example, if the interest is 2003 Asian students, only their 10 columns are highlighted. However, with the other 140 columns muted in the background, easy comparisons can be made. The user might then click on the White menu and have 20 columns highlighted or mute the 10 prior Asian columns first.

The run charts, scatter diagrams, and histograms compare data from year to year to year. Many rebel against this comparison, stating it is not accurate because different students took the test each succeeding year. The accuracy of this concern lies in the fact that one cannot accurately compare one year to another year. They are different students. However, with trend data one can accurately compare from year to year in spite of the fact that they are different students. When two years of data are compared, one has a 50 percent chance that any change (positive or negative) is the result of luck, not program or personnel. When a change occurs two years in a row beyond the baseline year, there's now a 75 percent chance that program or personnel caused the change, but still a 25 percent chance it was luck. After three years of movement in the same direction, finally there is an 87.5 percent chance that the change can be attributed to personnel or program. The possibility that the change occurred by chance is down to 12.5 percent. (Unfortunately, about the time school districts can have some certainty, state decision-makers change tests, causing districts to again have no basis for certainty. When a "leader" has ranking in mind, it matters not if the test is changed every year; any test will do. However, when leadership desires continuous improvement, consistency in testing is a necessity.)

THE BOTTOM LINE

Another analysis of norm-referenced exams is the answer to a simple yes/no question: "Based upon the prior year's norm- (or criterion-) referenced exams, are this year's eighth-graders more prepared for high school than any other prior class of eighth-graders from _____ school?" This question is asked of principals regarding their oldest students.

Reading	Yes	No
Mathematics	Yes	No
Language	Yes	No
Science	Yes	No

| History | Yes | No |
| Geography | Yes | No |

I call this simple yes/no chart "The Bottom Line."

"The Bottom Line," when graphed, gives district leaders insight into where leadership regarding improved student learning is happening within their districts. Figure 23.12 gives a view of improvement from schools. At which schools is the most improvement occurring? On the sample graph, three schools are providing most of the school-generated improvement— the one with it's all-time best in all five subjects, one in four subjects, and one in three subjects.

The second bottom-line graph studies the district by subject; superintendents need significant leadership both in the schools and in the curriculum offices. In the example shown in Figure 23.13, the most improvement is taking place in science. All can learn from the person(s) providing this leadership.

COHORT

Even though year to year to year comparisons are valid, there are also good reasons to follow a group of students, referred to as a *cohort,* as they move through the grades. When cohort analyses provide insights that can be used to generate hypotheses for improvement, they must be pursued.

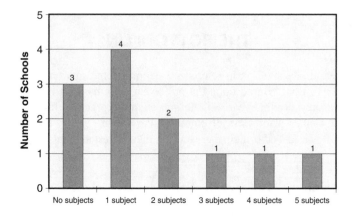

Figure 23.12   "The Bottom Line": How many schools did their all-time best in science, math, social studies, reading, and language?

Figure 23.14 is for the class of 2010 with five years of data. When viewed electronically, the viewer can view several subjects at once, muting all but one at a time.

I can see no reason for the argument of cohort versus year to year to year data. Both give insight into the system. All graphs can be used to blame somebody or can be used to ask questions that lead to the solutions necessary for higher achievement.

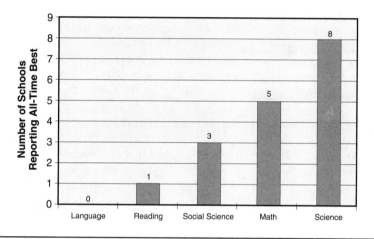

Figure 23.13   "The Bottom Line": which subjects had their all-time best?

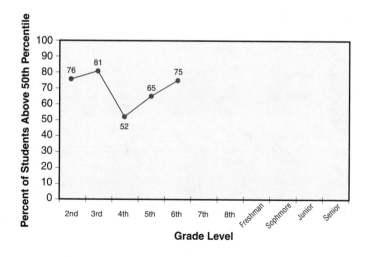

Figure 23.14   Class of 2010: mathematics.

PARETO CHART

At the opposite end of the graph spectrum from the run chart is the Pareto chart for item analysis. Pareto charts rank errors from most common to least common and give a running total by percentage. Figure 23.15 is a Pareto chart composed of all errors made by a district's third-graders on a norm-referenced math test. The students made 5204 errors in computation, 4713 errors in number sense, down to 627 errors in fractions. The numbers above each column display these totals.

The sloping line provides a running percentage. In Figure 23.15, 18 percent of the district's math errors were in computation. The first three columns, when added up, equals 48 of the errors. Now educators can set some instructional priorities for the upcoming year. Not every portion of the curriculum can be given "top-billing," so the Pareto chart is invaluable for establishing plans.

Another Pareto example is Figure 23.16. The district merely counted the number of students who scored below the 25th percentile on each of the state's 12 assessments. Readers can see that 43 percent of the students were either in sixth- or eighth-grade language or reading. Again, priorities are displayed.

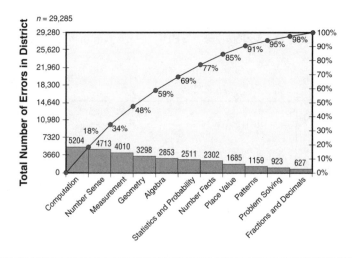

Figure 23.15 District erors on third-grade Mathematics test.

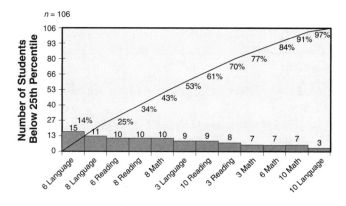

Figure 23.16   Number of students below 25th percentile.

STUDENT CHARTS

Run charts, scatter diagrams with overlays, and Pareto charts are useful for helping students to see their individual progress. The run chart plots their percentile scores from year to year. The scatter diagram, one per subject, shows the students how they compare with other students at their school. The Pareto chart provides an individual item analysis.

CONCLUSION

Larry Lezotte wrote in an article entitled "Learning for All" how he saw the possibilities with modern technology and responsibilities.[1]

> . . . *If the system is doing what is needed, it should be possible for a superintendent to use a computer to track an up-to-date student performance record, and tell the student's parents how well their student is doing, relative to the mastery of the district's intended curriculum.*
>
> *If the superintendent can do this, for any student at any time, she could be able to do the same thing for any aggregation of students, large or small. Likewise, anyone between the superintendent and the student, with a legitimate reason to do so, could also access the learning system. The school principal could monitor learning for individuals or groups of students in the school. The*

teacher could constantly monitor his students. The school-to-work coordinator or the director of the science curriculum for the district could also monitor the mission for the affected students or curricular areas.

Chapter 23 was written to describe the details regarding Dr. Lezotte's statement.

Together, the run chart, scatter diagram, web, control chart, histogram, "The Bottom Line," the cohort, and the Pareto chart provide the necessary graphed data to create insight. This insight becomes hypotheses for a better future. Each of the graphs can be electronically prepared for the district, school, grade, classroom, or student level. Administrators who assure that this level of insight is provided for their staffs are going a very long way toward Dr. Deming's fourth-generation management, where everyone is pursuing a common aim.

First generation	I'll do it myself
Second generation	Do it the way I tell you
Third generation	M.B.O.—management by objectives
Fourth generation	Everyone working toward a common aim

ENDNOTE

1. L. Lezotte, "Learning for All," *Journal for Effective Schools* 1, no. 1 (fall 2002): 8.

24
The Report Card of the Future is Here

A s I wrote in the first edition of *Improving Student Learning,* ideally student progress would also be reported on a student web. Figure 24.1 is a proposed student report card web that would help students and parents see a bigger picture of student learning. I envision the web as the cover of the student portfolio.

Each subject has one diameter on the web; the top radius is for performance measured on a continuum and the bottom radius is the essential information measured by counting. Note, however, that not all subjects are represented on the web; the figure is merely a concept, not a final product. Clearly, the most difficult aspect of having such a student report card is getting communities to agree on the performance levels and information to be learned by transition grades such as 5, 8, and 12. Once this is determined, students can be assessed at year's end and an appropriate dot placed on all radii. Connecting the dots, using a different color for each school year, will easily communicate to parents and students the progress in learning.

A well-designed reporting system informs parents, as precisely as possible, about two aspects of their children's education: expectations and progress toward meeting expectations. Expectations are communicated the first week of a course, both the essential information and the performance standards.

The second reporting responsibility is to tell parents how their children are progressing toward meeting the standards. Do I have a reasonable expectation that my child will meet the year-end standards? What about the standards for elementary school? Is my child on target to meet middle and high school standards? Grades communicate neither what is to be known or if it is learned.

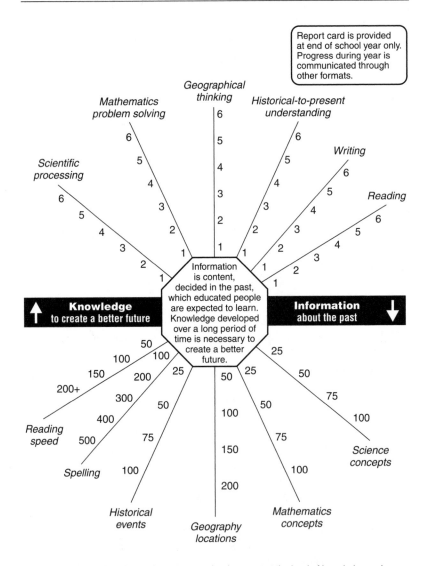

The ends of the radii on the student report card web represent the level of knowledge and information expected at the end of grade five. Information is measured like a track-and-field event: by counting. Knowledge is measured like a gymnastics event: by measuring against a continuum, from lowest to highest quality.

Figure 24.1 Student report card web.

The web, or radar, chart is a perfect tool for a report card. Figures 24.2 through 24.4 are from Columbia Elementary (a K–2 school) in Rochester, Indiana. The outer circles state the expectations at the end of each school year. They are the only school that has communicated to me their implementation of the concept in the first edition. It was implemented for the 2002–03 school year.

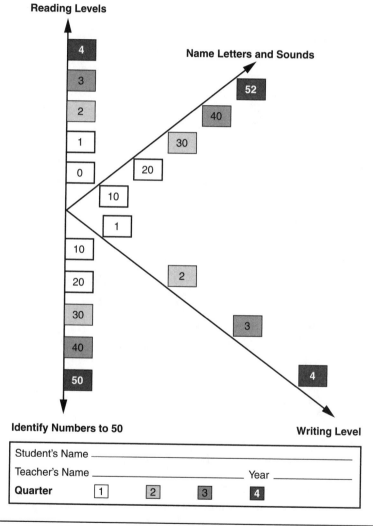

Figure 24.2 Kindergarten web: Columbia Elementary.

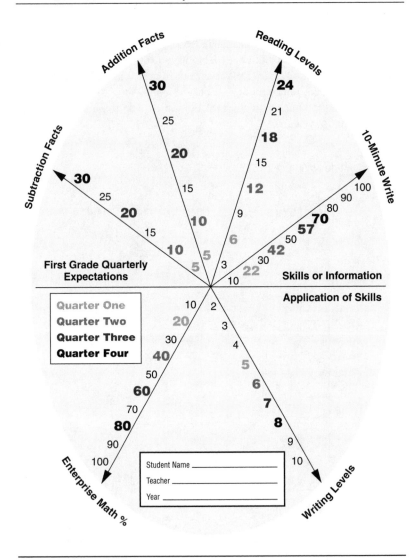

Figure 24.3 First grade web: Columbia Elementary.

The web for kindergarten (Figure 24.2) (in the shape of the letter K—clever, don't you think?) states the expectations for the end of the year in reading, letters and sounds, writing, and counting. The first grade (Figure 24.3) and second grade (Figure 24.4) webs also state expectations by the end of the year. The faculty has agreed on expectations for the quarters also,

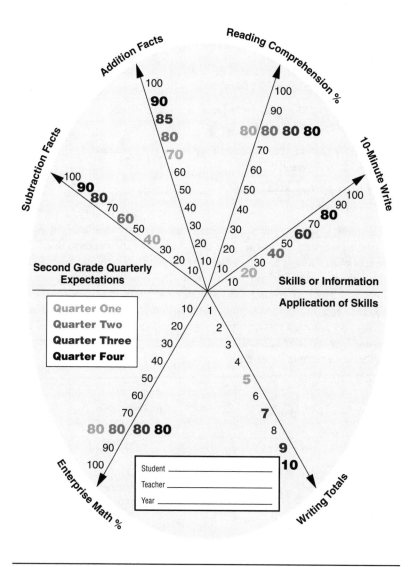

Figure 24.4   Second grade web: Columbia Elementary.

so they can share with parents even more precisely regarding progress. For example, for first-grade reading levels they are expecting level 6 at the end of the first quarter, level 12 at semester, level 18 at the third quarter, and level 24 by the end of the year.

Parents were very impressed with the web report card. Some comments were:

"Radar web was interesting! Provided a better understanding
of progress against the standards."

"I especially liked the circle graph because it gave a clear
picture of all areas of study."

"I really like the radar graphs; they make it a little easier
to understand."

"I liked the web grade scale. It seemed a little more
informative."

It matters not whether schools take my original thought of an annual addition to the web with expectations at the end of elementary, middle, or high school as listed or they take Rochester's adaptation of quarterly adding to the web. The point is that parents and students know precisely the expectations and progress toward the expectations. Also, the reporting is balanced between information (letters, sounds, and numbers) and performance (reading and writing). It is my opinion that readers will implement this concept much more from Columbia School's actual example than from my hypothetical example in the first edition.

Section VIII

Conclusion

Chapter 25
Conclusion

Acceptance of the contents of this book depends upon the answer to one question: are the problems nations are facing, in regards to education of its youth, caused mostly by the workers or the system? People who believe the workers (teachers and administrators) are generally the problem suggest the following solutions: (1) threaten job loss, (2) incentives, (3) embarrassment in the newspaper, (4) tougher credentialing laws, (5) more inspectors, and (6) general disdain for those who have chosen to dedicate their professional lives to the development of youth.

The premise of *Improving Student Learning* is that when every educator does his or her best, little significant improvement in student learning will happen. The problems of education are buried deep in the very fabric of education culture. *Improving Student Learning* attacks these root causes of educational frustration—permission to forget, poor psychology, wrong statistics, and other system defects that create loser students. *Improving Student Learning* is written for people willing to stop blaming workers and determined to change the culture of education.

From 1992 until 2000, the concepts of this book were developed in the Enterprise School District of Redding, California. This was step one. Five books were published describing the theory and practice. The first edition of *Improving Student Learning* was published in 1997 and was followed in 2000 by four books authored by Enterprise teachers. The books are *Continuous Improvement in the Mathematics Classroom* by Carolyn Ayres, *Continuous Improvement in the Science Classroom* by Jeffrey G. Burgard, *Continuous Improvement in the History and Social Science Classroom* by

Shelly C. Carson, and *Continuous Improvement in the Primary Classroom: Language Arts* by Karen R. Fauss.

The second step of this process was to determine if the theories worked outside of one school district where the superintendent (me) was extolling the virtues of continuous improvement and Dr. Deming. The second edition of *Improving Student Learning* documents the fact that the theories and practices work in all environments—urban to suburban and preschool to graduate school. Dr. Deming was right.

The third step of continuous improvement, for future writing, is to describe the process that has taken place to change the cultural norms of education. Students should no longer be given permission to forget, no longer be subjected to practices that cause them to lose their innate desire to learn, and no longer have athletic statistics applied to a nonathletic event (learning). When Dr. Deming was asked how many people were required to change an organization, he replied (surprise) the square root. If this is true, then America needs 125 school districts (square root of approximately 15,000 school districts) who have successfully implemented continuous improvement, as described in this book. Again, if Dr. Deming's square root is correct, this would change American education's culture for good because the rest of the nation would follow. Maybe a process for formal documentation of progress is needed, but for now I must meet the deadlines of this second edition.

Changing the culture of education will take the help of government leaders, journalists, ministers, school board members, unions, business leaders, and educators themselves. These individuals and organizations must be willing to stop pointing fingers and work to fix the system. Any readers who would like to share documentation of cultural change, as it applies to the content of this book, are invited to do so at www.fromLtoJ.com .

Section IX

Appendixes

Appendix A

Analytic Scoring Guides

Analytic Scoring Scale		
Understanding the Problem	0:	Complete misunderstanding of the problem.
	1:	Part of the problem misunderstood or misinterpreted.
	2:	Complete understanding of the problem.
Planning a Solution	0:	No attempt, or totally inappropriate plan.
	1:	Partially correct plan based on part of the problem being interpreted correctly.
	2:	Plan could have led to a correct solution if implemented properly.
Getting an Answer	0:	No answer, or wrong answer based on an inappropriate plan.
	1:	Copying error; computational error; partial answer for a problem with multiple answers.
	2:	Correct answer and correct label for the answer.

Source: NCTM, *How to Evaluate Progress in Problem Solving,* 1987. Used with permission.

Focused Holistic Scoring Point Scale

0 Points

These papers have one of the following characteristics:
- They are blank.
- The data in the problem may be simply recopied, but nothing is done with the data or there is work but no apparent understanding of the problem.
- There is an incorrect answer and no other work is shown.

continued

continued

Focused Holistic Scoring Point Scale

1 Point

These papers have one of the following characteristics:
- There is a start toward finding the solution beyond just copying data that reflects some understanding, but the approach used would not have led to a correct solution.
- An inappropriate strategy is started but not carried out, and there is no evidence that the student turned to another strategy. It appears that the student tried one approach that did not work and then gave up.
- The student tried to reach a subgoal but never did.

2 Points

These papers have one of the following characteristics:
- The student used an inappropriate strategy and got an incorrect answer, but the work showed some understanding of the problem.
- An appropriate strategy was used, but—
  a) it was not carried out far enough to reach a solution (e.g., there were only two entries in an organized list);
  b) it was implemented incorrectly and thus led to no answer or an incorrect answer.
- The student successfully reached a subgoal, but went no further.
- The correct answer is shown, but—
  a) the work is not understandable;
  b) no work is shown.

3 Points

These papers have one of the following characteristics:
- The student has implemented a solution strategy that could have led to the correct solution, but he or she misunderstood part of the problem or ignored a condition in the problem.
- Appropriate solution strategies were properly applied, but—
  a) the student answered the problem incorrectly for no apparent reason;
  b) the correct numerical part of the answer was given and the answer was not labeled or was labeled incorrectly;
  c) no answer was given.
- The correct answer is given, and there is some evidence that appropriate solution strategies were selected. However, the implementation of the strategies is not completely clear.

4 Points

These papers have one of the following characteristics:
- The student made an error in carrying out an appropriate solution strategy. However, this error does not reflect misunderstanding of either the problem or how to implement the strategy, but rather it seems to be a copying or computational error.
- Appropriate strategies were selected and implemented. The correct answer was given in terms of the data in the problem.

Source: National Academy Press, *Measuring Up,* 1993. Used with permission.

Appendix B
Dave Bell's Essential Rhythm Skills Patterns

ESSENTIAL RHYTHM SKILLS PATTERNS 1

Sequence adapted
from Edwin Gordon
Learning Sequences in Music

Usual Duple & Combined

Dave Bell
Winton Woods High School
Cincinnati, Ohio
bell_d@hccanet.org

ESSENTIAL RHYTHM SKILLS PATTERNS 2

Sequence adapted
from Edwin Gordon
Learning Sequences in Music

Usual Triple Meters

Dave Bell
Winton Woods High School
Cincinnati, Ohio
bell_d@hccanet.org

Appendix C
Carlisle, Pennsylvania Standards Attainment for Second-Grade Math

NUMBERS, NUMBER SYSTEMS, AND NUMBER RELATIONSHIPS: (2.1.2)

1. Students will count using whole numbers between one and 980. (2.1.2, A)

2. Students will count by twos, threes, fives, and 10s when given a starting number between one and 100. (2.1.2, A)

3. Students will be able to write whole numbers from 101–999. (2.1, B-2)

4. Using pictures, students will be able to write fractions for ½, ⅓, and ¼. (2.1.2, B)

5. Students will be able to write any given number between one and 99 several ways. (2.1.2, C)

6. Using only two addends, students will write as many addition problems as possible to represent the same number. (2.1.2, C)

7. Students will write as many subtraction problems as possible to represent the same number. (2.1.2, C)

8. Students will draw shapes and divide them into ¼. (2.1.2, D)

9. Students will put different coins under $1.00 together and tell the total value. (2.1.2, E)

10. Students will show more than one way to represent an amount under $1.00. (2.1.2, E)

11. Students will identify odd and even numbers on a hundred board. (2.1.2, F)

12. Students will state the ordinal position of objects in a line to 20. (2.1.2, G)

13. Students will read and write any two- or three-digit number. (2.1.2, I)

14. Students will write a two- or three-digit number and state which numeral represents the ones, which represent the tens, and which represents the hundreds. (2.1.2, I)

15. Students will put three or more two- and three-digit numbers in the correct order. (2.1.2, I)

16. Students will write all of the numbers of a fact family in addition and subtraction –11 to 20. (2.1.2, L)

COUNT USING WHOLE NUMBERS (TO 10,000) BY ONES, TWOS, THREES, FIVES

1. Write the numbers from 9075 to 9085.
   9075, _____, _____, _____, _____, _____, _____, _____,
   _____, 9084

2. Skip count by twos from 740 to 750.
   740, _____, _____, _____, _____, 750

3. Skip count by threes from 403 to 421.
   403, _____, _____, _____, _____, _____, 421

4. Skip count by fives from 8015 to 8050.
   8015, _____, _____, _____, _____, _____, _____, 8050

5. 934, 936, 938, 940, 942 This is an example of:

   a. Counting by ones

   b. Counting by twos

   c. Counting by threes

   d. Counting by fives

USE FRACTIONS TO REPRESENT QUANTITIES

1. Write a fraction for the shaded part. _____

2. Write a fraction for the shaded part of the group. _____

3. Write a fraction for the unshaded part. _____

4. Write the fraction for the shaded part of the group. _____

5. What is the fraction for the shaded part of the group?

   a. $\frac{5}{10}$

   b. $\frac{5}{14}$

   c. $\frac{7}{1}$

   d. $\frac{5}{12}$

Appendix D

Fenneman and Wurth's Parent Letter Regarding Dolch Sight Words

Dear parents,

Attached is a list of the Dolch Basic Sight Words (most commonly used words in reading) that we will be learning throughout the year. Every two weeks, fifteen words will be randomly selected to read aloud. The students' progress will be graphed individually and as a class. The students will not be expected to know all of these words when we first begin. By the end of the year, our goal for the students is to be able to read most or all of the words. Many of these words are already in our reading vocabulary lists.

Thank you very much.

Mrs. Patricia Fenneman
Mr. Marty Wurth
Clarksville Elementary
Clarksville, IA 50619

and	can	are
come	funny	go
he	is	like
jump	look	my

Appendix E
Shelly Carson's
U.S. History Facts

U.S. HISTORY FACTS FOR
FIFTH GRADE (PARTIAL LIST)

1. (5.1.1) The *natural environment* is earth and its physical attributes.

2. (5.1.1) *Folklore* is the traditional beliefs, legends, customs of a group of people.

3. (5.1.1) *Economics* is the science of the production, distribution, and consumption of goods and services.

4. (5.1.2) *Government* is the rule or authority over a country, state, or district

5. (5.1.2) *Latitude* is the distance north or south of the equator, measured in degrees.

6. (5.2) *Longitude* is the distance east or west on the earth's surface, measured in degrees from a meridian that runs through Greenwich, England.

7. (5.2) An *expedition* is a journey for some special purpose such as exploration, scientific study, or military purposes.

8. (5.2) A *compass* is an instrument for showing direction, consisting of a needle or compass card that points to the north magnetic pole.

9. (5.2) *Sextant* is an instrument used by navigators, surveyors for measuring the angular distance between two objects.

10. (5.2) An astronomical instrument that was once used for measuring the altitude of the sun or stars is an *astrolabe*. (It was later replaced by the sextant.)

11. (5.2) *Seaworthy* means that something is fit for sailing on the sea.

12. (5.2) A *chronometer* is a clock or watch that keeps very accurate time.

13. (5.2) A *Protestant* was a member of the Christian church other than the Roman Catholic and Eastern churches.

14. (5.2) *Reformation* was the religious movement in Europe in the 1500s that wanted change in the Roman Catholic Church.

15. (5.2) The *Triangle of Trade* was a route on the Atlantic Ocean between America, the West Indies, and Africa.

16. (5.3) *Fur trade* was an industry that allowed for the natural resources of fur to be sold or traded for other resources.

17. (5.3) An *alliance* is a union formed by mutual agreement, especially to protect or further mutual interests.

18. (5.3) A formal agreement, especially one between nations, signed and approved by each nation is a *treaty*.

19. (5.3) The *Pequot War* was a war between English settlers and the Pequot Indians fought in 1637.

20. (5.3) The war beginning in 1675, between 1675 English colonists and Native Americans, was called the *King Philip's War.*

21. (5.3) *Powhatan Wars in Virginia.*

22. (5.3) *French and Indian War* was fought between France, with allied Indian nations, and Britain and its colonists, for control over North America.

23. (5.3) *Trail of Tears* was a forced movement of Cherokees in 1838 and 1839 to land west of the Mississippi River.

24. (5.4) The study of the earth's surface, climate, continents, countries, peoples, industries, and products is *geography.*

U.S. HISTORY FACTS FOR EIGHTH GRADE (PARTIAL LIST)

General Terminology

1. A *rural* area is the area outside the city.

2. A product that is brought into the country is an *import*.

3. One specific point of view is called a *perspective*.

4. A nation with one ruler is called a *monarchy*.

5. The way a specific group of people live their lives, and their common beliefs and values is their *culture*.

6. A *primary source* document is a document that is written at the time the even occurred.

7. Another word for *commerce* is business.

8. Land claimed in the name of another nation is called a *territory*.

9. A tax placed on exported goods is called an *excise* tax.

10. A tax or duty placed by the government on imported goods is a *tariff*.

11. The right to vote is referred to as *suffrage*.

12. To be under absolute rule is *tyranny*.

13. *Democracy* is a government run by the people, where the supreme power is given to the people.

Government Documents

14. The document that secures individual rights and declares independence from Britain is the *Declaration of Independence*.

15. The *Magna Carta* was an influential English document, written in 1215, that limited the power of one ruler.

16. The *Mayflower Compact* established a form of self-government for Plymouth Colony.

17. William and Mary, king and queen of England, signed the *English Bill of Rights* in England in 1689, limiting their power.

U.S. HISTORY FACTS FOR 11th GRADE (PARTIAL LIST)

General Terms

1. *Capitalism* is an economic system where private owners produce goods and services, within a competitive realm, for profit.

2. (11.1) *Federalism* is a government where the authority is divided between the state and national governments.

3. (11.6) The government is separated into three branches of government, referred to as the *separation of powers*.

4. The *separation of church and state* is a principle in the first amendment that states that the government will take no action or interfere with the practice of religion.

5. (11.4) The actions a nation takes in relationships with other nations is *foreign policy*.

6. A *fiscal policy* is a plan relating to a nation's financial state.

7. (11.9) The idea that the nations throughout the world must rely on each other in such areas as trade, communication, and transportation is called *global interdependence*.

8. (11.9, 11.10) *Cultural pluralism* is a culture's ability to coexist and contribute to society without losing their own identity.

9. (11.4) The opposition to war and the refusal to fight under any circumstance is called *pacifism*.

10. (11.5) *Socialism* is a political structure that favors controlling property and income and that wealth should be distributed to everyone.

11. (11.5) The spreading of beliefs or ideas to help a specific cause and hurt the opposing causes is called *propaganda*.

12. (11.9.3) A *stalemate* is a situation in which neither side in a conflict is able to gain an advantage.

13. (11.11) A movement of attention to non-European cultures in areas such as education is called *multiculturalism*.

Appendix F

Jenny Bushman's Grammar/The Sentence and Its Parts

1. The *subject* of the sentence is who or what the sentence is about.

2. The *predicate* of the sentence is what is said about the subject.

3. The *verb* is the simple predicate. Three types include *physical action, mental action,* and *state of being* (linking).

4. A *helping verb* helps the main verb make a statement or express action.

5. *Compound subjects* are two or more subjects that share the same verb.

6. *Compound verbs* are two or more verbs that share the same subject.

7. A *conjunction* joins words or groups of words.

8. *FAN BOYS* is a mnemonic for the main conjunctions (for, and, nor, but, or, yet, so).

9. A *declarative sentence* makes a statement and ends with a period.

10. An *interrogative sentence* asks a question and ends with a question mark.

11. An *imperative sentence* tells or requests someone to do something and ends in period.

12. An *exclamatory sentence* is used to express feeling and ends in an exclamation point.

13. The *subject* of a sentence does not have to come at the beginning of the sentence.

15. A *run-on sentence* occurs when two or more sentences are written as one.

16. A *noun* names a person, place, thing, or idea (quality).

17. A *common noun* is the name given to a whole class of persons, places, things, or ideas.

18. A *proper noun* is the name of a particular person, place, thing, or idea.

19. A *direct object* is a noun (or pronoun) that tells whom or what after the action of a verb. The usual pattern is S V DO.

20. An *indirect object* is a noun (or pronoun) that appears after certain action verbs, telling to or for whom or to or for what the action of the verb is done. Pattern is S V IDO DO.

21. A *predicate noun* is a noun in the predicate that explains or identifies the subject.

22. A *singular noun* names one person, place, thing, or idea.

23. *Plural noun* names more than one person, place, thing, or idea.

24. A *possessive noun* shows who or what owns something.

25. A *pronoun* is a word that takes the place of a noun or another pronoun. There are three forms: subject, object, and possessive.

26. *Subject pronouns:* singular—I, you, she, he, it; plural—who, you, they.

27. *Object pronouns:* singular—me, you, her, him, it; plural—us, you, them.

28. *Possessive pronouns:* singular—my, mine, your, yours, her, hers, his, its; plural—our, ours, your, yours, their, theirs.

29. A *possessive pronoun* shows possession or ownership.

30. The noun that a pronoun stands for is called the *antecedent* of the pronoun.

31. Pronouns that do not refer to a particular person or thing are called *indefinite pronouns.*

32. *Transitive verbs* are verbs that have a direct object.

33. *Intransitive verbs* are verbs with no direct object.

34. A *linking verb* connects, or links, the subject with a word in the predicate that modifies or renames the subject.

35. A *verb phrase* consists of the main verb and one or more helping verbs.

36. A *verb* must *agree* with its subject in *number* and *tense.*

37. The *three tenses of a verb* are past, present, and future.

38. The *three principal parts of a verb* are present, past, and past participle.

39. An *adjective* is a word that modifies a noun or pronoun.

40. A *predicate adjective* is an adjective that follows a linking verb and describes the subject of the sentence.

41. The *comparative form* compares one person or thing with another.

42. The *superlative form* compares a person or thing with more than one other.

43. A *demonstrative pronoun* points out a specific person or thing (such as this, that, these, those).

44. A *demonstrative adjective* is when "this," "that," "these," or "those" is used as a modifier.

45. An *adverb* modifies a verb, an adjective, or another adverb.

46. A *preposition* is a word that relates its object to some other word in the sentence.

47. The *object of a preposition* is the noun or pronoun following the preposition.

48. A *prepositional phrase* is a group of words that begins with a preposition and ends with a noun (object).

49. A *prepositional phrase,* like an adjective or adverb, modifies a word in the sentence.

50. An *interjection* is a word or short group of words used to express feeling.

Appendix G

Kerry Newman's Triangle Math Assessment

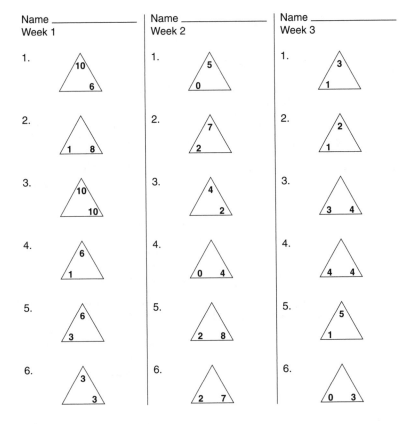

Name _____
Week 1

1.

2.

3.

4.

5.

6.

Name _____
Week 2

1.

2.

3.

4.

5.

6.

Name _____
Week 3

1.

2.

3.

4.

5.

6.

Appendix H

Jeff Hoseley's American Government Concepts

(PARTIAL LIST)

American Government students will be taught the following concepts. At the conclusion of the course, successful students will know:

Unit 1: Organization and Structure of Governments

1. The Code of Hammurabi contributed to the formation of our government by providing written laws which applied to everyone.

2. Magna Carta contributed to the formation of our government by limiting the absolute power of government.

3. The Mayflower Compact contributed to the formation of our government by showing that citizens could create a government that served their interests.

4. The Declaration of Independence contributed to our government by stating that the people should rule, not be ruled.

5. The Articles of Confederation contributed to the formation of our government by showing the need for a strong central government.

6. The roots of democracy were established by the ancient governments of Greece and Rome.

7. The ancient governments of England all contributed to the formation of our government by establishing the basic notions of ordered government, limited government, and representative government.

8. Democratic nations usually participate in free economic systems.

9. Dictatorships and communist nations tend to place more controls on their economic systems.

10. The purpose of government is to protect citizens' rights while managing national interests.

11. The six purposes of the United States government, listed in the Preamble, are: provide a more perfect union, establish justice, ensure domestic tranquility, provide common defense, promote general welfare, and secure the blessings of liberty.

12. The Virginia and New Jersey plans, leading to the Connecticut Compromise, demonstrate the importance of both equal and proportional representation.

13. The Constitution, including the Bill of Rights and all other amendments, is the basic document that guides our government.

14. The Bill of Rights, the first 10 amendments of the Constitution, define basic rights and liberties guaranteed to all citizens of America.

15. The Constitution is based on the principles of popular sovereignty, separation of powers, checks and balances, limited government, and federalism.

16. The government operates under the premises of due process, rule of law, and equal protection under the law.

17. Due process is the premise that the government cannot deprive individuals of life, liberty, or property without proper notice of impending actions as stated in the 14th amendment.

18. Rule of law is the premise that no one or thing is above the law.

19. Equal protection is the premise that everyone is treated the same under the law as stated in the 14th amendment.

20. The federal government is divided into three branches: executive, legislative, and judicial.

21. The qualifications for president, senator, and representative are stated in the Constitution.

Appendix I
High School Special Education Vocabulary List

(PARTIAL LIST)

1. Rarely
2. Considerate
3. Approach
4. Momentous
5. Impressed
6. Shudder
7. Arrogant
8. Obviously
9. Gratifying
10. Befuddled
11. Display
12. Pause

1. Not very often
2. Thinking about the feelings and needs of others; thoughtful
3. To go near
4. Very important
5. To have a positive effect on the mind or feelings of another person
6. To shake because of horror or disgust
7. Showing more pride and self-importance than is deserved
8. Acting in a way that is easy to see and understand
9. Causing someone to experience pleasure or satisfaction
10. Confused
11. An exhibit or eye-catching presentation of objects.
12. To stop for a short time

13. Peer	13. To look closely at something
14. Inquire	14. To ask or request information
15. Stammer	15. To repeat sounds and syllables over and over during speech
16. Blushing	16. To become red in the face because of embarrassment
17. Crimson	17. A deep red color
18. Application	18. A form that is filled out when seeking a job
19. Suggest	19. To propose a possible solution or something to consider
20. Explain	20. To provide information so that something will be understood
21. Stroll	21. To walk in a slow manner
22. Snugly	22. Firmly and comfortably
23. Protect	23. To guard from harm
24. Secure	24. To fasten safely
25. Adjust	25. To change something until it fits
26. Dubiously	26. With doubt or suspicion
27. Sway	27. To tilt to one side
28. Swerve	28. To turn aside from a straight line
29. Flail	29. To move or swing something around (such as arms)
30. Avoid	30. To keep away from
31. Plump	31. Having a full and rounded form
32. Dimple	32. A slight indentation (dent) on the skin
33. Remain	33. To continue doing something
34. Willowy	34. Tall, graceful, and thin
35. Determined	35. Sticking with a decision
36. Famished	36. Very hungry

Appendix J

Steve Denny's Essential Skills for Pre-Calculus

(PARTIAL LIST)

1. Evaluate functions using f(x) function notation.

2. Determine if a given graph is a function.

3. Give the Domain of a function from its graph or equation.

4. Give the Range of a function from its graph or equation.

5. Find a rule for function composition f(g(x)).

6. Evaluate composed functions—f(g(a)).

7. Find the inverse of a set of paired coordinates.

8. The x-variable is usually independent while the y-variable is usually dependent upon the x-variable.

9. An inverse is a switching of the x- and y-variables.

10. Find the inverse of a given equation.

11. Determine if the inverse of a relation is a function.

12. Determine if a given function is odd, even, neither or both.

13. Determine if a given function is continuous.

14. Find the slope of a line given two points.

15. Recognize positive and negative slopes from a graph.

16. Understand that slope is a measure of a rate of change.

17. Write the equation of a line in standard form.

18. Write the equation of a line in point-slope form.

19. Write the equation of a line in slope-intercept form.

20. Algebraically convert a given linear equation into another form.

21. Find the slope of a line given an equation in slope-intercept form, standard form or point-slope form.

22. Write the equation of a line that is parallel to a given line.

23. Write the equation of a line that is perpendicular to a given line.

24. Recognize the family of functions called linear functions by equation or shape of graph.

25. Recognize the family of functions called quadratic functions by equation or shape of graph.

26. Recognize the family of functions called cubic functions by equation or shape of graph.

27. Recognize the family of functions called quartic functions by equation or shape of graph.

28. Recognize the family of functions called higher-order polynomial functions by equation or shape of graph.

29. Recognize the family of functions called trigonometric functions by equation or shape of graph.

30. Recognize the family of functions called rational functions by equation or shape of graph.

31. Recognize the family of functions called inverse trigonometric functions by equation or shape of graph.

32. Recognize the family of functions called reciprocal trigonometric functions by equation or shape of graph.

33. Recognize the family of functions called exponential functions by equation or shape of graph.

34. Recognize the family of functions called logarithmic functions by equation or shape of graph.

35. Recognize the family of functions called radical functions by equation or shape of graph.

Appendix K
Mary Kaser's Chemistry Post-Lab Assessment Rubric

5 (20–18)	**Complete *and* thorough** (3 focal questions [see below] are fully answered; *1–2 minor errors in responses;* detail in math and writing evident; *1–2 spelling/grammar/mechanics errors*)
4 (17–16)	**Incomplete *or* not thorough** (1 or more focal questions not fully answered; *3+ minor errors in responses or 1–2 major errors;* lack of detail in math and writing; *3+ spelling/grammar/mechanics errors*)
3 (15–14)	**Incomplete *and* not thorough** (1 or more focal questions not fully answered; *3+ minor errors in responses or 1–2 major errors;* lack of detail in math and writing; *3+ spelling/grammar/mechanics errors*)
2 (13–12)	**Not handed in when due, *but* by 3 pm, same day** (Post-labs are normally due at the beginning of whichever section you attend the day I collect it, even if you are attending a different section because of conflict)
0 (11–0)	**Not handed in by 3 pm *or* copied** (All involved students will receive a 0, even if only some parts are identical)

The focal questions of a post-lab are as follows:

What did you observe? After an introductory sentence or two, describe the data and observations that you recorded. An organized table is preferred for numerical data, but observations can be listed. Include units and correct significant figures.

What do they mean? Questions and/or calculations assigned from your text or a handout are designed to help you make sense of your data. Answer them in order, numbering as you go. Questions should be answered in sentences. Problems should show all work (using dimensional analysis when appropriate) and include units. Round answers appropriately, using significant figure rules whenever measured quantities are part of the problem.

What did you learn? Class results and sources of variability should be taken into consideration when writing a short conclusion. In addition, the more connections you can make between your labwork and current (and previous!) text material, the more deeply you will learn chemistry. Think hard and write thoughtfully. Consider both concepts and skills. A paragraph or two would be appropriate.

Your post-lab must be word-processed and saved on disk!

Appendix L
Lloyd Roettger's Graduate Research Essential Facts

(PARTIAL LIST)

(1.04/01)
In contrast to empirical or theoretical articles, review articles: define and clarify a problem; summarize previous investigations; identify relations, contradictions, or inconsistencies in the literature; and suggest steps for future research.

(1.04/02)
A report of an empirical study usually includes an introduction and sections called Method, Results, and Discussion.

(1.04/04)
When writing a report of original research, the sections should be arranged by chronology in the experiment.

(1.04/05)
A research report usually includes an introduction and sections called Method, Results, and Discussion.

(1.06/01)
The title of the report must identify the specific variables investigated and the relation between them.

(1.07/01)
The abstract of an article should offer a brief evaluation of the material in the body of the manuscript, be a concise and specific report on the content of the article, and be written in the passive voice whenever possible.

Appendix M

Hope Showley's Essential Music "Fun" Facts

(PARTIAL LIST)

1. What are the closed vowels?

2. What are the open vowels?

3. What is a modified vowel?

4. What is a dipthong?

5. What does it mean to stagger breathe?

6. What is meant by vocal placement?

7. What is the symbol for a treble clef?

8. What is the symbol for a bass clef?

9. Make a staff.

10. What does the time signature 4/4 mean?

11. What does the time signature 3/4 mean?

12. What does the time signature 6/8 mean?

13. What is the choral pyramid?

14. Write a quarter note; how many beats does it get?

15. Write an eighth note; how many beats does it get?

16. Write a half note; how many beats does it get?

17. Write a whole note; how many beats does it get?

18. Write a sixteenth note; how many beats does it get?

19. Make a quarter rest; how many beats does it get?

20. Make an eighth rest; how many beats does it get?

21. Make a half rest; how many beats does it get?

22. Make a whole rest; how many beats does it get?

23. What are the eight solfege syllables?

24. What is a unison interval?

25. What is an octave?

26. Name a minor third.

27. Name a major third.

28. Name a perfect fourth.

29. Name a perfect fifth.

30. Name a major 6th.

31. What is the devil's interval?

32. What is an interval?

33. What is a chord?

34. What is a triad?

35. What does ritard mean?

36. What does legato mean?

37. What does marcato mean?

38. What does staccato mean?

39. Make a staccato mark.

40. What does crescendo mean? Make the symbol.

41. What does decrescendo mean? Make the symbol.

42. What does poco a poco mean?

43. What does a tempo mean?

44. What does tutti mean?

45. Make a repeat sign.

46. What does p mean?

47. What does mp mean?

48. What does pp mean?

49. What does f mean?

50. What does mf mean?

Appendix N
Debi Molina-Walters'
Science Lab Rubric

Science Lab Write-Up
Grading Rubric

Name _____

6	5	4	3	2	1
Exemplary	**Excellent**	**Acceptable**	**Almost Acceptable**	**Needs Work**	**Missed It**
Your work exceeds expectations. You have included all information in a remarkable way and one in which someone else can redo the lab and understand the steps completely.	Your work is very throughly completed and shows an excellent progression of thought. Each step of the write-up demonstrates excellent detail.	You have created a thoughtful write-up and worked through the thinking process with minor difficulty. Each step of the write-up demonstrates good detail.	You have completed each step of the lab write-up. Your explanations are on the right path, but could be strengthened with a clearer explanation, more detail, or a graphic. Your organization could use more work.	Your explanation of your thinking process is incomplete or not entirely clear. You may have left out some steps that make it hard for someone else to follow. Some parts are missing or unclear.	Your work is very unclear and/or steps are missing. Your write-up does not follow lab format.

Categories:

		Your Scores	Possible Score
Purpose	(Complete and clear statement of problem in your own words)	Score: _____	5
Hypothesis	(Prediction or guess about the results of the lab)	Score: _____	5
Materials	(All material needed for the lab must be listed in a vertical, numerical format)	Score: _____	5
Procedure	(Directions must be written in a step-by-step, detailed format to complete the investigation. Think of the procedure as a recipe.)	Score: _____	5
Results	(Collect detailed information through observations and display the data in an insightful way.)	Score: _____	5
Conclusion	(A paragraph explaining what the student learned from the lab. Reflect on hypothesis and results.)	Score: _____	5
	Bonus for creative and descriptive title	Score: _____	1

27–30 = A
24–26 = B
21–23 = C
18–20 = Redo
0–17 = Redo

Total Score: [ ] [30]

Appendix O

Carolyn Ayres'
Sample Math Problems

1. Mrs. Ayres has a piece of licorice. Please measure it in inches. If the licorice is divided up among 5 people, how many inches will each person get?

2. Terica had 60 cents. She wanted to share it equally with herself and three friends. How much would each person get?

3. Warren is designing a new toy to look like a porcupine. He has 4 porcupine bodies (marshmallows) and 33 quills (toothpicks). If every porcupine has the same number of quills, how many will each porcupine have?

4. Katie, Amber, Jennifer, Roy, Nick, and Jared want to finish off a box of Cheerios. There are only 72 Cheerios left. How many will each person get if they share equally?

5. There are 18 airplane seats. Sitting in those seats are 7 children and 6 adults. How many seats are empty?

6. Megan had 15 buttons on her dress. She lost 7, but her mom gave her 8 new buttons. How many buttons does she have now?

7. Amber had a flower garden with 9 beautiful blue flowers. Each flower had 4 delicate petals. She wondered how many petals that was all together. What did Amber find out?

8. There were 7 monsters in the movie. Each monster had 5 legs. How many legs were there?

9. It was fall and almost all of the leaves had fallen to the ground. The schoolyard had 8 trees. Each tree had only 3 leaves left. How many leaves were left on trees?

10. At Alta Mesa School there are 8 fish aquariums. Each aquarium has 5 fish. How many fish live at our school?

11. The bus has 48 seats. 15 girls and 17 boys are on the bus. How many empty seats are there?

12. In the pasture are 6 horses. How many legs are there? How many ears? How many noses? If you go to visit the horses, how many legs? Ears? Noses?

Note: Students should understand the language of the problem, but have difficulty with the mathematics. Too often students struggle to understand the problem, but once the language is understood, the math is simple.

Appendix P
Physical Education Blank Run Charts

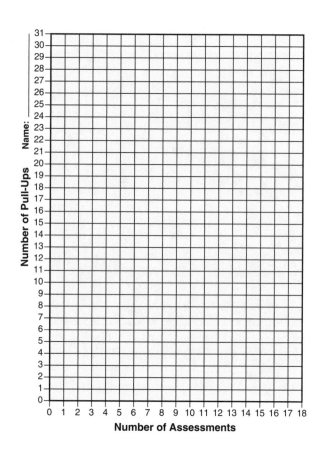

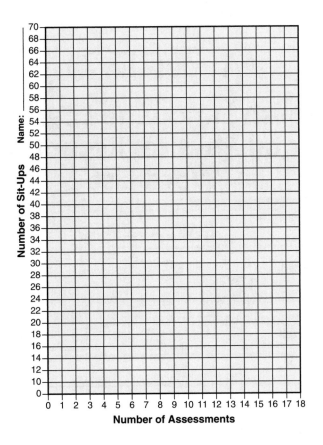

Name: _____

Number of Sit-Ups

Number of Assessments

Appendix Q

English Language Learners: Total Physical Response Word List

(PARTIAL LIST)

Actions	Nouns	Others
1. stand	16. shoulder	38. your
2. sit	17. head	39. and
3. walk	18. ears	40. my
4. turn	19. eyes	41. to
5. stop	20. mouth	42. up
6. sing	21. nose	43. down
7. touch	22. chest	44. around
8. smile	23. arm	45. the
9. jump	24. feet	
10. point to	25. leg	
11. skip	26. hands	
12. hop	27. fingers	
13. pick up	28. chair	
14. put down	29. table	
15. put	30. wall	
	31. desk	
	32. door	
	33. window	
	34. pencil	
	35. book	
	36. ball	
	37. marker	

continued

continued

Actions	Nouns	Others
46. dance	60. neck	84. on
47. frown	61. hips	85. a
48. rub	62. knees	86. now
49. write	63. stomach	87. me
50. erase	64. elbows	88. top of
51. draw	65. chin	89. bottom of
52. fold	66. forehead	90. with
53. throw	67. toes	91. red
54. catch	68. eyebrows	92. yellow
55. look at	69. cheek	93. blue
56. show	70. wrist	94. green
57. hit	71. ankles	95. purple
58. cut	72. hair	96. white
59. color	73. fingernails	97. orange
	74. bell	98. brown
	75. pen	99. pink
	76. eraser	100. black
	77. name	101. grey
	78. chalkboard	102. big
	79. paper	103. little
	80. notebook	
	81. floor	
	82. bell	
	83. scissors	

Appendix R
Mary Bohr's
Writing Power Points

Name _____ Date _____ Points __/10

WRITING POWER POINTS

Organization—3 Points
1. Hook at *beginning*
2. *Middle* with details
3. *Ending* that doesn't just stop

Style: Explosive Word Use—1 Point
1. *Wow words*
2. *Show me*—don't tell me (similes and metaphors)
3. *Dialogue*

Sentences—2 Points
1. *Run-ons and fragments*—few or no errors
2. *Paragraph form*—few or no errors

Editing—4 Points
1. Capitals
2. Usage—subject/verb agreement
3. Punctuation
4. Spelling

Appendix S
Marlane Parra's Speech Articulation Web

Inner circle moving outward:
0—Can't produce phoneme
1—Can imitate phoneme
2—Can produce phoneme in isolation
3—Can produce the phoneme in a word

4—Can produce phoneme in a sentence
5—Can produce phoneme in a conversation during therapy
6—Can produce the phoneme in spontaneous conversation

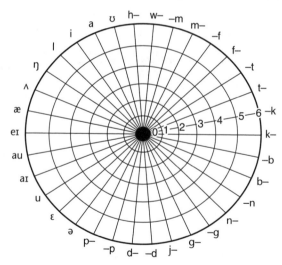

Expected articulation skills for an average developing four-year-old.*

*Based on norms from the *Arizona Articulation Proficiency Scale: Revised* by Janet Barker Fudala, MA; Western Psychological Services, Los Angeles, CA, 1970.

International phonetic alphabet: –k is final position; k– is initial position

Appendix T

Jeff Burgard and Shelly Carson's Writing Rubric for Science and History

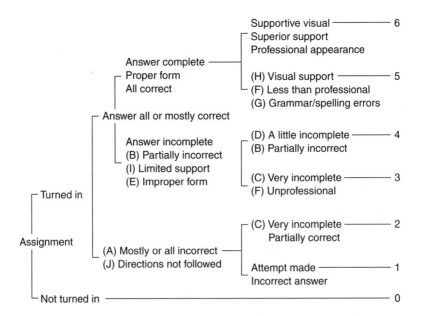

Error Key

A. Assignment is mostly or all incorrect.
B. Assignment is partially incorrect.
C. Assignment is missing a lot
   of required information
D. Assignment is missing a little
   required information.
E. Assignment is in improper form.

F. Assignment is lacking professional appearance.
G. Assignment has grammatical and/or
   spelling errors.
H. Answer lacks visual support, or visual
   doesn't help clarify the answer.
I. Assignment lacks support or evidence.
J. Assignment directions were not followed.

Appendix U

Dave Brown's 3-D Design Rubric

Name ———————————————————————— Rubric #: ————

Craftsmanship
(Neatness of technique)
5—exceptional technique; has verve;
4—strong technique; needs to be a little neater.
3—technique is satisfactory; needs to be neater; some areas are unrefined or overworked;
2—technique is weak; needs improvement; many areas are unrefined or overworked;
1—technique is poor and haphazard; most areas are unrefined or overworked; needs time and effort on your part.

peer	self	teacher

Conceptualization
5—exceptional communication of an idea or feeling; has verve;
4—strong communication of an idea or feeling; some connections between the sculpture and what it is intended to communicate could be improved;
3—satisfactory communication of an idea or feeling; all connections between the sculpture and what it is intended to communicate could be improved;
2— communication of an idea or feeling is weak; much improvement is needed;
1—lacks communication of an idea or feeling; more effort and reflection on your part is needed;

peer	self	teacher

What Idea or feeling are you trying to communicate?

Name of Peer Evaluator:

——————————————————

I have discussed my evaluation with the artist!

——————————————————
signature

Creativity
5—exceptional expression of idea or concept; innovative and original; has verve;
4—artwork reflects development of ideas and thoughts; need to take more risks; don't play it safe;
3—artwork reflects problem as given; very little original thought; needs spark of creativity; what more could be done to make it more original?
2—needs original thought; try brainstorming;
1—needs to be your idea, not a copy from the Internet, a magazine, or another student;

peer	self	teacher

Elements of Design:
(Parts of art)
Line, shape, form, value, texture, space and color;

Principles of Design:
(Organization of parts)
Balance, rhythm and movement, contrast, emphasis, proportion and unity;

———————————— creates
(element)
an interesting sense of

———————————— in my
(principle)
sculpture.

Design
5—exceptional growth in understanding and implementation of elements and principles of design; makes connections; has unity; has verve;
4—strong growth in understanding and implementation of elements and principles of design; need to make more connections between elements and principles of design; needs better unity;
3—satisfactory growth in understanding and implementation of elements and principles of design; needs connections between elements and principles of design; needs unity;
2—needs growth in understanding and implementation of elements and principles of design; lacks connections between elements and principles of design; needs unity;
1—poor and haphazard growth in understanding and implementation of elements and principles of design; needs practice with and thoughtful consideration of the elements and principles of design;

peer	self	teacher

Rubric Score:

Explain design statement:

Name _____ *Shelly Baumeister* _____ Rubric #: _____

Craftsmanship
(Neatness of technique)

5—exceptional technique; has verve;

4—strong technique; needs to be a little neater.

3—technique is satisfactory; needs to be neater; some areas are unrefined or overworked;

2—technique is weak; needs improvement; many areas are unrefined or overworked;

1—technique is poor and haphazard; most areas are unrefined or overworked; needs time and effort on your part.

peer	self	teacher
4.9	5	4.9

Conceptualization

5—exceptional communication of an idea or feeling; has verve;

4—strong communication of an idea or feeling; some connections between the sculpture and what it is intended to communicate could be improved;

3—satisfactory communication of an idea or feeling; all connections between the sculpture and what it is intended to communicate could be improved;

2— communication of an idea or feeling is weak; much improvement is needed;

1—lacks communication of an idea or feeling; more effort and reflection on your part is needed;

peer	self	teacher
5	5	5

What Idea or feeling are you trying to communicate?

confusion and being truthful

Name of Peer Evaluator:

Danielle Connelling

I have discussed my evaluation with the artist!

Danielle L. Connelling
signature

Creativity

5—exceptional expression of idea or concept; innovative and original; has verve;

4—artwork reflects development of ideas and thoughts; need to take more risks; don't play it safe;

3—artwork reflects problem as given; very little original thought; needs spark of creativity; what more could be done to make it more original?

2—needs original thought; try brainstorming;

1—needs to be your idea, not a copy from the Internet, a magazine, or another student;

peer	self	teacher
5	5	5

Elements of Design:
(Parts of art)

Line, shape, form, value, texture, space and color;

Principles of Design:
(Organization of parts)

Balance, rhythm and movement, contrast, emphasis, proportion and unity;

Line _____ creates
(element)

an interesting sense of

rhythm & movement in my
(principle)

sculpture.

Design

5—exceptional growth in understanding and implementation of elements and principles of design; makes connections; has unity; has verve;

4—strong growth in understanding and implementation of elements and principles of design; need to make more connections between elements and principles of design; needs better unity;

3—satisfactory growth in understanding and implementation of elements and principles of design; needs connections between elements and principles of design; needs unity;

2—needs growth in understanding and implementation of elements and principles of design; lacks connections between elements and principles of design; needs unity;

1—poor and haphazard growth in understanding and implementation of elements and principles of design; needs practice with and thoughtful consideration of the elements and principles of design;

peer	self	teacher
4.9	5	5

Rubric Score:

5

Explain design statement:

Using lines with the wire I created rhythm and movement supporting my theme of confusion.

Appendix V

Dave Brown's Pottery One Concepts

(PARTIAL LIST)

STAGES OF CLAY

1. Slip is the first stage of clay. It is liquid clay, and can be used for decoration or poured into forms made of plaster (slip casting).

2. Plastic is the second stage of clay. The clay is soft, and bendable.

3. Leather hard is the third stage of clay. The clay has hardened, still bends slightly before cracking, and feels like leather.

4. Bone dry is the fourth stage of clay. The clay has dried completely, and is very fragile. When the clay is bone dry, it is ready to be fired.

5. It is best not to work with bone dry clay for these two reasons:

   a. It breaks easily

   b. The clay dust produced from bone dry clay is bad to breathe

6. Before clay is fired, it is called greenware.

7. After the clay has been fired the first time, it is called *bisqueware*.

8. After the clay has been glazed and fired, it is called *glazeware*.

9. Three ways of increasing the plasticity of clay are:

   a. Aging the clay

   b. Adding water to the clay

   c. Wedging the clay thoroughly

10. To join two pieces of clay together, you must scratch and attach. This roughs up the clay surface, and helps hold the clay together.

11. Wedging is the main method of preparing clay for use. It distributes the water through the clay, and gets out any air bubbles.

12. If cracks appear in the clay while you are working, you can moisten your fingertips and rub over the cracks to recompress the clay.

13. To keep your clay project from drying too quickly, you should spray your project, and wrap it tightly in plastic.

14. If the clay has trapped air, or the walls are too thick, steam cannot escape rapidly enough, and your project will explode during the firing.

15. The five main methods of building pottery are: *pinch, coil, slab, wheel,* and *slip casting.*

16. The three main methods of making coils are:

    a. Rolling

    b. Squeezing

    c. Extruding

17. The three reasons you should join and smooth coils out on the inside of a coil pot are:

    a. To structurally hold the pot together

    b. To hold water

    c. To provide a visual contrast with the textured exterior

18. To make a coil pot get wider, place the coils toward the outside edge of the coil form.

19. To make a coil pot more narrow, place the coils on the inside edge of the form.

20. If the diameter of a coil form gets too wide, cut a wedge (or dart) out of the rim and reconnect the wall. This will bring the form in.

21. Coil pots should be dried slowly because each connection is a potential crack.

Appendix W

Tim Sheppard and Nancy Hunter's Math Fact Families

(PARTIAL LIST)

①	②	③	④
2 + 2 = 4 4 − 2 = 2	2 + 3 = 5 3 + 2 = 5 5 − 2 = 3 5 − 3 = 2	2 + 4 = 6 4 + 2 = 6 6 − 2 = 4 6 − 4 = 2	2 + 5 = 7 5 + 2 = 7 7 − 2 = 5 7 − 5 = 2
⑤	⑥	⑦	⑧
2 + 6 = 8 6 + 2 = 8 8 − 2 = 6 8 − 6 = 2	2 + 7 = 9 7 + 2 = 9 9 − 2 = 7 9 − 7 = 2	2 + 8 = 10 8 + 2 = 10 10 − 2 = 8 10 − 8 = 2	2 + 9 = 11 9 + 2 = 11 11 − 2 = 9 11 − 9 = 2
⑨	⑩	⑪	⑫
3 + 3 = 6 6 − 3 = 3	3 + 4 = 7 4 + 3 = 7 7 − 3 = 4 7 − 4 = 3	3 + 5 = 8 5 + 3 = 8 8 − 3 = 5 8 − 5 = 3	3 + 6 = 9 6 + 3 = 9 9 − 3 = 6 9 − 6 = 3
⑬	⑭	⑮	⑯
3 + 7 = 10 7 + 3 = 10 10 − 3 = 7 10 − 7 = 3	3 + 8 = 11 8 + 3 = 11 11 − 3 = 8 11 − 8 = 3	3 + 9 = 12 9 + 3 = 12 12 − 3 = 9 12 − 9 = 3	4 + 4 = 8 8 − 4 = 4
⑰	⑱	⑲	⑳
4 + 5 = 9 5 + 4 = 9 9 − 4 = 5 9 − 5 = 4	4 + 6 = 10 6 + 4 = 10 10 − 4 = 6 10 − 6 = 4	4 + 7 = 11 7 + 4 = 11 11 − 4 = 7 11 − 7 = 4	4 + 8 = 12 8 + 4 = 12 12 − 4 = 8 12 − 8 = 4

㉑ 4 + 9 = 13 9 + 4 = 13 13 – 4 = 9 13 – 9 = 4	㉒ 5 + 5 = 10 10 – 5 = 5	㉓ 5 + 6 = 11 6 + 5 = 11 11 – 5 = 6 11 – 6 = 5	㉔ 5 + 7 = 12 7 + 5 = 12 12 – 5 = 7 12 – 7 = 5
㉕ 5 + 8 = 13 8 + 5 = 13 13 – 5 = 8 13 – 8 = 5	㉖ 5 + 9 = 14 9 + 5 = 14 14 – 5 = 9 14 – 9 = 5	㉗ 6 + 6 = 12 12 – 6 = 6	㉘ 6 + 7 = 13 7 + 6 = 13 13 – 6 = 7 13 – 7 = 6
㉙ 6 + 8 = 14 8 + 6 = 14 14 – 6 = 8 14 – 8 = 6	㉚ 6 + 9 = 15 9 + 6 = 15 15 – 6 = 9 16 – 9 = 6	㉛ 7 + 7 = 14 14 – 7 = 7	㉜ 7 + 8 = 15 8 + 7 = 15 15 – 7 = 8 15 – 8 = 7
㉝ 7 + 9 = 16 9 + 7 = 16 16 – 7 = 9 16 – 9 = 7	㉞ 8 + 8 = 16 16 – 8 = 8	㉟ 8 + 9 = 17 9 + 8 = 17 17 – 8 = 9 17 – 9 = 8	㊱ 9 + 9 = 18 18 – 9 = 9

SAMPLE QUIZ

Name ______________________ Week **4**

Date ____________

⑮ 3 + 9 = ____	(59) 6 × 5 = ____	㊱ 9 + 9 = ____	㊶ 2 × 6 = ____
(61) 40 ÷ 5 = ____	⑫ 9 – 3 = ____	㉔ 12 – 7 = ____	㉝ 16 – 9 = ____

Appendix X

Dee Lovejoy's World Map Locations

Continents and Landforms	Countries
1. North America	26. Canada
2. South America	27. United States of America
3. Europe	28. Mexico
4. Asia	29. Columbia
5. Africa	30. Brazil
6. Australia	31. Argentina
7. Antarctica	32. Chile
8. Greenland	33. Great Britain
9. Iceland	34. Germany
10. Madagascar	35. France
11. Isthmus of Panama	36. Spain
12. Yucatan Peninsula	37. Portugal
13. Antarctic Peninsula	38. Italy
14. Baja California	39. Turkey
15. Aleutian Islands	40. Israel
16. Bering Strait	41. Egypt
17. Strait of Magellan	42. Saudi Arabia
18. Cape Cod	43. India
19. Cape of Good Hope	44. Afghanistan
20. Central America	45. Russia
21. Andes Mountains	46. China
22. Himalayan Mountains	47. Japan
23. Alps	48. Philippines
24. Ural Mountains	49. Indonesia
25. The Sahara	50. New Zealand

continued

continued

Bodies of Water	Map Features, Language
51. Arctic Ocean	76. Equator
52. Atlantic Ocean	77. Prime Meridian
53. Indian Ocean	78. Arctic Circle
54. Pacific Ocean	79. Antarctic Circle
55. Southern (Antarctic) Ocean	80. Tropic of Cancer
56. Gulf of Alaska	81. Tropic of Capricorn
57. Gulf of California	82. Map Title
58. Caribbean Sea	83. Scale
59. Mediterranean Sea	84. Compass Rose
60. North Sea	85. North Pole
61. Aegean Sea	86. South Pole
62. Arabian Sea	87. Eastern Hemisphere
63. Red Sea	88. Western Hemisphere
64. Persian Gulf	89. 40 N. Latitude
65. Sea of Japan	90. 40 S. Latitude
66. South China Sea	91. 100 E. Longitude
67. Coral Sea	92. 100 W. Longitude
68. Tasman Sea	93. 20 S, 40 W
69. Black Sea	94. Map Key
70. Caspian Sea	95. Inset Map
71. Hudson Bay	96. Type of Projection
72. Lake Victoria	97. International Dateline
73. Amazon River	98. Map Symbols
74. Nile River	99. National boundary line
75. Bering Sea	100. National capital

Appendix Y

Judy Flores' Math Weeklies

Name _____

Enterprise Weekly
Grade 2 Week 16

Enterprise Weekly
Grade 2 Week 16

1. Circle the shape that does NOT have 4 sides. `K(A1c)`

☐ ▭ △ ▯ ■

6. Write 912 in expanded form. `2(N2c)`

_____ + _____ + _____ = _____

2. 10 students were asked if they liked milk or chocolate milk for lunch. 7 students liked chocolate milk better and 3 students liked milk. Draw pictures to show what they liked. `K(S2b)`

7. Fill in the missing numbers. `2(N7c)`

4 , 8 , 12 , _____ , _____ , _____ , _____ , 32

8. What fraction of the square is colored in? `2(N11a)`

Answer: _____

9. Measure the length of the fence in the units shown below. `2(M1)`

The fence is about _____ units long.

3. Build 41 using the least amount of Base Ten Blocks. `1(N7c)`

How many tens? _____ How many ones? _____

4. Match the word to the symbol. `1(A3)`

+   equals

−   subtract

=   add

5. What time is it? `1(M4a)`

The time is _____ .

10. Patrick drew 12 cards from the deck and his results are shown below. On the back of this paper, show how you could keep track of what cards he has in his hand. `2(S1)`

5 9 6
4 10 2
2 A 8
6 3 7

Name _____

1. The store was selling a 6-pack of Coke for $1.86. If 6 of you shared the cost to each get a can, how much would each person need to pay? `3(N12)`

Answer: _____

2. What time is it? `3(M12)`

The time is _____.

3. Which fraction is represented by letter B? `4(N5)`

Answer: _____

4. Graph the points. `4(M5)`

x	y
0	2
1	3
2	4
3	5
4	6

5. A class counted the number of raisins in the small snack size boxes: `4(S2b)`

24, 26, 21, 20, 23, 27, 22, 25, 24

What is the median number of raisins? _____

6. What decimal is found at letter a? `5(N5c)`

Answer: _____

7. `5(N6)`

263
x 471

8. `5(A2a)`

3 x n = 21

n = _____

9. Match. `5(M4)`

_____ cubic units   A. area

_____ inches/centimeters   B. perimeter

_____ square units   C. volume

10. Nancy's bus mileage log for week 14: `5(S1b(1))`
Monday: 20 miles
Tuesday: 30 miles
Wednesday: 25 miles
Thursday: 40 miles
Friday: 35 miles

What was the mean average for miles driven each day?

Answer: _____

Appendix Z
Jean Wilson's Much Ado about English
Parkersburg High School,
West Virginia
Sophomore Edition

WRITING STRATEGIES (PARTIAL LIST)

1. *Voice*—The style a writer uses so the reader can hear a human personality in his or her writing. Use sentence structure, diction (word choice) and tone to share your style.

   a. *Passive voice*—The subject receives the action. This is a weaker style of writing. (Not *Tom Sawyer* was written by Mark Twain.)

   b. *Active voice*—The subject is performing the action. *Mark Twain wrote* Tom Sawyer.

2. *Narration*—Tells a story or recounts an event.

3. *Exposition*—Presents information or explains a process.

4. *Description*—Paints a colorful picture of a person, place, thing, or idea using vivid, sensory (using the five senses) detail.

5. *Persuasion*—Meant to change the way a person thinks.

   a. *Logical appeal*—Reasons, facts, statistics, and expert opinions to support a point.

   b. *Emotional appeals*—Uses vivid examples, details, and strong language to arouse the audience's feelings.

   c. *Ethical appeals*—Reinforces the writer's sincerity, sense of fairness, and reliability

6. *Purpose*—The specific reason a person has for writing; the goal of writing.

7. *Brainstorm*—The process of writing down ideas and comments in any order without attention to sequence, logic, and sentence structure. Quantity, not quality, is important here!

8. *Stages of writing process*—

   a. *Prewriting*—Planning ideas for writing

   b. *Shaping*—Organizing, outlining, and structuring ideas with an audience in mind

   c. *Drafting*—Composing and concentrating on organization, development, and fluency

   d. *Revising*—Rearranging, and clarifying; checking sentence variety and correct usage

   e. *Proofreading*—Correcting grammar, spelling, and punctuation

9. *First-person point of view*—One of the characters tells the story in his/her own words.

10. *Third-person point of view*—The story is told by only one character in the story (limited point of view) or the narrator might be an all-knowing (omniscient) observer who describes all characters and actions in the story.

11. *Thesis statement*—An specific statement that is the controlling idea of the essay; it defines the boundaries of the subject of the essay.

12. *Topic sentence*—The main focus of a paragraph.

13. *Supporting details*—Used in writing to prove, explain, or describe a topic using examples, anecdotes, or facts.

14. *Closing*—The summary or final part of a piece of writing; in a paragraph, the last sentence; in an essay, the last paragraph in the essay.

15. *Repetitive information*—Words that uselessly repeat information that is already given need to be omitted. (*Not* This is an ancient castle from days long ago. *Better* This is an ancient castle.)

Index